All across Africa, thoughtful Christians are crying out for guidance on how to apply their faith to public affairs. Our God  d right relationships in society and commerce se things, and so have Christian thinkers dov so many African preachers have so little to say about it, and how does this body of teaching apply to the African scene? Dr. Boyo addresses these questions with this timely and strategic book. May it be read widely. May it be put to good use.

Joel Carpenter, PhD
Nagel Institute for the Study of World Christianity,
Calvin University, Grand Rapids, Michigan, USA

This important book is part of a growing number of African voices speaking back to colonial and missionary forces that have been so influential in framing Africa's history. It is a deeply researched and biblically balanced reflection on African political theology today. Evangelicals around the world, and especially in the United States, have much to learn from this conversation.

William Dyrness, D'Théol
Senior Professor of Theology and Culture,
Fuller Theological Seminary, Pasadena, California, USA

The sustained confluence between the African Christian faith and its growing influence in Africa's social life on the one hand, and manifestation in Africa of a strand of politics that pulls back, dictates, and demeans on the other hand, continue to confound African Christian thought. How do we deal with this apparent anomaly that has changed the shape of Africa's social life? How did this debilitating social order germinate and thrive right under the watchful eyes of the church and its agents, or did the African church become a willing ally of the political elites?

In this book, Prof. Bernard Boyo offers a definition of the relationship between theology and politics, but more importantly, he reminds us of the innovative interplay of the two as practiced by the churchmen of Africa's yesteryears – John Henry Okullu, Alexander Muge, David Gitari, Manases Kuria, and Timothy Njoya. We know that the theology and practice of these churchmen motivates for greater contemporary contribution, although in their time they contributed directly to Kenya's second liberation. Additionally, this is a case for Africa's rising voice in theological definition.

I highly recommend this book for curious graduate students, churchmen, and students of religion and politics. It is a handy conversation for those who seek to hear and engage with Africa's current voice in the much-debated area of church and politics.

James Kombo, PhD
Associate Professor of Systematic Theology and Vice Chancellor,
St Paul's University, Limuru, Kenya

Context is critical for authors writing on any theme in African societies. Context shapes the political theologies and engagements of many African people and societies. Bernard Boyo's book *The Church and Politics: A Theological Reflection* achieves this very well by thoroughly illuminating African social, political, and theological engagements in historical, colonial, and post-colonial African societies. A leading African theologian and practitioner, Professor Boyo reflects on an area that is not very well researched. Using exegetical analysis as well as his own personal reflections and observations of the African social-political scene, he articulates the role of African-grounded political theology to produce an excellent book that also privileges African peoples' voices as they do theology and create theology in a highly contested socio-political, religious, and theological space. I highly endorse this wonderfully written and multi-disciplinary book to theological and academic libraries in Africa and beyond. I also highly recommend it to students of African theology, politics, religious studies, political science, history, anthropology, and many other disciplines.

Damaris Seleina Parsitau, PhD
President, African Association for the Study of Religions (AASR)
Former Director, Institute of Women Studies (IWGDS),
Egerton University, Kenya

The Church and Politics

HIPPOBOOKS

The Church and Politics

A Theological Reflection

Bernard Boyo

HIPPOBOOKS

Published 2021 by HippoBooks, an imprint of ACTS and Langham Publishing.
Africa Christian Textbooks (ACTS), TCNN, PMB 2020, Bukuru 930008, Plateau State, Nigeria.
www.actsnigeria.org

Langham Publishing, PO Box 296, Carlisle, Cumbria, CA3 9WZ, UK
www.langhampublishing.org

ISBNs:
978-1-83973-414-4 Print
978-1-83973-467-0 ePub
978-1-83973-468-7 Mobi
978-1-83973-469-4 PDF

British Library Cataloguing-in-Publication Data
A catalogue record for this book is available from the British Library

ISBN: 978-1-83973-414-4

Cover & Book Design: projectluz.com

Contents

Foreword

The Church and Politics brings to the surface the continued importance that religion holds in African life, not only in terms of numbers of believers, but also regarding the varieties of religious experiences and its links with politics. Coinciding with the wave of democratization and globalization efforts on the continent, a notable growth of the public presence of religion and its political referents in Africa is being witnessed. Alongside "development," religion will remain a hot issue in the future political trajectory of the continent. Its renewed presence in public spheres has also led to new understandings of what religion means and how it figures into both nation building and identity politics. This will prolong the challenges associated with the role and status of religion in the "secular state model" found in most African countries. Can these states, while "besieged" by believers, maintain neutrality among diverse worldviews, and if so, how?

The book analyzes historical, political, and sociological dimensions in order to investigate the African experience of the non-secular and its persistence. It is argued that since the independence of most of the African states, there has been a systematic political endeavor to secularize society. However, the macro-economic situation and politico-religious conflict has served to favor the strengthening of a communitarian experience and to counteract the process of secularization. The two forces seem to go for an equilibrium to allow for mutual existence of the state and the theological proponents of the essence of society.

The two main areas in the book broadly cover: (1) The Problem in African Political Engagement and (2) the Theological Approaches to Politics. In here you will find Trends in African Political History, Characteristics of Traditional African Politics, Contemporary Issues in African Politics, Political Theological Thought, The Bible and Politics, and Politics and Praxis.

As a professor of theology, Boyo's specialization in *contextualization* is what makes me believe that he is the right fit to articulate and decipher a theological perspective of politics in Africa. I have no doubt that this will be a valuable book for reference in discussions related to politics and theology in both Christian and non-Christian circles.

In conclusion, I echo the words of Dr. Voddie Baucham, a cultural apologetic who has waded through life and landed in Christ, the solid Rock.

The Bible does speak to every issue in life, and our political issues are informed by our theology. There's no such thing as a politician or a political issue that is not theological. You cannot do politics without theology! So we have to break this false dichotomy.

I am therefore privileged to welcome you to this great book, *The Church and Politics: A Theological Reflection*. My final advice to you is to be open-minded, have an enduring fortitude as you go through the book and you will find it a treasure!

Professor Laban Peter Ayiro PhD, MA, MSc, Med, Bed
Professor of Research Methods and Statistics
Senior Fulbright Scholar
Vice-Chancellor, Daystar University

Preface

Numerous books and articles have been published and consultations and seminars held on the general area of the relationship between religion and politics, but not much theological reflection has been done to give a clear biblical view of politics in Africa. There are virtually no theological publications addressing politics in Africa, particularly from a biblical approach. This lack can be attributed partly to the focus among pastoral clergy and theologians on preaching sermons rather than publishing.[1] There is thus a great need for African theologians to engage more in writing and publication so as to inform and guide citizens more appropriately on their roles and responsibilities in politics.

This book seeks to help fill the void in African literature on this area of study. It is hoped that it will serve as a textbook for students in institutions of higher learning where there are very few or no African textbooks on this subject. At the same time it is hoped that religious leaders will find it a suitable reference guide in their ministries and service to society, and that it will help individuals who enter politics to be civil and forthright politicians.

---

1. Gideon Gichuhi Githiga, *The Church as the Bulwark against Authoritarianism: Development of Church and State Relations in Kenya with Particular Reference to the Years after Political Independence 1963–1992* (Oxford: Regnum, 2001), 7.

Introduction

Should Christians be involved in politics? Are they under a moral obligation to do so? Are there any theological foundations guiding Christian sociopolitical engagement? What does the Bible have to say about political matters? Why do different groups interpret the Bible's teaching on this subject differently? That is one set of questions we need to be asking.

There is also another subset of questions we need to ask. There are many African politicians who profess to be Christians. They attend church and actively participate in church life, but their faith appears to have little to no impact on their political engagement. Why not? Why don't we hear their voices raised in response to the issue of corruption that plagues Africa? Since they are in positions of leadership, and such evils are perpetrated on their watch, can the Kikuyu proverb *gutiri muici na mucuthiriria* ("There is no difference between the thief and the looker-on") be applied to them?

These are the types of questions we will be looking at in this book as we investigate the role of Christians and seek biblical guidance on how to live and to govern within a democracy, or whatever form of government prevails in your region.

A. Politics and Problems

Some of the social issues in Africa are so well known that there is little need to repeat them. There are few democratic governments in Africa. Instead we have authoritarian governments and dictatorships established by coups-d'état, rampant tribalism, manipulation of votes, and rigged elections. The rule of law is equally elusive in many African countries. Instead there is rampant injustice, bribery, corruption, land-grabbing, and mass evictions. Civic administrations are plagued by poor governance, which leads to weak social structures paralyzing public systems and rendering services inadequate. Thousands endure grinding poverty, while many more live as "displaced persons" and refugees.

If, instead of looking at general patterns, we look at individual countries, we see xenophobia in South Africa, civil wars in Congo and the Central African Republic, postelection violence in Kenya, dictatorial authoritarianism in Zimbabwe, Uganda, and Rwanda, as well as religious extremism in Nigeria.

Terrorism now poses a major threat to the continent as a whole. As Prosper Mushy says, "The ever increasing number of atrocities perpetrated by terror gangs in the African continent is a great cause for alarm. Incidents such as kidnappings, rampant bombings, destruction of property and the killing of innocent civilians among other acts of violence and bloodshed show that terrorism in Africa is real."[1] Where does the African turn for a reprieve?

With all these problems, there is plenty of scope for Christian involvement in politics. And there have been Christian leaders in Africa who have spoken out boldly against sociopolitical evils perpetrated by their governments. Think of Desmond Tutu and Allan Boesak in South Africa; Henry Okullu, Alexander Muge, and Timothy Njoya in Kenya; Janani Luwum in Uganda; and most prominently Albert Luthuli, a leader in the Africa National Congress and recipient of the Nobel Peace Prize. Luthuli was a Methodist lay preacher who opted "for secular politics rather than ecclesiastic chieftaincy as a means by which to serve the people."[2] There have also been cases where church representatives and religious bodies, such as the Christian Association of Nigeria (CAN), the National Council of Churches of Kenya (NCCK), and the South African Council of Churches (SACC), have shouldered civic duties and responsibilities that have informed government policies and practices within their individual contexts.

These examples raise other pertinent questions regarding individual and communal responsibility. What are the boundaries of tolerance, and how should we respond individually and as a community to religious extremism and radicalization? How can we as Christians be relevant in matters of good governance and administration? What do we have to say when dealing with issues of justice and human rights? Unless we think about these things, we will have nothing to say when confronted by political elites who insist that there must be a great divide between church and state and between religion and politics – even when such a divide is a Western construct that is alien to African, and biblical, thinking.

---

1. Prosper Mushy, "Terrorism in Africa: The Response of Theology," *African Ecclesiastical Review* 57, no. 1–2 (June 2015): 4.

2. Scott Everett Couper, "'When Chief Albert Luthuli Launched "Into the Deep"': A Theological Reflection on a Homiletic Resource of Political Significance," *Journal of Theology for Southern Africa* 130 (March 2008): 82–83. Couper asserts that "Luthuli grounded his political statement with a theological foundation using a title and the same concluding sentence: 'The Road to Freedom is via the Cross.' . . . Luthuli communicated that the basis and impetus for politics is a calling from God to serve others. To his faith-based community, Luthuli communicated that through politics, one implements faith."

B. Theology and Politics

Some may ask what a discipline like theology, which talks about God, has to say about the practical issues of political life on earth. This question portrays a clear lack of understanding of the nature of theology and of what theologians do. Theologians look at the self-revelation of God to the people he has created. Their aim is to expose the ugliness of life without God with a view to pointing people to the beauty of the abundant life that he intended for his entire creation. Thus theologians need to understand the perceptions, beliefs, and practices of the people for whom the theology is intended, and need to explain the kind of lifestyle humans ought to live in light of God's revelation. Theology must, therefore, always be grounded in the context of people and their experiences in real life. Clemens Sedmak puts it this way: "Doing theology is a way to attend to the wounds of our time. There are the wounds of ignorance and stupidity, the wounds of broken promises and unrealized dreams, the wounds of innocent suffering and guilt, the wounds of open questions and burning concerns. We all do theology as wounded healers, as people in need of healing and comfort, and as people who can share the life-giving strength of our wounds."[3]

That is why Bishop Henry Okullu, for instance, argues strongly that "churches . . . have an historic mission, which is to assist in the definition, validation and articulation of just political, economic and social objectives."[4] But such talk must be honest, and must not be merely a moral cloak over naked political ambition. Bishop Tutu acknowledged this danger:

> Many were somewhat skeptical, believing that I was really a politician masquerading as an archbishop, and that come liberation I would emerge in my true colors as I entered politics full-time. They did not believe me when I said I am involved politically because of my faith and not because of some political ideology. They began to think that I just might have been speaking the truth when I did not take public political office, and especially when I did criticise Madiba and his government.[5]

For historical reasons that will be addressed later in this book, most of the leadership in the African church, particularly in evangelical churches,

---

3. Clemens Sedmak, *Doing Local Theology: A Guide for Artisans of a New Humanity* (Maryknoll, NY: Orbis, 2002), 9.

4. John Henry Okullu, *Quest for Justice: An Autobiography of Bishop John Henry Okullu* (Kisumu, Kenya: Shalom, 1997), xv.

5. Desmond M. Tutu, "Dark Days: Episcopal Ministry in Times of Repression, 1976–1996," *Journal of Theology for Southern Africa* 118 (March 2004): 39.

has tended to focus exclusively on caring for spiritual needs and has had very little to do with the social life of the people. This is a problem that needs to be addressed.

C. Politics and Culture

Every society has its own cultural framework that defines its lifestyle and identity. This framework embraces not only artifacts and rituals, but also the beliefs, practices, and institutions that the community draws from to make sense of everyday life. While culture is passed on from generation to generation, it is also affected by people's exposure to new ideas and their experiences. It follows that there is a multiplicity of diverse cultures, with significant similarities and differences.

It goes without saying that politics is entrenched in the cultural structure of a people's existence and thus cannot be conceived outside a given cultural context. So it is not enough for Christians who are interested in politics to simply know the Scriptures. An understanding of "the fundamental elements of politics requires the religious sources of knowledge found in Scripture, theology, church history, and Christian experience. It also requires corroborating and expanding insights from political theory, sociology, anthropology, economics, psychology, and secular history."[6]

As Christians we are called to be the salt, light, and leaven that infiltrates and transforms society by resisting every form of evil. Sound biblical theology is crucial to the way African Christians approach this task. But too often the theology we are taught arises from a Western worldview that is ill informed about the intricacies of the African context. The result is that erroneous and irrelevant conclusions are made. For African Christians to be relevant in dealing with local issues that affect their individual contexts, their theology must be appropriately contextualized with a view to illuminating practically the needs of the continent.

Thus the first part of this book focuses on highlighting the African political context in which we live out our faith. We shall discuss some cardinal requirements of an African political theology that hinge on relevance and validity within a context that is highly communal and ethnic yet endeavor to have biblical anchorage. Because our present is always influenced by our past, we will look at both precolonial and colonial political structures, and see

---

6. Stephen Charles Mott, *A Christian Perspective on Political Thought* (New York/Oxford: Oxford University Press, 1993), 7.

how they have shaped present-day politics in Africa and the church's present understanding of its role. We will see how this history has contributed to many of the problems that plague us today.

But it is not only historical events that shape our politics. So does our distinctively African worldview which is rooted in our long-standing African cultures with their diversity, communalism, tribal affiliations, and the like. Unless we understand the influence of such factors, we cannot critique them, seeing both their strengths and their weaknesses. We cannot suggest practical ways to deal with issues such as tribalism in politics if we do not have a deep understanding of how they work on the ground, how they manifest themselves, and why they have endured for so many centuries.

Some of Africa's problems today spring from the conflict between these ancient elements of the African worldview and elements that have entered Africa only in recent centuries. Concepts such as the nation state and democracy run counter to many ancient principles. Often these concepts exist as a veneer on older ways of exercising power.

Another problem that has come with modern centuries is the rise of extreme poverty in Africa. In the past, Africans may not have been wealthy, but there was far less of a divide between the rich and the poor. Urbanization has led to the rise of massive slums; so how should the issues surrounding wealth and poverty be understood in political terms, and how do we as Christians set about finding the needed political solutions to alleviate and ideally to end the existence of slums?

After this thorough review of the African context, we will turn to the various theological options for engagement put forward by missionaries, evangelicals, liberation theologians, and African theologians. Here, too, we will look at the strengths and weaknesses of each option, recognizing that they too arose within particular historical and cultural contexts. Liberation theology, for example, arose in the context of oppression in South America and was then taken up in Southern Africa and used to challenge the apartheid system. But recognizing that the context within which a political theology arises shapes its view of God and of salvation will also mean that we need to examine our own views. To what extent are our own political opinions simply the product of our experiences?

Recognizing the danger of a selective reading of Scripture and of proof texting, we will then turn to exegetical analysis in an attempt to understand both Old Testament and New Testament political thought. Our goal will be to ensure that Christian involvement in politics is established on a solid biblical foundation.

Once that foundation has been laid, we will turn at last, in the final chapter of the book, to issues of praxis such as elections, governance, and corruption. By developing a mature understanding of these matters, Christians can move to the forefront in demonstrating the proper application of democratic principles in politics while bringing vices to the attention of the ruling authorities and working to constructively address the social ills that have crippled and impoverished African society as a result of poor governance.

Part One

The Problem in African Political Engagement

The African political context is characterized by numerous problems and challenges which continue to plague the various political contexts in the continent. This situation is, for the most part, wrought by a leadership that fails in its political responsibility of exercising just and righteous governance. Along with numerous civic agencies, political players have not only increasingly been agents of oppression, but have perfected skills and legalities of abetting injustice and numerous political malpractices. Like sharks in the waters that prey on unsuspecting victims for personal indulgence and satisfaction, these forces are relentless proliferators of sociopolitical problems in Africa. The church, for its part, in its abnegation of politics, has failed to be the conscience of society in giving appropriate direction on sociopolitical issues. In this regard it not only lacks a political theology but also has abdicated its role and responsibility of addressing the vices brought about by poor politics. In its theology, the church seldom speaks to the sociopolitical issues that have crippled the life of many civic contexts in the continent. Thus the church fails to be true to its calling as Christ's agent in his redemptive act to all the nations. This section attempts to decipher the contours of the problem of African political engagement with a view to pointing out possible requirements of an African political theology of the church.

In our discussion of this problem, we will first discuss selected components that are vital for proper engagement in the sociopolitical affairs in the African context. These are important aspects as they are not only contextual but central to understanding the African way of life, and they are also core to the Christian faith. At the same time, we will argue that these requirements have in a sense contributed to the problem, either by being misunderstood, ignored, or misused. The African heritage, in its diversity, has also been a key contributing factor to shaping the African way of life and politics. Since the future is influenced by the past, we shall look at the sociopolitical structure prior to the Western influx and domination of the continent which will set the scene for our understanding of where we have come from as a people. The impact of colonialism, coupled with the missionary factor, has far-reaching implications for African sociopolitical theology that characterizes the life of the church today. This historical approach is critical because "the ever changing mosaic of religious, economic, social and political factors that have lain and overlain the African continent since its earliest history, must be integrated in a new hermeneutics for visualizing the interaction between faith and culture within the African Christianity."[1] African culture, in general, is characterized by values and emphases that are central to a holistic view of life in which all dimensions of human existence are interrelated and inseparable. These are traditional characteristics that we will need to consider as they are central to the perennial problems that have bedeviled African politics. Along with these, we shall also look at contemporary issues that have compounded the African political structure, often negatively.

First we will look at the requirements of an African political theology.

---

1. Stan Chu Ilo, "Contemporary African Cultural Values: A Challenge to Traditional Christianity," *African Ecclesiastical Review* 49, no. 3–4 (Dec. 2007): 185.

1

Requirements of an African Political Theology

There are many aspects that could be identified as key to African sociopolitical engagement. In this section we will focus on three that we deem to be significant, although they are not exhaustive, and nor would they be considered the only requirements of an African political theology. But before we look at them, it is imperative that we delineate the use of the term "politics." "Politics" is a concept derived from the Greek word Πολιτικά, which according to Aristotle relates to the management of the affairs of a city. However, we need to note that political science theory did not originate with Aristotle, as earlier statesmen and philosophers, including Socrates, had applied the term in numerous ways.[1] According to Aristotle, the uniting of villages to form a single community necessitates the formation of a state to manage the basic needs of human life for the good of the affairs of the populace.[2] In this respect, then, politics relates to the management of the affairs of citizens who belong to a particular state in which human beings by nature find themselves and enjoy the good of life in its fullness.[3] According to Aristotle, it is only within a political community that human beings can live "the good life," implying that politics and human existence are intertwined. James Skillen observes that according to Plato and Aristotle, "the most complete realization of mature human community is to be found in the well-ordered polis, the political community, or what we usually refer to as the Greek city-state."[4] Skillen contrasts this view

---

1. Aristotle, *Aristotle's Politics*, trans. Benjamin Jowett (Oxford: Clarendon, 1967), 3.
2. Aristotle, *Politics*, 28.
3. Aristotle, 28.
4. James Skillen, *The Good of Politics: A Biblical, Historical, and Contemporary Introduction*, Engaging Culture (Grand Rapids, MI: Baker Academic, 2014), 18.

with the biblical view, which he says is incompatible with both the modern as well as the ancient Greek understanding.[5] Hoelzl and Ward discuss the Hebrew and the Christian Scriptures as the twofold root of politics.[6] In this book, we will be using the term "politics" to refer to the civil administration or governance of a society or community. But given that the function of good governance is to address issues and problems that arise within a community, we will inevitably have to address social issues as well. These issues are diverse and touch on every aspect that affects the well-being of the entire society, both negatively and positively.

The first requirement of an African political theology, then, is *relevance and validity*. A sociopolitical theology that is relevant and valid ought to take cognizance of all aspects of a people's ethos, values, and way of life, understanding how they relate and their ramifications. Essentially, the aspects that contribute to politics should be authenticated in order to articulate a theology that meaningfully impacts society. In the same vein there is need to understand the nuances of traditional and cultural beliefs that impinge on the Christian worldview. Another requirement is *communalism and ethnicity*. These are key features that characterize African life. They are, as we shall argue, cardinal components that will contribute to understanding the African sociopolitical structure: vital features of the African heritage without which deciphering the kernel of the African socio-structural framework would be impossible. Considering that we are talking about a Christian theology, it is also imperative for African political theology to be *biblical*. The reading, understanding, and application of biblical truth must be the guiding factor of African political theology. This implies seeking an informed understanding of what God is doing in the sociopolitical structures of the lives of his people as he reveals himself in the person of Christ.

These are the requirements of an African political theology that is pragmatic regarding the African political context that is characterized by tenacious problems and challenges which, although replicated in other contexts, are rampant in Africa. The negative expressions of these cardinal tenets and their

---

5. Skillen, *Good of Politics*, 19.

6. Michael Hoelzl and Graham Ward, eds., *Religion and Political Thought* (London: Continuum, 2006), 2. They say that "both the Hebrew and the Christian Bibles provided sources for the *legitimation of power*; the exercise of political power was based upon biblical authority. While, on the other, there is the classical Greek tradition that has given us basic classificatory *concepts* in political science as well as a definition of the *political* itself." And, further, note that "although modern understandings of democracy bear little direct relation to the classical Greek *polis*, nevertheless the category of democracy as defined in the context of Aristotle's typology of government remained a benchmark until the nineteenth century."

impediments to a meaningful engagement in politics must be understood and decried. This is a task that the church in Africa must engage with in order for its political theology to be relevant and valid.

A. Relevance and Validity

A number of African theologians, such as John Mbiti, who was brought up in a mission church, have been at the forefront in advocating for authentic Christianity in light of the realities of African life and cultural values. Mbiti puts it very well: "There is no permanent home for foreign Christianity in Africa. Africans are taking the Christian message very seriously. We want to keep it in our continent. So our churches will have to struggle to retain this message, to make it our own and to let it make us its own."[7] It is only then that the Christian faith will be truly African, since "Authentic African Christianity can only evolve out of the interaction of the Gospel of Jesus Christ with the total life of the people."[8]

Cultural values and practices are rich in portraying African authenticity, which is a key component that political theology should utilize. Generally, there should be minimal recital of creeds "following the tradition from some Churches of the West – African Christians are more at home in dancing their faith, in celebrating their faith, in shouting their faith (through jubilation), singing their faith, being possessed by the Holy Spirit of their faith and demonstrating the frontiers of their faith."[9] This is where the African communal perspective of life must be embedded within the articulation of theology if Christianity is to make any meaningful inroads into the heart of African existence. The use of proverbs, fables, riddles, wisdom sayings, and narration of stories is one of the primary means by which Africans express their self-understanding, thereby displaying the "great richness and wealth in their culture, language, traditions and customs."[10] The political theology of the church in Africa should therefore utilize such aspects that depict the reality of the African worldview.

In order for it to be relevant, a valid political theology must relate to the current African setting. Quite often the theology espoused by the church

---

7. John S. Mbiti, *Bible and Theology in African Christianity* (Nairobi: Oxford University Press, 1986), 19.

8. Mbiti, *Bible and Theology*, 19.

9. Mbiti, 127.

10. Joseph G. Healey and Donald Serbertz, *Towards an African Narrative Theology* (Nairobi: Paulines Publications Africa, 1996), 17.

has been found wanting as it has focused on issues that do not address the current needs of the people. This has often been the case due to the church's conformity to inherited historical theological traditions. The church should, therefore, reevaluate its political theology particularly with regard to Christian engagement in politics. In general, the church in Africa lacks a valid and clearly articulated political theology in its doctrine. Churches have not been keen to prioritize engagement with the sociopolitical scene as part of their ministries.[11] This may be attributed to a lack of ingenuity on the part of the church in breaking away from the influences associated with its historical roots. It is imperative, then, that the church, in its theology of politics, seek not only to scratch where it itches, but also to scratch where it ought to itch! The church in Africa's laissez-faire attitude and approach to the sociopolitical affairs of the people must be abhorred and promptly reversed.

Generally, most churches in Africa either replicate or react to the theological perspectives of missionary Christianity which emphasized personal faith in Christ and obedience to ecclesiastical stipulations. The focus was essentially evangelistic: conversion of souls with an eschatological stance. African cultural values were relegated to the periphery through the colonial history in which, "across Africa, over the course of several decades, the cultures of many communities were pushed into irrelevance. The wisdom-keepers were dismissed as sorcerers and witches, and what they knew about their communities – the ceremonies, symbols, stories, dances, folklore – died with them."[12] The evils associated with African social structures included "the dangers of devil worship, [which were] originally promulgated by Christian missionaries in Africa to characterize African minds and natures as vulnerable to evil and in need of being saved, [and] came to be explicitly politicized and integral to state governance."[13] Church and state relations in Africa were thus polarized by this kind of theological hiatus. This situation created an unwarranted dichotomy which, along with other contemporary developments and challenges, requires urgent theological reflection and response by the

---

11. Jesse Ndwiga Kanyua Mugambi, *Democracy and Development in Africa: Role of the Churches* (Nairobi: All African Conference of Churches, 1997), 28–29.

12. Wangari Maathai, *The Challenge for Africa* (London: Arrow, 2010), 40.

13. James Howard Smith, "Making Peace with the Devil: The Political Life of Devil Worship Rumors in Kenya," in *Displacing the State: Religion and Conflict in Neoliberal Africa*, ed. James Howard Smith and Rosalind I. J. Hackett (Notre Dame, IN: University of Notre Dame Press, 2012), 49–50. Smith notes that "the state ought, with some success, to define itself as both Christian (rooted in values that were in some way Christian as opposed to being pagan or savage) and secular (predicated upon science – especially scientific agriculture, psychiatry, and cultural anthropology)."

church.[14] Albert Luthuli's sociopolitical theological perspective provides a good illustration here. His "political decisions were primarily motivated by theological beliefs . . . that through politics, one implements faith . . . Luthuli proclaimed that one is a mere extension of the other; neither of the two can be separated. In his sermon and, to a lesser extent in his political statement, Luthuli utilised the hermeneutic lens of typological re-enactment to convey his justification."[15] This unnecessary dichotomy between the sacred and secular dimensions of life must therefore be confronted and addressed with a view to reaching a holistic and integral view of life.

The African context looks for solutions to sustain life in the midst of insufficient and unevenly distributed resources. For sociopolitical theology to be relevant in Africa therefore means confronting powers of evil in the public square, such as political dictatorship, corruption, mismanagement of public wealth, and greed that increases poverty.[16] This implies that the validity of political theology in Africa will be attested by its relevance in addressing the people's questions and problems with a "theological result [that] will make the most sense for dealing with the situation at hand."[17] Valid aspects of African customs, cultural expressions, beliefs, and practices should characterize this theology.

Another requirement for African political theology encompasses ethnic and communal affiliations which characterize African sociopolitical life.

B. Communalism and Ethnicity

Ethnic identity is a strong bond that characterizes African communities. It is also a major factor that defines the African sociopolitical terrain and which the effective theology of the church ought to be sensitive to. The term "community" has "different meanings."[18] It is "a unified organism, a living body,

---

14. Philip Jenkins, *The Next Christendom: The Coming of Global Christianity* (New York: Oxford University Press, 2002), 11.

15. Scott Everett Couper, "'When Chief Albert Luthuli Launched "into the Deep"': A Theological Reflection on a Homiletic Resource of Political Significance," *Journal of Theology for Southern Africa* 130 (March 2008): 82–83.

16. Andrew Mullei, *The Link between Corruption and Poverty: Lessons from Kenya Case Studies* (Nairobi: Africa Centre for Economic Growth, 2000), 29.

17. Robert J. Schreiter, *Constructing Local Theologies* (Maryknoll, NY: Orbis, 1985), 74.

18. Eric Masinde Aseka, *Transformational Leadership in East Africa: Politics, Ideology and Community* (Kampala: Fountain, 2005), 12.

whose members are united by a common, shared life."[19] Assurance of one's welfare, security, and protection underlies ethnic belonging and identity. There is a sense in which trust is elicited from tribal ties and affiliations. Essentially, then, we cannot ignore the centrality of such a key sociopolitical and cultural component. Indeed "the impact of culture, religion, . . . in their various forms [on] the development of styles of leadership and national political cultures is a critical question."[20] Africans are intrinsically bound by communal values and "worth that demands duties and obligations to one another."[21] Strong ties to traditional cultural beliefs and values shape Africans' practices and more so their religious and sociopolitical affiliations. Specific cases can be drawn from countries such as Zambia, Nigeria, South Africa, Rwanda, Burundi, Uganda, and Kenya, which have experienced tribal-instigated flare-ups.

Attachment to culture, for instance, is foundational for many Africans who continue to value their traditional beliefs and practices which shape their identity. This may be attributed to the belief articulated in the Swahili proverb *mwacha mila ni mtumwa* ("someone who abandons his or her culture becomes a slave"). It is unfortunate, as Joseph Galgalo observes, that "African Christians are first Africans and then Christians, or just Christians, who also happen to be Africans and . . . although Christianity is widely followed, yet it often comes a poor second to the African Traditional Religion . . . It is only when conflicts or competition of sorts arises, that we can tell with certainty where [the] true loyalty of the African adherent lies."[22] This authenticates our argument that such communal attachment to culture requires a proper biblical evaluation with a view to developing an African sociopolitical theology that not only addresses the negative dimensions but also eradicates the undue dichotomy of separating African values of humanity from the core tenets of Christianity. This is a continuing challenge for the church to address. However, it will not be until the Christian faith has penetrated the core of African existence that it will be able to address the real and felt needs of Africans and will consequently be owned by them.

One of the strongest ties of community is ethnic affiliation. "While there is no universally accepted definition, ethnicity is generally characterized as a

---

19. B. J. van der Walt, *When African and Western Cultures Meet: From Confrontation to Appreciation* (Potchefstroom: Institute for Contemporary Christianity in Africa, 2006), 147.

20. Aseka, *Transformational Leadership*, 12.

21. Aseka, 116.

22. Joseph D. Galgalo, *African Christianity: The Stranger Within* (Eldoret, Kenya: Zapf Chancery Africa, 2012), 6.

sense of groups belonging, based on ideas of common origins, history, culture, language, experience and values . . . Most definitions of ethnicity emphasize 'the sharing of a "culture," the most notable aspect of which is language.'"[23] In most cases the identity of a given community is defined by ethnicity: a people group who speak the same language and share a common cultural history. Traditionally, they would be affiliated to a common ancestor with a shared religious heritage. Such a group would be identified as a tribe, clan, family, and house or home, signifying a very strong bond of belonging and identity. When those who share such identity meet at home or in the streets, or assemble in large gatherings, they speak in their mother tongue. The mother tongue, or the vernacular, is the language in which African people communicate most effectively, particularly as they use riddles and proverbs whose nuances are difficult if not impossible to replicate in another language. The significance of the vernacular as a unifying language has led to some scholars calling for its use in African Christianity. Two of the most notable Ghanaian African theologians, Kwame Bediako and John Pobee, have made a sustained argument for the significance and use of the vernacular as a unifying tool.[24] The significance of the use of mother-tongue or vernacular language in African societies is also deeply entrenched in African oral literature.[25] Their argument is hinged on the notion that the vernacular is not merely a cultural tenet but a theological necessity. While it may be argued that the vernacular unites a people group, the diversity of most contemporary African societies, coupled with the influence of education, poses a challenge for such calls. Nevertheless, this is the wealth of the diversity of African heritage which gives pride to the bond of unity that characterizes African communities.

Understood from this perspective, then, ethnicity is not in any way negative but rather a positive component that manifests community and identity. It is a rich and enviable aspect that gives credence to the bond of unity that characterizes most African societies. Any attempt to understand and engage meaningfully in the African sociopolitical framework must speak to this cardinal facet. Consequently, African political theology must be attested through interaction with the reality of African communal and ethnic

---

23. Graham K. Brown and Arnim Langer, "The Concept of Ethnicity: Strengths and Limitations for Quantitative Analysis," in *Ethnic Diversity and Economic Instability in Africa: Interdisciplinary Perspectives*, ed. Hiroyuki Hino (Cambridge: Cambridge University Press, 2012), 57.

24. Kwame Bediako, *Christianity in Africa: The Renewal of Non-Western Religion* (Edinburgh: Edinburgh University Press, 1995).

25. Ngugi wa Thiong'o, *Mother, Sing for Me: People's Theatre in Kenya* (London: Zed, 1989).

expressions. We must observe, though, that ethnic identity is not uniquely traditional as contemporary society, particularly the younger generation, has less affinity with their parental languages and seldom speaks in the mother tongue.

Ethnic identity and communal affiliations have been key factors in determining political alliances, thus creating an unwarranted politics of suspicion and mistrust in most African countries. Tribal attachment is a key cultural tenet that dictates virtually all aspects of a sociopolitical nature, especially when it comes to voting patterns and political appointments, or even appointment to particular civil or government responsibilities. Negative ethnicity or tribalism has been one of the major contributing factors to the violence witnessed in a number of African countries from time to time.

It is indeed unfortunate to see "how the essence of ethnicity has been transformed from a malleable cultural identity in the past to an antagonistic political solidarity protective of territory and supposed group interest today."[26] There are documented cases "both at national and local level, [where] politicians are known to have used historical land issues and ethnicity to whip up communities against each other in order to raise more votes."[27] Most people are lured to these tribal cleavages because they "assume that having a member of their own ethnic group in a position of power will increase their access to patronage resources."[28] Professional politicians have taken advantage of ethnicity to continue in their maneuvers of self-sustenance and propagation. It is sad to note how, because "the current national leadership is . . . driven by selfish interests and the pursuit of power through ethnic and regional mobilization, the political and economic elite do not endear hope to the people. At another level, the communities are themselves divided on the basis of clan and ethnicity as they struggle over meager resources."[29] Unfortunately, negative ethnicity[30] and a communal tendency have also been witnessed in

26. Bethwell Allan Ogot, "Essence of Ethnicity: An African Perspective," in Hino, *Ethnic Diversity*, 91.

27. Saida Yahya-Othman and Joseph sinde Warioba, *Moving the Kenyan Constitution Review Process Forward: A Report of the Fact-Finding Mission to Kenya* (Kampala: Fountain, 2007), 27.

28. Daniel N. Posner, *Institutions and Ethnic Politics in Africa* (Cambridge: Cambridge University Press, 2005), 91.

29. Kimani Njogu, *Youth and Peaceful Elections in Kenya* (Nairobi: Twaweza Communications, 2013), 5.

30. Eunice Kamaara, "Towards Christian National Identity in Africa: A Historical Perspective to the Challenge of Ethnicity to the Church in Kenya," *Studies in World Christianity* 16, no. 2 (2010): 128.

religious circles, sadly even in the manner in which the church manages its affairs. A number of churches and denominational groups, especially the Africa Independent/Indigenous Churches, are ethnic or tribal communities. Some even use their ethnic vernacular languages during worship services, thus closing out anyone who does not belong. Such negative semblance of the tribe, especially in our public and religious entities, needs to be challenged. However, human ethnic affiliations in and of themselves portend no evil and are a source of individual identity and belonging as derived from God's intent and purpose in creation. In this sense, theology must always uphold the supremacy of the Bible as it is read, interpreted, and applied within the African context. This is crucial because "in the Scriptures God stands revealed plainly as the author of nature, as the sustainer of human institutions (family, work, and government), and as the source of harmony, creativity, and beauty."[31] This implies that the political theology of the church must be based on a relevant reading, understanding, and interpretation of the Bible for the community of God's people of all ethnic affiliations.

C. Biblical

The reading of the Bible in Africa dates back to the first century AD. The articulation of early Christian theology was primarily an African endeavor. Charles Copher captures this notion: "Even before that portion of the Bible known as the Hebrew Scriptures, the Old Testament of the Christians had reached its final form around the year 100 A.D., [and people from] Africa [and] Jerusalem [were] reading from a version of those Scriptures that had been produced in the African city of Alexandria, Egypt."[32] It is unfortunate, though, that the manner in which some Africans have read, interpreted, and used the Bible in the past was influenced largely by the political chauvinism of the West. For instance, "the interpretation of the Bible among West Africans and their dispersed relatives was influenced by their white enslavers, especially with reference to the so-called, unbiblical curse upon Ham and other passages that could be used to uphold the enslavement of Black peoples."[33] This trend has since changed as African Christians read, in their languages, understand, and apply the Bible from their own context and perspective. The Bible is therefore

---

31. Mark Noll, *The Scandal of the Evangelical Mind* (Grand Rapids, MI: Eerdmans, 1994), 4.

32. Charles B. Copher, "The Bible and the African Experience: The Biblical Period," *The Journal of the Interdenominational Theological Center* 39, no. 1 (2014): 59.

33. Copher, "African Experience," 60.

a core source of authority for African Christians' understanding of their faith and practice. A number of theologians have written on the centrality of the Bible in Africa and have observed the diverse ways in which Africans read the Bible and the impact it has on their lives.[34] Although there is no unanimity on how the Bible is interpreted, for Africans the Bible is the word of God and is often read within their experiential context, giving "a spiritual haven for physical problems like economic hardships, political turmoil, social unrest and supernatural problems."[35] This is not to say that the Bible is an escapist tool that gives solace and thus endorses the perpetuation of human problems. It is rather a confirmation of the African holistic view of life where God is at the heart of an individual's life and speaks practically to all facets of life.

For political theology to be engaged in a relevant, viable, and authentically African context it must be centered on the Bible. How to bring the Bible to the fore is, however, one of the challenges facing the church in Africa today. The dilemma is always associated with the balance between biblical authority and other sources of authority. At the same time, Africa comprises different generations that are characterized by diverse values and interests. The older generation emerged from and is still deeply rooted in its respective African cultural traditions whose customs, values, and practices not only are held dear but also give identity to the individual within the community. The younger generation is shaped by the contemporary postmodern relativism that has less regard for traditional and cultural tenets and values. An authentic political theology has to take cognizance of and speak effectively to each of these generations.

The Bible should be read and applied in such a way that it speaks to these generations and the diversities of their worldviews and philosophies. Thus "theology in Africa today . . . has its own peculiar sets of circumstances in which it operates, and as such it seeks to work out its own solutions to deal with those peculiar contexts."[36] The Bible must be at the core of the development of a political theology that speaks to the uniqueness of the African context and its peoples. It addresses issues and questions that are embedded within the very core of African existence: poverty and corruption,[37] sickness, drought, lack

---

34. John S. Mbiti, *Bible and Theology in African Christianity* (Nairobi: Oxford University Press, 1986), 42.

35. Emmanuel Adow Obeng, "The Use of Biblical Critical Methods in Rooting the Scriptures in Africa," in *The Bible in African Christianity: Essays in Biblical Theology*, ed. H. W. Kinoti and John Mary Waliggo (Nairobi: Acton, 1997), 17.

36. John Parratt, *Reinventing Christianity: African Theology Today* (Grand Rapids, MI: Eerdmans, 1995), 24.

37. Mullei, *Corruption and Poverty*.

of and denial of basic social and civil services, injustice in the distribution of resources such as land and property ownership, favoritism, nepotism and lack of disbursement of legal justice, as well as bribery due to greed and bad political governance. These are issues facing most communities in Africa today, and the church must have a clearly defined theological rationale that does not relegate its responsibility to other institutions and organizations whose interests fall short of the divinely ordained biblical mandate. In this respect, then, a viable political theology must address from a biblical perspective such issues that the community grapples with.

The church in Africa is thus faced with "a clamant demand for an interpretation of the Christian faith in a sanguine hope that such an interpretation, when produced, would provide the means of bringing home to Africans the truths of the Christian gospel in an idiom related to the African situation."[38] Desmond Tutu echoes this:

> A truly relevant theology was one that addressed the issues of a particular community. There could therefore be no final theology, since the questions, the contexts, were forever changing. A theology that was of any use should not, certainly initially, be striving after universal validity, but should, in a sense, glory in its inbuilt obsolescence as determined by the scandal of its particularity. It should answer the questions raised by this community in this specific setting. It must forever be trying to make sense of the existential conundrums of this group, the life and death issues raised there, with the ultimate reference point being the revelation of God in our Lord and Saviour Jesus Christ.[39]

The articulation of this theology calls for decisiveness on the part of the church in separating its focus from external encumbrances and the African cultural context. This tension creates a dilemma, as illustrated through a graphic picture of "Mumo," a graduate of a Bible school in Africa who is torn between two worlds:

> [One world is] the world of Christian faith represented by the Bible he studies, the church where he worships, and a special religious vocabulary filled with words that blaze with personal meaning, words like, "born again," "justified," "Spirit-filled," and

---

38. Parratt, *Reinventing Christianity*, 14.

39. Desmond M. Tutu, "Dark Days: Episcopal Ministry in Times of Repression, 1976–1996," *Journal of Theology for Southern Africa* 118 (March 2004): 32.

above all, "saved." Mumo was ushered into this new world of
faith . . . in a dramatic conversion experience. This is the world
of Christ, the gospel, the Spirit. It is a world of light which fills
him with great peace and satisfaction . . . [The other world is]
the world of African culture represented by the name he bears,
the ancestry to which he belongs, and the headlines of the daily
newspaper, alive with political, economic, intellectual and social
pulsations. The vocabulary of this world is filled with words
like "tradition," "spirits," "development," "poverty," "cultural
authenticity," "selfhood" and "non-alignment." He was ushered
into this world of culture twenty-five years ago at his birth. It is a
world of richness, a black richness, like dark, fertile soil.[40]

His dilemma relates to his struggles with the crisis of the "yawning gap between
the two worlds he loves. His search is for a theology which bridges the chasm
between his Christ and his culture. His search is for an African evangelical
theology, a theology which bridges this gap by applying the truths of the world
of the lordship of Jesus Christ, as taught in the Scripture, to the world of African
culture, issues and problems."[41] The Bible should therefore be understood
through the grid of African reality for this reality to be reflected in the light
of the truth of the Bible.

Each theology is shaped by the social structures and values it encounters
in any given context. In this respect, the church will have to grapple with
the influences that inform its hermeneutics. In teaching, understanding, and
interpreting the Bible, the church ought to draw principles that will help
in guiding its theological conclusions and practices. Such an approach will
demand that, although influenced by traditions, the church will wrestle with
the scriptural text, in its entirety, as the only basis upon which any meaningful
theological discussion can emanate. By so doing, the church will be wary of
adopting irrelevant and unauthenticated theologies drawn from contexts whose
issues are significantly different from those facing its own setting. The Bible
is, therefore, a requirement for the development of African political theology.

A relevant political theology must arise out of a truly Christian and
African mind that reads and engages the Bible with African values and cultural
concepts. One reality the church cannot ignore is the integration of biblical
truth to specific cultural contexts. As Robert Schreiter says, "Only a theology

---

40. "What Is African Evangelical Theology?," editorial, *East Africa Journal of Evangelical Theology* 2, no. 1 (1983): 1.

41. Editor, "African Evangelical Theology," 1.

firmly rooted in a culture can be genuinely prophetic in that same culture . . .
Prophecy is effective when it reorganizes knowledge already part of the culture.
To stand completely outside is to be ignored. Thus the more contextually
rooted a theology, the more acute can be its prophetic voice and action."[42]
This implies that a biblically based political theology must be socially and
culturally authenticated for it to be valid and relevant for the church in Africa.

Due to the complexity of the contemporary structure and composition of
the African church, coupled with the ever-changing sociocultural and political
context, developing the church's theology must be an ongoing process. This
theology must be true to the biblical text and at the same time sensitive to the
diversity of the different cultures constituting the African populace. Schreiter is
right in saying that "the dramatic increase in the number of cultures now making
up the church, all seeking a Christian identity, compounded by their struggles
to be freed from socioeconomic and political oppression, gives a particular
urgency to developing a greater sensitivity to theology and its context."[43] It is
imperative, therefore, that the church understands the complexity of its own
political context. Church leaders, pastors, and theologians need to work with
civic leaders and interact on a daily basis with the people in their struggles
as they seek to make ends meet, visiting and talking with them in all sectors
of life: at home, in hospitals, prisons, workplaces, at social venues, and in the
marketplaces. This is an important approach, since "the place in the social
structure in which one works is an important part of the theologian's life,
greatly influencing what he or she thinks about a given question. No theologian
can legitimately think he or she knows another situation without honest
dialogue with concrete believers who live in that particular social location."[44]
Our concern here is that the African church should develop a well-rounded
theology that will not only address concrete issues in a truly African manner
but is also informed by an authentic reading, understanding, interpretation,
and application of the Bible. This kind of theology is to be owned by the people
whom it addresses so that they can identify themselves as part of what God
is doing in the life of his church. In this way, the church will be visible on the
sociopolitical scene of its context. It is only then that we can talk of an effective
political theology of the church in Africa that is biblical.

---

42. Clemens Sedmak, *Doing Local Theology: A Guide for Artisans of a New Humanity*
(Maryknoll, NY: Orbis, 2002), 16–17.

43. Schreiter, *Constructing Local Theologies*, 75.

44. Sedmak, *Doing Local Theology*, 96.

2

Trends in African Political History

The African political context is intricately connected with the history that shaped the lives of the people in ancient Africa. As is true in other contexts, African history has contributed greatly to the present reality of which the church is a part and which it needs to interrogate.[1] This history displays the fabric that has woven Africans' way of life with regard to their cultures, religions and beliefs, family ties, and tribal as well as ethnic affinities which contribute to shaping their identity. Diverse factors contributed to the making of African history, and more so to the African political context. In our discussion of the political context, we shall look at trends that contributed to the formation of this political history. Among the key factors that have impacted African political structures is colonialism. In order to appreciate the impact of colonialism we will look first at slavery and its effect in the sociopolitical and racial disparagement that accompanied it, both among African societies as well as between African and European societies. We shall then look at the precolonial history, which will give us an idea of the traditional African political structure that existed prior to the advent of colonialism. The different African tribal groups had their own way of life that demonstrated their polity, beliefs, and values. This is the structure that the arrival of Western domination subjugated and utilized in its colonial and Christianization missions.

Colonialism affected the African context in many ways, and these effects continue to shape African life today. Colonialism is an important period because it introduced new sociopolitical systems and ways of thinking that shook the cohesiveness of society and created animosity among the various ethnic groups, as we shall discuss. This animosity gave rise to antagonism and

---

1. Clement Chinkambako Abenguni Majawa, "Church as Conscience of the State: Christian Witness in Politics for the Transformation of Africa," *African Ecclesiastical Review* 56, no. 2–3 (n.d.): 152.

resistance, which resulted in the formation of freedom-fighting movements such as the Mau Mau in Kenya. Colonialism was also instrumental in the founding of Christianity, which became closely associated with Western civilization. Colonialism and Christianity with its Western structures have together greatly shaped the prevailing sociopolitical context in virtually all African countries. An understanding of colonialism, therefore, provides a perspective on the postcolonial structure in which Africans, after independence, inherited the colonial way of life which was regarded as sophisticated and civilized, with its plethora of evils. This is reminiscent of stories that were told of African leaders, who would be described, in a derogatory way, as whites with a black skin.

Numerous historical trends have contributed to the diversity of politics in modern Africa. In this sense, African countries have very varied political structures, such that we cannot talk of African politics as a single entity. It would also be misleading to say that African countries have a similar political system or share the same political history, since there are several systems and they are varied and unique.[2] Most studies on African history have focused on the period after the European onslaught, yet a proper trajectory of African history goes back to the vast precolonial history. This distortion may be attributed to the fact that the historical accounts were written by Europeans, since Africans disseminated information orally, which also explains the fact that the accounts had a Christo-European bias.[3] This is well captured by Philip Curtin:

> The importance of pseudo-scientific racism for the study of African history lies in the fact that racism was most prominent at precisely the period when Europeans conquered and colonized Africa. The colonizers who had the best opportunity to investigate the African past, assumed (as a by-product of their racial attitudes) that Africa could have no history worth investigating. When European historians wrote about Africa, they usually confined their study to the activity of their own people. Thus what passed for African history was really only the history of Europeans in Africa. Some of it was good history, and some bad, but it left the impression that no other history of Africa was known – or could be discovered.[4]

---

2. Chris Allen, "Understanding African Politics," *Review of African Political Economy* 22, no. 65 (1995): 301–2.

3. Friday M. Mbon, "Response to Christianity in Pre-Colonial and Colonial Africa: Some Ulterior Motives," *Mission Studies* 4, no. 1 (1987): 43.

4. Philip D. Curtin, *African History* (New York: Macmillan, 1964), 4.

The precolonial period gives us a view of a continent that was characterized by diverse ethnic ties that were fluid and flexible, whereby individuals or whole communities could be assimilated into other ethnic groups, adopt and adapt their practices, beliefs, and values, and easily blend in and become amalgamated.[5] The colonial political system utilized some of the structures of the African cultural values, although in general it was not constructed from an African worldview. It is necessary for authentic African historical experiences to be brought out more clearly in such a way that the pains and struggles, joys and celebrations, of our ancestors and the intricate structure of our heritage can speak to our present, for "until the lions tell their tale, the tale of the hunt will always glorify the hunter."

One precolonial trend that impacted the political structure of Africa was the seventeenth- and eighteenth-century transatlantic slave trade.

A. Slavery and the Slave Trade

When the history of Africa is told, Europe must feature because of the many interweaving connections between the two continents. Europe has shaped Africa in many ways, but the introduction of the slave trade made the greatest impact on sub-Saharan Africa.[6] Understanding the significance of the transatlantic and trans-Saharan slave trade is crucial for understanding the African political context because of the impact of the slave trade on the political scene and the socioeconomic life in the region. It is important to note, though, that some African countries already had systems of domestic servants who could pass as local slaves hired as laborers. However, although Curtin argues that a form of "slave trade within Africa existed before Europeans appeared,"[7] there is no sustained empirical study that shows slavery to have been a formative structured framework among the traditional African societies. Martin Klein, for instance, alludes to the fact that most African societies on the coast of Upper Guinea had no practice of slavery until it was introduced by the transatlantic trade.[8] Also, among the tribal groups of Congo, African slavery had different manifestations. Most of the slaves were those who had

---

5. Patrick Chabal, *Culture Troubles: Politics and the Interpretation of Meaning* (Chicago: University of Chicago Press, 2006), 114–15.

6. Curtin, *African History*, 21.

7. Curtin, 43.

8. Martin A. Klein, *Slavery and Colonial Rule in French West Africa* (Cambridge: Cambridge University Press, 1998), 41.

been captured in warfare, while others were criminals, debtors, or those "given away by their families as part of a dowry settlement."[9] This intra-African slavery entrenched in certain cultural practices and relationships would later be translated into a catastrophic global genocide of Africans, sanctioned by the custodians of the ideals and values of Christianity.

The Portuguese arrived in Congo in the fifteenth century first as missionaries, but later, when they discovered the enterprising trade of slavery, their initial mission was abandoned altogether. Hochschild states that slave fever seized the Portuguese in the kingdom of the Congo, to the extent that

> the lust for slave profits engulfed even some of the priests, who abandoned their preaching, took black women as concubines, kept slaves themselves, and sold their students and converts into slavery. The priests who strayed from the fold stuck to their faith in one way, however: after the Reformation they tried to ensure that none of their human goods ended up in Protestant hands. It was surely not right, said one, "for persons baptized in the Catholic church to be sold to peoples who are enemies of their faith."[10]

The brutality of slavery in the Congo was further escalated by the Belgian King Leopold II, who was also driven by greed for money (through brutal and extensive slave trading) and power, while masquerading as an antislavery crusader. Through treacherous and conniving wit and political stratagems, King Leopold II acquired control of the vast central African Congo Basin and set up his capital at Boma, a major seaport center of slave trading. Capitalizing on the explorations of John Rowlands, better known as Henry Morton Stanley, the first explorer to cross the continent of Africa from the east to the west coast, King Leopold II signed "treaties" with hundreds of Congo Basin chiefs giving him "a complete trading monopoly, even as he placated European and American questioners by insisting that he was opening up Africa to free trade. More important, chiefs signed over their land to Leopold, and they did so for almost nothing."[11] Just as in other African contexts, during colonialism the chiefs entered into some form of agreement with the Europeans, not knowing that they were transferring to them the full rights of ownership of their land.

---

9. Adam Hochschild, *King Leopold's Ghost: A Story of Greed, Terror, and Heroism in Colonial Africa* (Boston: Houghton Mifflin, 1998), 10–11.

10. Hochschild, *King Leopold's Ghost*, 10.

11. Hochschild, 71.

This was a precursor of the many examples of European subjugation of Africa that led to the dehumanization of its people.

Scholars debate the material importance of slavery and its ensuing impact. There are those who, like Philip Curtin, argue that the effect of slavery was political and that it was not purely an economic activity that benefited slave merchants and suppliers alike. While the political effect was important, by and large slavery was about economic gains, not because slaves were of more economic value than other items of trade, but because of the supply and demand at both ends of the trade: Europeans needed a labor force[12] and Africans needed provisions of weapons and other commodities for warriors and servants of the state.[13]

The Ashanti tribe, for instance, was one of the best-organized and intractable communities the British Protectorate had to deal with along the African Gold Coast that was involved in slave trading. Known for their human sacrifice as part of their traditional religious practices, the Ashanti tribe were also notorious for inflicting heavy defeats on their foes.[14] The British quest for the abolition of the slave trade which had benefited the Ashanti was met with stiff opposition. One of the chief abolitionists was Sir Charles MacCarthy, who repudiated the Ashanti tribe for their atrocities toward other tribes. When the Ashanti invaded the Fanti tribe, MacCarthy marshalled some white men to join Fanti natives to fight against the Ashanti, but he was deserted by his allies and eventually killed. Maxwell observes, "The Ashanti were most impressed by his effort – no Briton had ever stood up to them before. So they cut off his head and took it home to Kumasi, where the skull was turned into a ceremonial drinking cup. The king used to swear oaths on it on particularly important occasions."[15] The economic drive that enhanced the slave trade would result in a significant contribution "to a complex process of political transformation."[16]

Prior to the transatlantic slave trade, slavery for provision of labor in the Mediterranean plantations had been a normal regional practice, making use of prisoners of war between Christians and Muslims. This acquisition of slaves would later become a global phenomenon due to economic factors and the complexity with which it manifested. The Europeans moved across

---

12. Philip D. Curtin et al., *African History: From Earliest Times to Independence* (London: Longman, 1995), 185.

13. Klein, *Slavery and Colonial Rule*, 37.

14. Leigh Maxwell, *The Ashanti Ring: Sir Garnet Wolseley's Campaigns 1870–1882* (London: Leo Cooper in association with Secker & Warburg, 1985), 10.

15. Maxwell, *Ashanti Ring*, 8.

16. Klein, *Slavery and Colonial Rule*, 39.

the Atlantic along with their plantation concept. The Spanish, Portuguese, and Dutch established vast plantations across South America and the Caribbean Islands.[17] Demand for labor in the plantations could not be met by the indigenous American Indian slaves, and this resulted in the importation of slave labor from Africa. Coupled with this was the ability of Africans to withstand tropical and hot climates, as well as their acquired immunity to certain diseases, such as smallpox, malaria, and yellow fever,[18] making them preferred as slaves. European explorations along the coastal regions of Africa enabled the opening up of trade routes in the interior and the establishment of slave trading ports along the coastal strip. There is evidence of an increased level of commercial activities along the coastal towns of the continent, where merchants exchanged goods with Africans and in return obtained slaves for Arab, European, Spanish, and American labor markets. The establishment of other industrial and commercial enterprises, including mining, spread the need for labor beyond the plantation complex. With the North America importation of the plantation concept, along with the concept of slavery from the South, the impact of the slave trade escalated to a global peak in the 1780s, resulting in a major outcry regarding the brutal atrocities meted out on the slaves. Most European countries gradually outlawed the trade until it was finally abolished, although the oppressive master–slave relationship lingered on during the generations that followed.[19] One of the impacts of slavery on African society was the fragmentation of ethnic and nation-state ties that colonialism would intensify with the political division of the continent along national state boundaries.

B. Precolonial Political Structure

Prior to the advent of Western domination of Africa, and especially the arrival of colonialism, African societies were characterized by communal or tribal sociopolitical structures through which members participated, directly or indirectly, in the governing of the community and the daily running of the society's affairs. Scholars debate the categorization of precolonial political

---

17. Curtin et al., *African History*, 185.

18. Philip D. Curtin, *Cross-Cultural Trade in World History* (Cambridge: Cambridge University Press, 1984), 207.

19. Curtin et al., *African History*, 186–87.

systems and structures.[20] While each group of people living in specific regions of Africa had a different socioeconomic system of survival and sustenance based on their locality and environment, generally African tribes were subsistence farmers, hunters, or gatherers. A number of those who were pastoralists moved from one region to another in search of pasture and safe havens.[21] The land was expansive, and population flow and migration from one region to another was common.

As a result, "different circumstances produced different societies with different traditions, customs and politics, and these societies rose, fell and adapted as the centuries passed."[22] Each of these societal groups had its own self-governing political structure that shaped its internal polity and sustenance and was characterized by features and values that became the essence of tribal politics. Whether organized as states or stateless, these African societies had political structures that derived from their contextual environment. They coexisted as individual communities with diverse sociopolitical and economic frameworks of leadership and governance.[23] The Maasai of Kenya and Tanzania, for instance, utilized the sociopolitical and cultural methods of "fission and fusion" that enabled them to be "formed and reformed, expanded and contracted."[24] These social structures enabled them to shape their cultural affinities, making it difficult for a person to be excluded from cultural community ties. It was very difficult for someone to depart from these formal and informal cultural structures, which were safeguarded by a strong leadership and oral tradition, without facing resistance and serious consequences.[25] Africans propagated their cultural values and self-sustenance through these oral structures. It would therefore be preposterous to assume

---

20. M. Fortes and E. E. Evans-Pritchard, *African Political Systems* (London: Oxford University Press, 1940).

21. Dorothy Louise Hodgson, *The Church of Women: Gendered Encounters between Maasai and Missionaries* (Bloomington, IN: Indiana University Press, 2005), 7.

22. Alex Thomson, *An Introduction to African Politics* (London/New York: Routledge, 2000), 9.

23. Eunice Kamaara, "Towards Christian National Identity in Africa: A Historical Perspective to the Challenge of Ethnicity to the Church in Kenya," *Studies in World Christianity* 16, no. 2 (2010): 129.

24. Hodgson, *Church of Women*, 7.

25. Gordon R. Mullenix and John Mpaayei, "Matonyok: A Case Study of the Interaction of Evangelism and Community Development among the Keekonyokie Maasai of Kenya," *Missiology* 12, no. 3 (1984): 332.

that Africa was a continent that lacked structures that inculcated knowledge and values that have continued to evolve.[26]

The various family groups, clans, and tribes were informally organized into "kingdoms" or "governments" that took care of their communal sociopolitical affairs as well as protecting their interests at any given time. Intercommunity conflicts were not based on territorial occupation but the economic advantages of acquiring gold, slaves, and livestock.[27] It should be observed, though, that prior to the advent of colonialism, these communities had their own political and social structures[28] which safeguarded the interests of each individual within the community. The kingdom of the Congo, for example, was a society that comprised diverse groups ranging from large and well-organized entities to small tribal groups that had no formal political structures, such as "the Pygmies of the Ituri rain forest, who lived in small bands with no chiefs and no formal structure of government."[29]

It is important to note that these structures had religious significance, since the physical and spiritual realms are inseparable in African cosmology. It is in this sense that the "patterns and the sanctions for political organizations were often derived from a religious cosmology and the mythology that expressed and supported it, and the political leader or head was the channel through which ultimate or cosmic forces operated for the welfare of the society."[30] African chiefs were the tribal kings who epitomized tribal identity and had many responsibilities, central to which was their religious function.[31] Among the Ghanaians of West Africa, for instance, the chief was vested with absolute authority over his people. There was a designated process of choosing a chief which involved the community. The chief was "chosen from a particular family – the royal family – of the tribe by the queen mother whose choice is approved by the elders of the land and the common people before he is installed . . . The chief is sometimes called the divine king because of the

---

26. Michael Omolewa, "Traditional African Modes of Education: Their Relevance in the Modern World," *International Review of Education* 53, no. 5 (Nov. 2007): 594.

27. Thomson, *Introduction to African Politics*, 11.

28. Ludeki Chweya, "Reversing Rural Poverty in an African Country: A Review of the Kenyan Policy Regime" (paper presented at the Development Policy Management Forum, Nairobi, 26 October 2006).

29. Hochschild, *King Leopold's Ghost*, 72.

30. Mbon, "Response to Christianity," 44.

31. Kwasi Addo Sampong, "Traditional Governance and Social Transformation through the Gospel in Ghana," *Ogbomoso Journal of Theology* 17, no. 3 (2012): 117.

sacredness of his person and his paraphernalia."[32] The stool on which the chief sat was a symbol of authority. The "Akans traditionally consider a stool as a symbol of the soul of society and the chief's stool as the soul or spirit of the nation. This is why the chief becomes sacred and is called Nana (Ancestor) as soon as he is *enstooled*. Also the chief's stool is believed to be a resting place as well as the symbol of the chief's soul."[33] Among the Yoruba in Nigeria, these chiefs, known as *oba*, were highly regarded, and each one "occupied the stool or throne of an area as a natural ruler, the custodian of tradition of his land and the father to all his citizens."[34]

One of the many sociopolitical structures found in Nigeria is the diversity of religious groups, particularly of Islamic background, who were inhabitants of the region in precolonial times. The establishment of the Sokoto Caliphate among the Hausa and Fulani tribes of Northern Nigeria can be dated as far back as the sixteenth century and was characterized by numerous ethnic and religious wars among various tribal communities. Most of these tribal communities experienced frequent raids from their neighbors besides numerous internal political wrangles and coups d'état. As the indigenous peoples of the Northern Nigeria region, the Hausa and Fulani tribes have historically been closely related in terms of their cultural, religious, and sociopolitical structure. One of the best-known groups is the "Sokoto" in northwest Hausaland, which was established as a camp in 1809 over a five-year period of the Islamic "jihad" of the sheikh.[35] Zakyi Ibrahim writes, "In 1804 C.E., Dan Fodio, a Muslim intellectual whose orthodoxy and zealousness are always highlighted, mounted an attack against the Hausa chiefs of Northern Nigeria, and together with his companions, established an Islamic state on Hausa/Fulani land in Nigeria."[36] Their zeal was driven by the need for religious reforms that focused on social issues, particularly family relationships and the place of women. The intertribal wars saw the establishment of many strongholds across the Fulani region. It was in this context that Dan Fodio, son of Bello, was appointed the *'āmil* or deputy for the area of Lajinge when he was about twenty-six years old. His responsibilities included safeguarding the area, expanding their territory through raids, and maintaining justice by upholding the law. He was "to avoid

---

32. Sampong, "Traditional Governance," 117.

33. Sampong, 118.

34. Rafiu Ibrahim Adebayo, "The Role of Traditional Rulers in the Islamization of Osun State (Nigeria)," *Journal for Islamic Studies* 7, no. 30 (2010): 61.

35. Murray Last, *The Sokoto Caliphate* (New York: Humanities Press, 1967), lix.

36. M. Zakyi Ibrahim, "Islam in Africa: The Impact of Dan Fodio's Reforms on the Muslim Family," *Hamdard Islamicus* 29, no. 2 (June 2006): 69.

insulting, striking, imprisoning or, above all, killing anyone without due process of law; to guard against bribes, illegal taxes and lavish spending; instead, he was to welcome righteous men and listen to their advice, to receive travelers and help the poor. Finally he had to obey the Caliph, and his people had to obey him or he would be replaced; his only purpose was to help in maintaining Islam."[37] From this list of duties, it is apparent that the elaborate precolonial structure of the Fulani Muslim state placed value on the maintenance of cohesion within the society, while respecting the rights of individuals. These are values replicated in traditional African societies that have, at their roots, a recognition of human worth. The modern religious extremism manifested by Boko Haram insurgents is a total contrast to the ideals of traditional Islam in Nigeria, as well as to African cultural mores.

The Caliphate had a well-established and well-defined leadership structure that the community was mandated to adhere to and accord due allegiance and obedience to, failure in which resulted in severe punishment including execution. Well-documented instructions were taught to members of the community in mosques or seminars. The community was categorized into ten groups, each with different roles and responsibilities for the well-being of all. The "real member" was supposed to be "guided not by the world but by God, giving up property, power and family for the life to come."[38] In this sense, then, the precolonial political structure demonstrated a society that was well organized and stratified, with tribal states that were well defined and coordinated their sociopolitical lives justly within their religious confines.

The kingdom of the Congo Basin is another precolonial African kingdom that illustrates the traditional African political structure. This kingdom spanned about 300 square miles, an area which today is occupied by several countries.[39] The kingdom may have existed since the twelfth century and had a variety of tribal groups, some with a structured system of clan elders vested with the election of the king, and others without formal structures. One of the structured groups was the Congo. The capital of this kingdom was situated on the "town of *Mbaaza* Kongo – *mbaaza* means 'court' – on a commanding hilltop . . . today just on the Angolan side of the Angola–Congo boarder."[40] In 1491, "an expedition of awed Portuguese priests and emissaries" arrived at "the court of the Kongo [sic] king [marking] the beginning of the first sustained encounter

---

37. Last, *Sokoto Caliphate*, 75–77.
38. Last, 59.
39. Hochschild, *King Leopold's Ghost*, 8.
40. Hochschild, 8.

between Europeans and a black African nation."[41] The king, ManiKongo, who was adorned with animal parts (zebra-tail whip, skins, and heads of baby animals), is said to have "dispensed justice, received homage, and reviewed his troops under a fig tree in a large public square. Whoever approached him had to do so on all fours. On pain of death, no one was allowed to watch him eat or drink. Before he did either, an attendant struck two iron poles together, and anyone in sight had to lie face down on the ground."[42] Save for the archaic display, there is an indication here that the Congo kingdom was also formidable and well defined, with a sociopolitical structure.

An understanding of the precolonial political structure and the wealth of the empires in Africa would be incomplete without mentioning one of the most discussed traditional African kingdoms that bore varying cultural symbols of authority, power, and dread. The Zulu kingdom was an "independent polity in southeastern Africa established by Shaka in the 1810s and ruled by his descendants until 1879."[43] The beginning of this kingdom is identified with Shaka kaSenzangakhona, who is said to have assumed leadership in the form of the Zulu chiefdom through the assistance of "neighboring Mthethwa paramount, Dingiswayo."[44] Shaka consolidated power and control after conquering the neighbors around him and establishing a vast and formidable kingdom that dominated the entire "region between the Phongolo and Thukela rivers."[45] In order to entrench himself in power, Shaka decisively edged out his close male relatives and elevated his distant kin to high positions, while surrounding himself with loyal, powerful generals and advisers who were not related to the ruling house.[46] The tensions created by this alienating tactic led to his assassination by two of his brothers in 1828.

The king sought to consolidate his authority and establish a new kingdom through the *amabutho* system, which entailed gathering young men and socializing them to identify the Zulu king as their ritual leader and the one to make decisions on their behalf with regard to their social life. They were to swear allegiance to him and the Zulu tribe. Shaka enforced the demands of his rule arbitrarily by creating fear among his subjects through "carefully managed

---

41. Hochschild, 8.

42. Hochschild, 9.

43. Carolyn Hamilton, *Terrific Majesty: The Power of Shaka Zulu and the Limits of Historical Invention* (Cambridge, MA: Harvard University Press, 1998), xi.

44. Hamilton, *Terrific Majesty*, 48.

45. Hamilton, 48.

46. Hamilton, 48.

displays of despotism and brutal justice at his court, using terror as the basis for absolute rule across a huge kingdom."[47] His frugal commercial enterprises only strengthened his polity, although different accounts by historians and early European explorers and traders who came into contact with the Zulu king depict him as a tyrant and monster.[48] The authority of the Zulu kingdom as seen in the installation of successive chiefs or kings was legitimated by the colonial powers that were bent on decimating the tribal states and their kings. This is illustrated, for instance, by the installation ceremony of Cetshwayo after the death of his father, Zulu King Mpande, in 1872, which "was presided over by Theophilus Shepstone, secretary for the native affairs (SAN) in the neighboring British colony of Natal."[49] The Zulu kingdom has continued to impact the sociopolitical life of the people of South Africa as well as their governments and South African politics as a whole. Even with such authority and power, the Zulu kingdom was still considered inferior by the British colony, typical of the colonial mindset across the continent, as we shall demonstrate in our discussion below. Precolonial Africa was therefore not a vast empty jungle, but had diverse communities with well-established political structures, albeit characterized by wars and different customs, beliefs, and practices with rules and regulations that helped maintain their polity.

As we have noted, the traditional values that characterized precolonial Africa were concerned with communal welfare. It would not be right to think, though, that these structures lacked the weaknesses and flaws that would negate the upholding of human value and dignity. Personal greed and desire for success is common to all humanity. However, establishing structures in order to dominate others was a foreign concept which disordered traditional African values. The influx of European colonizers in Africa with their incipient Western mindset "superimposed on top of these precolonial institutions new state organizations borrowed from the Western historical experiences that are identified with today's African countries."[50]

The colonial masters did, however, utilize the precolonial political African structures and systems, albeit with a new Western focus and an intent to dominate African sociopolitical life. Upon arrival in Yorubaland in Nigeria, for example, "the colonial masters met a well-organised and well-established

---

47. Hamilton, 50.

48. Hamilton, 148.

49. Hamilton, 72.

50. Nicola Gennaioli and Ilia Rainer, "Precolonial Centralization and Institutional Quality in Africa" (paper, 2005).

system of government and so allowed the status quo to remain with minor modifications. They coopted the 'obas' into the colonial government system, especially when they had shortage of administrative personnel."[51] This African chiefdom mentality continues to characterize modern politics in Africa today, where leaders behave like traditional chiefs. The negative side of this is that since traditional chiefdom was not a temporal or a term office, African leaders cling to power with the support of their kith and kin, who rally massive support behind them. In the same way, some church leaders have unfortunately tended to assume similar chiefdom authority over their individual congregations, commandeering autocratic authority. Chiefs were not questioned; thus leaders in our societies can do what they want with impunity. Traditional chiefs owned everything; thus political leaders (modern chiefs) do whatever they can to amass great wealth. Due to the dynamism of African cultures, the influence of Western domination through colonialism had very different effects on these traditional African structures.

C. Colonial Political Structure

The colonial period in Africa was relatively short but it had an immense effect in restructuring the African way of life in every aspect, ranging from internal and local politics to international relations and policies. Tribal boundaries were realigned with the introduction of hegemonic state territories, and human relations were aligned with the new societal interests driven by strong political and economic ties to the state. African countries were gambled for gold, diamonds, and other natural resources by Western settlers, explorers, and missionaries alike. Missionaries preached the gospel and introduced Western education systems[52] and health care practices, but, ill-informed, they disdained the diverse wealth and cultural values of African sociopolitical structures. Africans therefore adopted colonial structures which were not only in conflict with, but actually destroyed, their traditional value systems. The missionaries were convinced that Africans needed to be liberated by Western culture from their native "uncivilized" cultural practices. Christianity therefore became the tool by which this cultural change would be effected. The colonizers' severe denunciation of African culture in favor of their Western practices is indicative of their narcissistic attitude and condescending approach to Africans and their values. Their attitude was heavily criticized by many African nationalists, who

---

51. Adebayo, "Role of Traditional Rulers," 61.
52. Omolewa, "African Modes of Education," 594.

saw it as a plot to undermine African human values.[53] This has significant implications for Christian missionary thought, a topic we shall engage with later in our discussion. Thus the colonial domination of the continent and consolidation of control over the Africans had far-reaching ramifications.

Colonial Domination

The colonial domination of Africa is a story of veiled and implicit wrongs committed by Westerners that led to African dispossession of their land. In South Africa, for instance, the Dutch and English carried out a major onslaught on the native South African Khoikhoi and San, who were easily decimated, and the militant Xhosas and Zulus, who fought fierce fights over two and a half centuries. While the Africans put up a spirited defense, the superiority of Western weapons prevailed over the valiant African warriors, leading to the defeat of Chief Bambatha in 1906 and the eventual occupation of African land by the white Europeans.[54] The preceding slave trade had already created major racial rifts between the white Europeans and the black Africans, paving the way for the machinations of white superiority. This wave of the political scramble for Africa swept through most African countries, bringing European settlers who acquired the prime fertile land, conveniently dispossessed the Africans, and established themselves through their home-based political powers.

The French colonial domination of West Africa was established with its first territorial administration in Senegal, with the first French governor being appointed in 1854; this became the first colony of France in West Africa.[55] The French West Africa federation comprised "seven territories – Senegal, Côte d'Ivoire, Niger, Dahomey (now Benin), French Sudan (now Mali), French Guinea, and Mauritania – as well as . . . Togo."[56] In order to entrench itself, the colony was divided into many small regions called *arrondissements* under the military command of French officers known as *commandants d'arrondissement*, with native chiefs, "the *bracks, burs* and *damels*." Further, the *arrondissements*

---

53. Robert Strayer, *The Making of Mission Communities in East Africa: Anglicans and Africans in Colonial Kenya, 1875–1935*. London: Heinemann; Albany, NY: State University of New York Press, 1978), 77.

54. Tandi Gcabashe, "From Luthuli to Mandela: The Struggle Goes On," *The Journal of the Interdenominational Theological Center* 16, no. 1–2 (1988–1989): 175.

55. William B. Cohen, *Rulers of Empire: The French Colonial Service in Africa* (Stanford, CA: Hoover Institution Press, 1971), 9.

56. Ruth Ginio, *French Colonialism Unmasked: The Vichy Years in French West Africa* (Lincoln, NE: University of Nebraska Press, 2006), 3.

were divided into *cercles* which were headed by traditional rulers known as *chefs de cercle*.[57] While this model was later modified, with new administrative units such as *commandants de cercle* introduced, it became the pattern for French colonial administration of black Africa and Madagascar.[58] The chiefs, as Ginio rightly observes, were intrinsically tied to African "tradition" more than to any other institution in French colonial discourse which was central to the distribution of power.[59] Each French *commandant de cercle* was given powers to "transform into reality on the local scene the schemes of his superiors either in the colonial capitals or in Paris."[60] Consequently, with the decree of the *Code de l'indigénat* on 30 September 1887, the colonial administrators were given executive and judicial powers to discipline "all 'natives' who were not French citizens,"[61] which they did with great brutality. This marked the introduction of colonial authoritarianism: pervasive and absolute rule with hostility toward local structures. The paternalist attitude of colonialism also emerged in the manner in which the French censored many social structures so as to limit the locals' identification with their masters.[62] This administrative structure indicates that the French utilized the precolonial African political structure but placed themselves in the highest rank in the pyramid of authority and power for ease of domination. The colonial prejudice of the French was clearly demonstrated by their belief that this conquest would bring about enlightenment and the humane administration of the colony, as indicated in words believed to have been spoken by the colonial administrator Faidherbe toward the end of his mission: "Our intentions are pure and noble, our course is just; the future cannot fail us."[63] This attitude was replicated among other European colonial regimes across the African continent, with their Christianizing intent that was often mixed with domination and exploitation of the vast wealth and natural resources of Africa which continued to embellish their own nations.

---

57. Ginio, *French Colonialism*, 11. Ginio observes that "this system of administration was built in a pyramidal shape; at the apex was the governor, at a lower echelon two to seven commandants, under each of this four or five regional chiefs, and finally the village chiefs; it was the system that was to be characteristic of French rule in West Africa, as the *cercle* itself was to become the unit of French territorial administration in West Africa" (12).

58. Cohen, *Rulers of Empire*, 57.

59. Ginio, *French Colonialism*, 117.

60. Cohen, *Rulers of Empire*, 67.

61. Cohen, 68.

62. Ginio, *French Colonialism*, 40.

63. Cohen, *Rulers of Empire*, 9.

The colonial domination of Kenya is yet another demonstration of the devastation the Africans endured. The first colonial settlers in the Kenyan "White Highlands" included Lord Delamere (1897), John Boyes (1898), and Sir Charles Eliot (1901), "first commissioner for British East Africa."[64] This British domination was instigated by the British government which invited settlers from England and South Africa to farm in the prime Highlands of Kenya that were purported to be vacant and unoccupied. Bishop Walter Carey says,

> The British Government said: "we can't afford to *maintain* the railway, we must have farmers to grow crops and provide paying freight for the railway." Therefore the British Government *invited* – nay *begged* – settlers to come out and build up farms. Many came, from England and South Africa. Today we are told that these settlers were cruel land-grabbers: oppressors of the harmless native and so on. Just a complete lie. If there were wrongdoers, it was the British government of those days, who by the advice of Sir Harry Johnstone and Lord Lingard *invited farmers* to come.[65]

The condescending and superior attitude portrayed by Carey in his statement is worth noting briefly. He argues that "the government assigned land to the settlers in this empty country, which is now a paradise of lovely fertile farms."[66] While it is not within the scope or interest of this book to analyze the validity of such claims, the bishop portrays Africans as foolish undignified brutes with no sense of good, and the remedy as being "to turn savages (in the mass) into law-abiding, hard-working, social-minded, yes, and Christian people. For (forget it, if you like, in England) Western civilization is based on Mosaic and Christian principles without which you will never build a true civilization, and if you betray these (as some seem increasingly anxious to do) we shall go back to decadence. Christian education is the only solution."[67] For Carey, Christianity is Western civilization communicated in Western culture and values. Western political style and values are the standard which any civilized government should uphold. Without taking due regard and consideration of Africans, the British government imposed its cultural values in the name of Christianizing Africa. Anything that negated their interests was barbaric and

---

64. Keith Cole, *Kenya: Hanging in the Middle Way* (London: Highway, 1959), 28.

65. Walter Carey, *Crisis in Kenya: Christian Common Sense on Mau Mau and the Colour-Bar* (London: Mowbray, 1953), 14.

66. Carey, *Crisis in Kenya*, 15.

67. Carey, 17.

savage. As expressed by one African, the missionary came to convert us to Christianity, and while we closed our eyes in prayer, he turned and grabbed our land. To this extent, then, as the Kikuyus would say, *Gutiri Mubea na Muthungu* ("There is no difference between the priest and the colonialist"), for it was the same white person who carried the Bible in one hand who had a gun in the other.

The sentiments of Carey contrast, however, with those of historian George Bennett, who argues that the Highlands was land belonging to the Kikuyus who, like others in the region, had encountered several disasters due to disease, drought, and locust invasion that resulted in a major famine threatening the survival of the people. The Kikuyus retreated to a safe haven for refuge and temporarily leased their land, in accordance with their African custom, to "an incoming fair-skinned people, Europeans with different ideas of land tenure." The British believed that they had acquired full rights of ownership. Only when the Kikuyus wanted to come back to their land did it dawn on them that these "red strangers" had already assumed full ownership and occupation by enforcing "their interpretation of the bargains made."[68] Similarly, Richard Cox argues that "during 1888 and 1889 a great smallpox epidemic, severe drought and a plague of locusts on top of earlier rinderpest, had combined to drive [the Kikuyu] out of the Fort Hall District and back to their homelands around Kiambu, near Nairobi. The white settlement started just after this and when the Kikuyu wanted to reoccupy the land they found it closed to them."[69]

Sentiments similar to Carey's were also aired by Sir Charles Eliot, in August 1903 when inviting the second wave of settlers to Kenya, demonstrating the characteristic view among the white settlers that Africans had neither culture nor civilization: "There can be no doubt of the immense progress made in rendering the civilization of the African at least possible, and it is a progress which need occasion no regrets, for we are not destroying any old or interesting system, but simply introducing order into blank, uninteresting, brutal barbarism . . . A large part of East Africa is a white man's country, suitable for European colonization."[70]

This is a clear indication that the motives of the West were all too often mixed with their own personal interests. When the British settled in Africa and established themselves, they passed legislation to preserve their rights,

---

68. George Bennett, *Kenya: A Political History* (London: Oxford University Press, 1963), 5–6.

69. Richard Cox, *Kenyatta's Country* (London: Hutchinson, 1965), 18.

70. Norman Leys, *Kenya* (London: Hogarth, 1924), 182.

such as a land board that was instituted to grant the Highlands to the white settlers.[71] Huge tracts of land were acquired as settler farms, while a few native reserves were established far from the European centers, but "native villages" were allowed on the settlers' farms in order for the black Africans to provide labor. Along with the land tenure, the British introduced other socioeconomic structures, such as the formal use of money, formal schooling for children, and "wage laboring." Such attempts by the "British administrators, settlers and missionaries to get Africans to do many of these novel things . . . were not readily or easily accepted."[72]

Such colonial derision met with a vehement reaction from African nationalists who were especially enraged by the occupation of their land.[73] This nationalism would later culminate in the struggle for African emancipation. The Africans were incensed because they had been robbed of their land and denied their rights, and this triggered major antagonism that impacted sociopolitical life as well as ecclesial developments that emerged during this period.

Cultural and Sociopolitical Antagonism

The relationship between the missionaries and African Christians has frequently been portrayed as harmonious, resonating with mutual trust, genuine communion, and true Christian fellowship. There was, however, another side, one characterized by continued conflict that threatened cohesiveness and which was precipitated by the prevailing sociopolitical and cultural conditions that led to the rise of nationalism. The underlying cause of the strained relationship was racial in nature. The kind of treatment the Africans received from the missionaries was similar to their treatment by the colonialists. Many of the factors that contributed to the ongoing antagonism between the Africans and the white Europeans were rooted in the Europeans' attitudes of superiority, paternalism, and condescension.

The relationship between white Europeans and locals was complicated by racial differences as well as by differences in cultural values and philosophical worldview. The Africans were still rooted to their traditional approach to issues and their cultural belief system – African Traditional Religion (ATR) –

---

71. Bennett, *Kenya*, 23.

72. Robert L. Tignor, *The Colonial Transformation of Kenya: The Kamba, Kikuyu, and Maasai from 1900 to 1939* (Princeton, NJ: Princeton University Press, 1976), 4.

73. Carl G. Rosberg and John Nottingham, *The Myth of "Mau Mau": Nationalism in Kenya* (New York: Frederick A. Praeger, 1966), 18.

which shaped their sociopolitical, economic, and religious life. The white Europeans – particularly missionaries, with their Western philosophical mindset and their objective to spread Christianity – established mission stations, hospitals, and schools, albeit with racial distinctions. In Nigeria, for instance, Christian missionaries had established many schools and churches in the north by 1960, and this resulted in hostility with the Muslim communities and ongoing suspicion on both sides.[74] The basic principles that governed the lives of the missionaries and the locals were distinct in intent and purpose, denting their relationships.

In Kenya, for example (similar scenarios were replicated in other countries in colonial Africa), the people, mainly Kikuyu, formed an organization called the Kikuyu Central Association (KCA)[75] whose aim was to fight for their rights.[76] This organization sought to unite the Kikuyu against white dominance through an oath-taking ceremony invoked through the "Kikuyu traditional symbols and magico-religious practices" whose intent was to guarantee the unity and commitment of the members to the intended purpose of their mission.[77] The movement grew quickly because of the shared feelings of resentment and the enduring pain of dispossession and alienation from their homeland.[78] Although the struggle by the Africans was political in nature, it also carried religious implications because the missions and the colonialists (government) were one and the same in the eyes of the Africans, as they were united against African customs, values, and practices. One of the traces of cultural nationalism is seen among the Kikuyu tribe who protested against the missionary opposition to African cultural practices such as female circumcision, non-burial of the dead, and *ngomas* (traditional dances).[79] These issues, and female circumcision in particular, brought about a bitter and enduring antagonism between the

---

74. Yushau Sodiq, "Can Muslims and Christians Live Together Peacefully in Nigeria?," *The Muslim World* 99, no. 4 (Oct. 2009): 650.

75. Donald L. Barnett and Karari Njama, *Mau Mau from Within: Autobiography and Analysis of Kenya's Peasant Revolt* (London: MacGibbon & Kee, 1966), 114.

76. Jomo Kenyatta, as secretary general of KCA, wrote a letter which was published in the *Manchester Guardian* on 18 March 1930 in which he articulated the aims of this organization. See Jomo Kenyatta, "Letter to *Manchester Guardian*, 18 March 1930," in Jomo Kenyatta, *Suffering Without Bitterness: The Founding of the Kenya Nation* (Nairobi: East African Publishing, 1968), 35.

77. Barnett gives a vivid depiction of the oathing ceremony in *Mau Mau from Within*, 116–21.

78. Barnett and Njama, *Mau Mau from Within*, 114.

79. There were numerous circulars prepared between the government, the mission, and the representatives of the Kikuyu (Kikuyu Central Association) on these cultural practices. See Rosberg and Nottingham, *Myth of "Mau Mau,"* 118. It may be of interest for the reader to

Kikuyu nationalists and the missionaries. The Kikuyus challenged the way the missionaries rejected the African cultural practices as unacceptable while seeing their Western values, practices, and social institutions as acceptable. The Africans were to abandon their cultural practices and adopt Western ones, since "Western culture and Christianity were identified together as an integral corpus of belief and practice; the rejection of one element in the whole was defined as a total rejection and hence as 'cultural atavism.'"[80]

The Kikuyus were open to embracing Christianity without the debilitating Western cultural traits. This amounted to questioning the authority of the missionaries and their motives in condemning African cultural practices, most of which were not in conflict with biblical teaching. In this respect, then, the authority of the missionaries was brought into disrepute, and a cultural nationalism emerged, spearheaded by the Kikuyu Central Association, whose call was not a rejection of Christianity but an attempt to preserve certain aspects of Kikuyu culture. Indeed, it seemed to them that it was not Christianity that was in danger, but Kikuyu culture, as the process of modernization deepened and spread across their country.[81] The Kikuyu demanded to have a selective process of the changes that their conversion to Christianity would bring about to their cultural values and practices. Some of these were not in contradiction to the teachings of the Bible, yet the missionaries and the colonial state were bent on imposing Western Christian civilization upon them. This is an interesting joining together of the church and the state which tended to emerge from a purely theological dimension that we will revisit in the later chapters of this book.

In a similar vein, Zablon Nthamburi posits that it was Kikuyu culture, and by implication their identity, rather than Christianity that was at stake. What for the missionaries was regarded as stubbornness or a "work of darkness" was essentially "a legitimate attempt to prevent the disintegration of their culture."[82] The African converts had been shielded from these "heathen" practices by being separated from the rest of the unbelieving community and settled in mission stations. Those who exemplified any kind of sympathy were branded hypocrites and excluded from church communion. The dispute over these

---

note that the Kikuyu, like all African tribes, express themselves through parables and riddles encrypted in their music and dance.

80. Rosberg and Nottingham, 105.

81. Rosberg and Nottingham, 112–13.

82. Zablon Nthamburi, ed., *From Mission to Church: A Handbook of Christianity in East Africa* (Nairobi: Uzima, 1991), 18.

issues became heated in the late 1920s when mission schools were rocked with disturbances as Kikuyu men were charged with "holding the Muthirigu song and dance," culminating in the murder of Hulda Stumpf of AIM (Africa Inland Mission) in Kijabe on 2 January 1930.[83] By the time the government had moved in and restored the situation, "the dispute [had] cost the CSM [Church of Scotland Mission] at Kikuyu 90 per cent of its communicants within the first month, while the AIM at Kijabe lost all but 50 of its 600 adherents."[84] The cultural and sociopolitical antagonism was detrimental to the interests of both the white missionaries and the Africans, resulting in major casualties in the wake of the struggle for independence.

It is worth pointing out, however, that while there appeared to be a cordial and good working relationship between the missionaries and the colonial government on a number of issues, most missionary movements were not supported or even funded by the state, even though they were involved with the sociopolitical issues of the societies among which they worked. The missionaries were concerned primarily with the preaching of the gospel and the establishment of mission stations, while the sole focus of the government officials was the establishment of the colony. However, a symbiotic relationship was, in most cases, necessary for each to achieve their intended mission.

African Resistance and Struggle for Independence

Africans became increasingly agitated by the racial segregation and denial of human rights by the colonial governments. The settlers and missionaries, on the other hand, sharing a common belief that the indigenous people were mentally and culturally inferior, persisted in their dissemination of Western civilization.[85] Although we will here focus on the Mau Mau revolt in the Kenyan context, we should note that other African countries had similar movements of resistance to colonial power in their own contexts. In his discussion of Mau Mau, Rob Buijtenhuijs alludes to the similarities and differences between "the three peasant revolts that [occurred] in colonial Africa (Madagascar, Kenya, Cameroun)."[86] It is ironic that the missionaries failed to see their

---

83. Rosberg and Nottingham, *Myth of "Mau Mau,"* 124.

84. Rosberg and Nottingham, 124.

85. Kamuti Kiteme, "The Impact of European Education upon Africans in Kenya: 1846–1940" (DEd diss., Yeshiva University, 1970), 96.

86. Rob Buijtenhuijs, *Essays on Mau Mau: Contributions to Mau Mau Historiography* (Leiden: African Studies Centre, 1982), 213.

own shortcomings, and yet they were rejecting traditional African customs wholesale. They took pride in the feats of Western civilization to transform "heathen" African life through trade, settlers, and government. This was mixed with their perception that these aspects were equated with Christianity and the transforming power of Christ on the darkness of African life.[87]

With the goal of attaining political freedom, the Mau Mau movement rose to the challenge of the time as a nationalist agenda. It must be understood that nationalism as it relates to the African context is distinct from nationalism in a Western context. M. Kilson quoting Diedrich Westermann observes that "nationalism has in its application to Africa not the same meaning as when applied to European countries. In Europe it is the desire of a nation to be united and to control all its members. In Africa it simply means independence from European domination."[88] The struggle for political freedom in Kenya, and in particular the formation of the Mau Mau freedom fighters, has been attested in many works.[89] This was a struggle not just for political freedom, but for emancipation from all forms of Western domination. The nationalists were also contending with the foreignness of the demands of missionary Christianity on Africans that had depersonalized them by insisting that they abandon their "indigenous modes of thinking, expression and action. The whole indigenous religious concept of the African people, most notably their view of the unity of the person, was to be put aside. The missionaries needed a clean break with the past for Christianity to be planted. All those who felt that they could be Christian and remain African were considered rebels and many of them left the Church. It was, for example, sin to use one's African name in Baptism."[90] This may explain why African Christians take up as their first (baptismal) names those derived from the West with foreign, and in many cases unknown, meanings for the bearer, rather than African names which almost always carry a descriptive meaning which links an individual to his or her environment and society.

---

87. H. Virginia Blakeslee, "Is a Curtain Falling on Africa?," *Inland Africa* 39, no. 1 (1955): 10–11.

88. M. Kilson, "The Analysis of African Nationalism," *World Politics* 10, no. 3 (1958): 484–97, quoting Diedrich Westermann, "Cultural History of Negro Africa," *Cahiers d'histoire mondiale* 4 (1957): 1003.

89. For a detailed discussion and clear analysis of the events that led to the formation of the Mau Mau revolt movement of 1952–1957, and the arrest, torture, and assassination of key African political activists leading to the independence of Kenya in 1963, see Barnett and Njama, *Mau Mau from Within*; and also chapter 9 of Rosberg and Nottingham, *Myth of "Mau Mau."*

90. John Henry Okullu, *Church and State in Nation Building and Human Development* (Nairobi: Uzima, 2003), 23.

African resistance to British colonial domination cannot be explained exhaustively in our discussion here. British brutality in Kenya was extensive and devastating, particularly for the tribes that were in close proximity to Nairobi.[91] While the Kikuyu was the tribe that was affected the most, the struggle was a "heroic resistance of Kenyan peoples of all nationalities."[92] The different tribal groups were all part of the struggle for independence, but the Kikuyu were at the forefront in organizing the strategic Mau Mau revolt whose members were bound by an oath; any deserters would be killed on sight. The Mau Mau struck both white settlers and Africans who betrayed the cause of their fellow Africans by collaborating with the colonialists. This is the category that Ngugi refers to as "*Sell-out*, a traitorous tradition whose highest expression was in the actions of the home guard, loyalist collaborators with the British enemy."[93] For the colonialists, the African fight for their land was perceived against the enduring patronizing attitude depicted in the following statement by Bishop Carey that is worth quoting at length:

> When the Kikuyus increased in numbers and didn't find their (badly cultivated) land sufficient, what was easier than to cast longing eyes at the lovely farms of the White Highlands and covet them! "Let's forget all about purchases, and empty lands now turned into a paradise by European capital, sweat and initiative; let's forget how the Europeans have given us hygiene, hospitals, protection, education; let us raise the cry of 'give us back *our* land: rid us of the oppressive settler, so that we can sprawl over their farms, and (for a few years till we ruin them) live in their houses and feed on their farms.'" Gratitude . . . is simply not in African nature . . . They have *no* equivalent terms for gratitude, love, honor, integrity, and virtue: such words don't exist in their language. Europeans have had to *invent* words for these.[94]

The sentiments leave a lot to be desired. Apart from the statements being untrue, Carey, just like his fellow white missionaries and settlers alike, came with a superiority complex, and with a very low opinion of Africans. This gives us a hint of the hatred with which the Europeans treated the Africans. While

---

91. Tignor, *Colonial Transformation*, 4–5.

92. Ngugi wa Thiong'o, *Moving the Centre: The Struggle for Cultural Freedoms* (London: J. Currey; Portsmouth, NH: Heinemann, 1993), 97.

93. Ngugi, *Moving the Centre*, 97.

94. Carey, *Crisis in Kenya*, 18.

we do not discount the fact that they brought Christianity – albeit clothed in Western civilization – they robbed Africans of their dignity, human worth, and value.

The years that followed World War II saw Kenyatta and other patriots unite and form national parties beginning with the Kenya African Union (KAU) in 1944. Kenyatta's return from a sixteen-year period of study and stay in the UK, from 1930 to 1946, saw him dive into the struggle for Kenya's freedom. He traveled across the country in order to make KAU an effective political organization that would fight for the equality of all races in Kenya.[95]

With the declaration of the state of emergency in October 1952 because of the Mau Mau uprising, Jomo Kenyatta, who was considered to be one of the key leaders of the Mau Mau rebel movement, "was detained together with some of his associates and later tried and convicted."[96] He was imprisoned for seven years, but the struggle continued, and upon his release in 1961 he went on to become the president of Kenya African National Union (KANU). He continued on to parliament, and "in June 1963, after the K.A.N.U. victory in the general election, he became Kenya's first prime minister, and in December 1963, its president."[97]

While we have focused primarily on the Kenyan struggle for independence by the Mau Mau, other countries in Africa had their own similar experiences. and their own mechanisms by which they dealt with colonial domination and liberated their people. The importance of our discussion of the historical-political context lies in the fact that it lays a significant foundation for understanding the problem of African political engagement and the mindset that shapes the political theology of the church in Africa. The partisanship of missionaries and their cooperation with colonial officials resulted in animosity among the Africans. This indicates that there was an underlying political theology of missionary Christianity whose influence on the contemporary African church needs to be meaningfully engaged with. It is necessary to understand why the African church in general has regarded politics with disdain as we reflect on the theology it inherited derived from the Western mindset. The struggle for emancipation provided a context in which mission was done, and at the same time paved the way for spiritual reflection and revival.

---

95. Bennett, *Kenya*, 119.
96. Cole, *Kenya*, 45.
97. Cox, *Kenyatta's Country*, 26.

Spiritual Awakening

In the wake of the rise of African nationalism, in which Africans stood firm against Western attempts to disintegrate their culture through Christianization, a number of African groups emerged and provided an alternative to the missionary establishments.[98] This period also marks the beginning of African Independent Churches which were expressions of Christianity within the framework of African cultural practices. Since Africans had come to faith in Christ, they wanted to retain the faith without the missionary garb, thus paving the way for the emergence of independent schools along with independent churches.[99] The rise of indigenous churches raised a number of questions for those who did not want to be fully detached from the founding missions. The continued relationship between the missionary-established African churches and the mission agencies was crucial since the churches owed their existence to the missions and did not want to sever the bond while they were still in their infancy. At the same time, the missions had established a number of projects that benefited the churches, such as hospitals, schools, and children's homes, which the churches were not yet prepared to run. Needless to say, the missions were advantaged, politically, under the colonial rule. At the same time, they were still in control, so to speak, of the theology and the doctrinal foundations on which the churches were based, since the theological institutions and Bible schools were still under their leadership and supported by them.

As a result, the spread and acceptance of Christianity through the missionary movement in Africa posed certain challenges of authenticity. The need for education and improvement of status may have been the attraction for many in accepting Christianity, and not because they had experienced a genuine conviction of faith. This resulted in external conformity to Christian practices, including church attendance, which was just a ritualistic outward show lacking inward commitment and transformation. It was for this reason that genuine African Christians distanced themselves from this lukewarm type of superficial Christianity. They "often lamented the Church's tepidity and yearned for a spiritual renewal. The Ruanda Mission, which was founded in the 1920s and run as a separate entity within the Anglican Diocese of Uganda openly denounced the 'Laodicean state of the Church of Uganda.'"[100] This

---

98. Nthamburi, *From Mission to Church*, 18.

99. Nthamburi, 18.

100. John Karanja, "Confession and Cultural Dynamism in the Revival," in *The East African Revival: Histories and Legacies*, ed. Kevin Ward and Emma Wild-Wood (Farnham: Ashgate, 2011), 144.

spiritual awakening, commonly known as the East African Revival, swept like a fire through the Central and East African region.

This movement had major sociopolitical impacts as African Christians turned to God in large numbers and demonstrated that Africans can truly be Christians, filled and moved by the Holy Spirit to go out and become witnesses of God's salvation.[101] The emphasis of this revival movement was conversion as "an overwhelming experience of brokenness at the cross, which provoked a public confession of sin. Previous Christian experience apart from this event was not recognized as '*kulokoka*' – the state of being saved."[102] Even with such a radical focus on the evangel, the movement was not fully palatable among evangelical leaders. This was because of its call "for African clergy and European missionaries to confess their sins and to come in brokenness to the Cross," a call that was received with much resentment among the church leaders and missionaries whose integrity and "the boundaries of propriety in their relationship with Africans had been unquestioned in a colonial milieu."[103] This movement also demanded that all converts and others who claimed to be Christians "compose a testimony, a narrative that contrasted the depravity in which they once lived with the new life they enjoyed as saved people."[104] We need to underscore that this revival movement called for the social equality of all people, such as clergy and laypeople, as well as Europeans and Africans, which had far-reaching political ramifications at that time. It met, however, with strong resistance from the politically instigated African nationalism, and this may have been the reason why revivalism was accepted by churches in the 1950s. As described by Ward, the movement kept away from

> militant anti-colonialism; nor did they have faith in a new world of African politicians and national politics. Balokole refused to take the oaths demanded of militant nationalists in the Kenyan Mau Mau movement of the 1950s. They refused to kill or expropriate the goods of Tutsi in the Hutu revolution in Rwanda. They refused to fall in with the Buganda nationalism of the Kabaka Yekka movement. For them *Yesu Yekka* – Jesus only – was the cry. But nor were they enthusiastic about a wider Ugandan nationalism.

---

101. Kevin Ward, "Introduction," in Ward and Wild-Wood, *East African Revival*, 4.

102. Ward, "Introduction," 4.

103. Ward, 5.

104. Derek R. Peterson, "Revivalism and Dissent in Colonial East Africa," in Ward and Wild-Wood, *East African Revival*, 105.

Nevertheless they did see themselves as modelling a non-racial, non-tribal, non-ethnic solidarity with those who were saved.[105]

This revival was a demonstration of the expression of Christianity within the African context, as it resounded with vibrant open-air evangelistic preaching, prayer meetings, Bible studies, and the boldness of people publicly confessing and repenting of their sins.[106] It was a movement with a great lesson for the Christian church in Africa, and for the mission movement in particular, as its success was a story in itself, indicative of how Christianity had not only been embraced but also become incarnate in African societies. The brotherly bond that was exhibited by the "saved ones" was a distinctive mark of the difference that Christ can make in the midst of racial animosity.

The impact of revivalism in Kenya, for instance, is clearly seen in light of the rise of the Mau Mau revolt. Numerous conventions for the deepening of spiritual life were held in Kenya from 1948 through the height of the Mau Mau uprising in 1952.[107] There was great tension between the revivalists and the Mau Mau, which can be attributed to the fact that "the revivalists boldly preached Jesus, whom the Mau Mau affirmed was a cunning European or Asian, incredible blasphemies being uttered against Him; the revival broke down racial distrust and separation, and called every believer 'brother' regardless of tribe or race."[108] In this respect, then, we can assert that the East African Revival movement had major sociopolitical and religious implications that affected the internalization of the faith by Africans as well as crystallizing the relationship of all believers, irrespective of their racial background. Indeed, the believers' faith was put to the test: "when a great falling-away occurred in Kenya, due to fear of Mau Mau terror, the bulk of those who maintained their witness cheerfully and fearlessly were the revived people. Many were tortured, and some were killed."[109]

Our discussion of the sociopolitical context during the colonial period and in particular the struggle for independence illustrates the feeling of Africans in general toward suppression by the white colonizers. The struggle for nationalism was not only for political reasons but also religious, in reaction to the mission-established organizations which were dominated and controlled

---

105. Ward, "Introduction," 5.

106. Okullu, *Church and State*, 23.

107. James Edwin Orr, *Evangelical Awakenings in Africa* (Pasadena, CA: Mission to the Academic Community, 1972), 181.

108. Orr, *Evangelical Awakenings*, 182.

109. Orr, 182.

by white people. Although the missions and the church claimed to maintain a nonpartisan stance toward this struggle, both abhorred the acts and practices of the Mau Mau freedom fighters. The missions, however, responded to a call by the government to provide pastoral ministry in prisons by sending pastors and evangelists to preach the gospel, so as to help convert jailed Mau Mau activists.[110] This became a precursor of prison ministry, in which chaplaincy became a cardinal duty.

The British forces were unrelenting in their efforts to stamp out the Mau Mau uprising in which thousands were killed, others imprisoned, and some gave themselves up. What is apparent is that the church did not regard the prevailing sociopolitical oppression of Africans by the colonial government as a justified cause for civil disobedience. On the contrary, in their view, the African demand was a desire for worldly possessions rather than desiring the eternal blessings that come with the knowledge of the saving work of Christ.

By standing up to oppression and demanding freedom, the nationalists were deemed to be rebelling against the authority of the government, which was seen to amount to rebellion against the divine Giver of that authority. The Mau Mau movement was thus seen as an expression of the Kikuyus' rejection of the saving work of Christ, as attested in Blakeslee's comment: "From the beginning, the light shining in dark places has produced the same results in all parts of the world. Kikuyu-land has been no exception. The majority of mankind love darkness rather than light, and light rejected brings judgment of one kind or another."[111] Such a statement clearly demonstrates that the events taking place were interpreted from a spiritual perspective in which the church was to step in and proclaim the gospel message in order to change the focus of the people away from worldly things (political freedom) to spiritual (eternal) ones. What we fail to see on the part of the missionaries, as well as the African Christians, is their responsibility to challenge the colonial government regarding the atrocities carried out on the Africans and on the need to disburse equal justice to all citizens without discrimination. The church failed to identify with the real and felt needs brought about by the social deprivation and political oppression of the very people whose souls it craved to win for Christ. This was a missed opportunity! The silence on the part of both the missionaries and African Christians amounted to an endorsement of the status quo – colonialism and its attendant repression of Africans. Although it is beyond the scope of our discussion here, an investigation is needed into how each African country

---

110. Blakeslee, "Curtain Falling," 11.
111. Blakeslee, 11.

that experienced colonialism finally attained liberation, and the implications that struggle had on the life of its people, and especially on the church and the expression of Christianity.

D. Postcolonial Political Structure

The colonial political structure made a significant impact on the sociopolitical scene in Africa, and this impact continues to be felt today. Our discussion of postcolonialism reveals stark traces of the historical colonial period. Postcolonialism refers to the period of time following colonial rule and it is characterized by obvious colonial traits and hangovers. The actual break between the colonial and postcolonial periods was fluid, although for most countries it may be associated with attainment of independence. Postcolonialism is a global phenomenon whose concern is "about the nature of our contemporary identity."[112] It is worth noting, though, that "the concept of postcolonialism has recently taken on a socio-cultural and political meaning."[113] The events that unfolded during the transition from European to African control of government posed major challenges to the relationship between the white settlers and Africans in all sectors of society. It had implications for both the political as well as the ecclesial shift in leadership from the control of white people to that of Africans. In this respect, we could argue that postcolonialism is a synthesis of the colonial political structures, with their Western biases, and African cultures.

While, for the most part, postcolonial Africa is characterized by numerous vices wrought by greed and poor political leadership, there are cases of national heroes who have been selfless and patriotic in their leadership styles and have positively impacted their countries and the continent as a whole. One of the renowned African leaders was Nelson Mandela, the first South African post-apartheid president, who

> revealed a truly human genius for *ubuntu* – the awareness that his life was inextricably bound up with the lives of all his fellow human beings, including his enemies. He was the great includer; nothing was too much trouble if he could cajole or charm an

---

112. Patrick Chabal, "The African Crisis: Context and Interpretation," in *Postcolonial Identities in Africa*, ed. Richard Werbner and Terence Ranger (London & New Jersey: Zed Books, 1996), 38.

113. Mabiala Justin-Robert Kenzo, "Thinking Otherwise about Africa: Postcolonialism, Postmodernism, and the Future of African Theology," *Exchange* 31, no. 4 (2002): 324.

opponent into friendship. This was a man who would not bend an inch in his determination to win freedom for his people, nor bow to the cruelty of his prison guards, yet who said to his comrades as soon as they arrived on the island, "Chaps, these Afrikaners may be brutal, but they are human beings. We need to understand them and touch the human being inside them, and win them." And they did.[114]

However, most postcolonial leaders who were heroes of independence in their countries became dictators and authoritarians who enriched themselves and impoverished their people.

The African postcolonial structure is compounded by multiple sociopolitical ills which degrade the concept of state sovereignty and make it "virtually a political fiction." There are economic problems as a result of greed and corruption, widespread insecurity, and politically instigated violence "fostered by foreign arms dumping; [the leaders'] retreat in practice from the populist promises of the early nationalist period after independence, often externally enforced; their impoverishing withdrawal from public welfare institutions, internationally sanctioned; [and] their proliferation of state salariat, frequently foreign-aid driven. Africa's debt crisis, its increasing economic dependence, its kleptocracies in collusion with extractive transnationals, the suborning of its postcolonial elites by global consumerism, all these complex realities across different parts of the continent invite the simplistic formulations of neo-colonialism."[115]

Political instability characterizes most African countries but, as noted by Patrick Chabal, "Africa is not just a continent of great political instability, it is also a continent where incompetence, greed and the lust for power have unleashed untold violence on ordinary men and women."[116] Most countries in postcolonial Africa have been victims of political wrangles and unrest that have in some cases degenerated into ethnic cleansing or genocide. In a number of cases, political competition and desire for control of power and wealth have created a politics of suspicion, particularly across ethnic or tribal differences, resulting in killings and assassinations. A Kenyan example is

---

114. Peter Storey, "Mandela, Nelson, 1918–2013," *The Christian Century* 131, no. 1 (8 Jan. 2014): 11.

115. Richard Werbner, "Multiple Identities, Plural Arenas," in Werbner and Ranger, *Postcolonial Identities*, 5.

116. Chabal, "African Crisis," 31.

the death of Tom Mboya on July 5, 1969 at the hands of a Kikuyu assassin, Isaac Njenga Njoroge, was seen by many Kenyans as a political assassination. Mboya's long political base in the labour movement, his acceptance by different ethnic groups and being Kenya's best spokesman of his day perhaps posed a threat to Kenyatta. His death sparked a number of political events. Out of guilt and recognizing the consequences to which the murder would lead, Kenyatta's henchmen appealed to the Kikuyu people to unite through the oathing exercise.[117]

Other African countries have their own examples of victims of political assassinations, most of whom are implicated as wanted criminals and eliminated in cold blood, while many simply vanish without a trace.

Tribal hostilities in postcolonial Africa have been a major cause of violence, as is well attested in the cases of Rwanda, Burundi, and South Africa.[118] Party politics and rivalries are largely inflamed by tribal or ethnic differences as the struggle for domination through leadership and control has become a perpetual phenomenon. In countries with multiethnic or different tribal communities, representation in the upper echelons of power has been a major cause of dispute and despondency, especially for the marginalized. The postcolonial structure in Africa can thus be regarded as neocolonialism, with black imperialists having replaced the white imperial colonial masters.

On the ecclesial scene, the postcolonial period has been a time when African theologians have been actively involved in the articulation of an understanding of the Christian faith in the form of African theology. The ecclesial ramifications of the relationship between church and state on the one hand and the missionary enterprise and the national church on the other are also critical aspects for consideration in relation to the political theology of the church. As Gerrie ter Haar observes, "After most African countries had gained political independence in the 1960s, the churches in Africa, too, embarked on a process of self-determination that gradually put the control of the churches in the hands of the Africans. This tilted the power balance from the 'mother'

117. Gideon Gichuhi Githiga, *The Church as the Bulwark against Authoritarianism: Development of Church and State Relations in Kenya with Particular Reference to the Years after Political Independence 1963–1992* (Oxford: Regnum, 2001), 53.

118. Chabal, "African Crisis."

to the 'daughter' churches, changing the relationship from a parent–child into a sibling relationship."[119]

The churches in different regions of the continent have responded differently to the sociopolitical issues of postcolonialism. Henrik Petersen observes, for instance, that "during the last decade historic churches in Eastern Africa have been engaged in discussions about national issues in different ways. Although some have taken the explicit stand to avoid engagement in politics, many historic churches have been more or less pulled into the public sphere due to their numeric sizes, which are significant in national matters since they involve millions of voters."[120] In South Africa, the church has continued to grapple with the postcolonial impact, as James Cochrane describes:

> If, therefore, we may regard South Africa as now being in a "postcolonial" condition, then it may be said that religion and its concern for human values and virtues has a high place on the agenda. The adoption of that political instrument of modernization which we call democracy, with its formal separation of the state from religion, has not meant the decline of religion at all, nor the removal of religion from the public sphere. The irony, in fact, is that the issues previously identified are driven more by the state than by the religious communities of South Africa in general. It is the state, particularly President Mbeki himself, which repeatedly pushes for a stronger response from religious communities to the challenges of our transformation out of apartheid to something more hopeful and just.[121]

On many occasions the church has dissociated itself from active participation in influencing the necessary political changes. The argument the church gives for its stand pertains to the church's position that its aim is the conversion of human souls through the proclamation of the gospel and not involvement in political affairs. For example, speaking at a church in Mbaraki, Mombasa, Kenya, the bishop of Africa Inland Church (AIC) dissociated the church from engaging in the succession issue of the next president prior to

---

119. Gerrie ter Haar, "African Christians in Europe: A Mission in Reverse," in *Changing Relations between Churches in Europe and Africa: The Internationalization of Christianity and Politics in the 20th Century*, ed. Katharina Kunter and Jens Holger Schjørring (Wiesbaden: Harrassowitz, 2008), 242.

120. Henrik Sonne Petersen, "Political Engagement of Historic Churches in Eastern Africa," *Svensk Missionstidskrift* 101, no. 1 (2013): 67.

121. James R. Cochrane, "Religious Pluralism in Post-Colonial Public Life," *Journal of Church and State* 42, no. 3 (Summer 2000): 445–46.

the 2002 elections. He argued that the work of a minister of God is "to preach so that people can come to Jesus," and therefore "God-fearing clergy ought to spread the word of God."[122] He stated that the church is neutral when it comes to matters of political affiliation and that its role is to pray for the country. This view emphasizes the spiritual aspect while minimizing the physical dimension of the church's gospel mandate to the whole world.

This stand suggests a noninvolvement stance that tends to send mixed signals on the part of the church. While some church leaders, including bishops, have ventured into active politics, other churches have clearly denounced such involvement. The involvement or noninvolvement of the church is not guided by a proper theological view but by momentary individual motives and aspirations. A good example is Africa Inland Church (AIC) in Kenya. The 2002 version of the AIC Constitution and regulations prohibits its pastors from getting involved in politics. Article XIII number 4 states that "a Pastor who enters politics shall relinquish his pastoral responsibilities. His Diocesan Church Council shall revoke his license or ordination and inform the Government Registrar. His license or ordination certificate shall be returned to the Diocesan Church Council. Such a person, who subsequently leaves politics, shall not be reinstated to a pastoral position. He shall not be eligible to hold a leadership position in the church for a period of at least five years."[123] This statement, much as it may be a deterrent to pastors who may want to enter politics, is made without evidence of biblical support or a theological rationale. The enforcement of this constitutional provision by the church in this respect seems to be indecisive. At the same time, it is ironic that such a statement should be made by a church which has benefited from past political regimes, since the second and longest-serving president of Kenya was a member of this church, and the church was favorably predisposed during his rule. Indeed, the participation of some of its pastors in elective politics illustrates how the church lacks a political theology.

One pastor narrated how he ventured into politics after due consultation with the relevant authorities of the church and assurance from them that his intention was welcome and would not affect his administrative duties in the church if he failed to make it to parliament. Just before the elections, the issue

---

122. Mathias Ringa, "AIC Neutral in Succession Debate, Says Head," *East African Standard* online, 2 September 2002.

123. Africa Inland Church – Kenya, *Constitution and Regulations* (Kijabe: Kijabe Printing Press, 2002), 16. Other earlier versions of the AIC Constitution do not have any reference on pastors or church leader's involvement in politics.

was raised at an executive meeting of the Central Church Council to the effect that it was not wise for a minister of the gospel to be involved in politics, yet he was still holding the certificates that belonged to the church. The council unanimously agreed, and the pastor's ordination certificate was confiscated. When the pastor failed to make it to parliament, he attempted to return to his job as promised, but all the leaders were opposed to the idea. After some time, a number of churches requested him to offer his services, and he made an appeal to the Central Church Office for the return of his certificate. A special church council (Baraza Kuu) met and faulted the decision that had been previously made by the executive to confiscate the certificate in the first place, since according to the church council, the church does not have a decisive statement in its constitution regarding the issue of political involvement. The pastor was given back the certificate, but not his administrative job, and continued with his pastoral ministry.[124] The other mention of politics is in the AIC-Kenya Constitution amended in 2018 which says: "To avoid conflict of interest, government administrators and politicians should not be elected as church leaders."[125] This shows that this church has no clear official scriptural or theological stand on political involvement that informs it practice. The absence of a such a definitive statement on the political involvement of the church is indicative of how uncertain the church is on the issue and highlights the lack of a clearly defined theology supported by Scripture.

Essentially, the church needs to be decisive and intentional in developing a sociopolitical theology that not only affirms biblical authority but also takes the whole Bible seriously. In being evangelical, the church must have a critical stance that does not give a blanket assent to the status quo or simply ignore it altogether. The church must have an ongoing sociopolitical involvement in which Christians exercise their obligation to critique the state, and at the same time they must be careful not to wed the church and the state. The role of the church in the political dimension is vital for a theology that attests to the kingship of God. For the church to be effective in its calling to be the agent of God's change in society, it cannot ignore, neglect, or put aside the political dimension of life. It must be the prophetic voice that consistently condemns wrongdoing by the state, while upholding its own distinctive moral authority. While there are many areas where the missionaries excelled in establishing the church in Africa, "it is perhaps in the political kingdom that the Western

---

124. Rev. David Mbuvi, interview by author, 6 August 2003.

125. *Africa Inland Church – Kenya Constitution Revised 2018* (Nairobi, 2018), 7, article VI on church leaders part A Spiritual Leaders number 6.

missionaries failed the young African churches most grievously. The lack of a prophetic voice, a consistent official critique of European class society, meant that no coherent social philosophy was handed on."[126] The way in which the church has continued to view politics negatively, and as an arena it should not meddle with, leaves a gaping hole in the theology of an institution that claims to be the representative of Christ in a world tainted with injustice.

Our discussion of postcolonial Africa and the challenges therein requires the church in Africa to reevaluate its stance and develop a political theology that is informed by Scripture and relevant to the African context. We need to bear in mind that the postcolonial context in which the church finds itself is compounded by diverse challenges that call for a "holistic" African worldview approach. A clear rationale for the manner in which Christians are to be involved in the political processes of their countries is necessary. This will also help in defining the place of the church as well as expanding its vision on such matters as global issues, the labor market, trade, technology, and the like, which seem to be critical in the contemporary African political context. The church in Africa and beyond needs to heed the wake-up call for action that clearly rings out across the continent and indeed the world at large, so that it can help redeem the integral values of human existence that are rapidly disintegrating and threatening the survival of the human race. Christianity is a life of contradictions of sorts. There is a great longing for a life of community and belonging, and yet individualism alienates us from each other. Society today is drunk with the spirit of consumerism and the desire to own more, even as poverty flourishes as more and more people are "socially abandoned to poverty and misery" in the backyard of the most affluent Christian societies. The church must wake up to the reality of its responsibility, for "at the heart of the social, economic, and political issues that rage around us are fundamental questions that challenge our most basic sensibilities."[127] These are realities that cannot be ignored as they are embedded within the core of human society, issues that reflect ongoing challenges that need to be revisited constantly.

---

126. R. Gray, *Christianity in Independent Africa* (London: Rex Collings, 1978), 243–44.

127. Jim Wallis, *The Soul of Politics: Beyond "Religious Right" and "Secular Left"* (San Diego/New York/London: Harcourt, Brace & Co., 1995), 6–7.

3

Characteristics of Traditional African Politics

In order to understand the politics of any given context, one needs to take into account the cultural dynamics and traditional authority[1] that guides the life of the people. This is so because a people's way of life is understood from the traditions, beliefs, and values that shape their practices. In the African context the characteristics of traditional African politics have shaped modern politics significantly. Many studies have been done on African political systems, giving details on how the kingdoms were formed and the relationships that existed between the rulers and their subjects, but there is very little study on how cultural traits are linked to kingship. The different people groups in Africa have distinct and unique traditions. Consequently, generalizations cannot be made regarding their values, beliefs, and practices – not even in any one given country. This notwithstanding, it is important to note that some of these traditional aspects that characterized African politics cut across the different tribal groups and peoples in different countries of Africa.

Since characteristics of traditional African politics have shaped politics in modern Africa, solutions to the problem of enduring political strife in most African countries might hinge on such traditional tenets. The legitimation of political authority in postcolonial Africa cannot ignore some of the inherited traditional approaches and practices.[2] The postcolonial realities of African politics have indeed been structured along these characteristics in many ways.

---

1. Donald I. Roy, "Chiefs in Their Millennium Sandals: Traditional Authority in Ghana – Relevance, Challenges and Prospects," in *Critical Perspectives in Politics and Socio-Economic Development in Ghana*, ed. Wisdom J. Tettey, Korbla P. Puplampu, and Bruce J. Berman (Leiden: Brill, 2003), 242.

2. Roy, "Chiefs in Their Millennium Sandals," 243.

One obvious feature of African polity is its diversity of cultures. As has already been mentioned, Africa does not have a single culture but multiple cultures with different values, beliefs, and practices. Each polity is guided by certain social logics that are byproducts of culture, be they informal or institutionalized. That being so, "culture cannot be dismissed as irrelevant . . . because it is the foundation on which not only formal, but also informal institutions arise."[3] The fact that traditional African politics has been characterized by a diversity of cultures is important for us to note as Africans are byproducts of their cultural heritage.

Tribal and communal affiliations also characterize traditional African politics. These affiliations are key, not only in defining the contours of African localities, but, more significantly, as the shapers of African identity. Politics is a highly socialized and socializing human entity that brings people together with both positive and negative repercussions. One resultant impact of communal and tribal affinity is relationships and roles pitting male and female against each other in a highly patrilineal society. The place of women in traditional African politics, although not widely publicized, was critical to the survival of society. The debates that dominate modern political circles regarding the marginalization or exclusion of women in politics may be, by and large, a foreign instigation that fails to appreciate the value of women in traditional African politics. The understanding of the place of women goes hand in hand with other values which were central to traditional African politics and are controversial in contemporary politics in Africa. These values include land and inheritance as well as property and wealth, and are at the heart of the economic stability of society; any political engagement must therefore understand how they shape the convictions and opinions of society. We have selected these characteristics for discussion as they are core to understanding African politics today, with all its opportunities and challenges to the African church and society as a whole.

A. Diversity of Cultures

One of the distinct aspects that characterizes the African context is the diversity of its cultures, with its effects on African life and, more significantly, on its political history. Each context has a history and tradition, based on the culture the people have grown up in, which shapes every aspect of their way of life

---

3. Göran Hydén, *African Politics in Comparative Perspective* (New York: Cambridge University Press, 2006), 7.

and their thinking patterns. For this reason, any viable theology must have an understanding of the context in which the traditions, culture, and other aspects that define a people's existence emerged. We use "culture" in its broad sense as meaning the way of life of a given people within their context and worldview, which includes their value systems, their "norms of behavior, sense of meaning and purpose, customs, social institutions and social and historical reference points, as well as the ways by which the values and mores of the culture are transmitted from one generation to the next, or from one group to another, by socialization, education and social communications."[4] The diverse cultures that form the African polity have contributed to differences and caused conflicts that continue to characterize African politics. While it may be argued that these diverse cultures reflect the wealth of African traditions, they have also disrupted African social cohesiveness. Therefore, an authentic theology of politics must be relevant to the culture and its dynamics of change and evolution.

While people groups may reflect commonalities in shared values and beliefs, political attachments and allegiance, they still retain their individual uniqueness. The sharing of values helps create bonds of unity for each cultural unit in a way that differs from one group to another. In this sense, then, we cannot talk of common African values, much as these may be positive. The differences that we have seen in the political arena demonstrate that politics is often driven by the diversity rather than the unity of Africa cultures. This may explain why there is no sense of a united Africa similar to what is seen in other contexts, for example, Americans.

Numerous attempts have been made to unite the African continent as a single political entity, but these efforts have not achieved much. Calls for such unity by the pioneer presidents within independent Africa, such as Léopold Sédar Senghor of Senegal with his concept of Negritude, the pan-Africanism of Kwame Nkrumah of Ghana, Jomo Kenyatta of Kenya, and Julius Kambarage Nyere of Tanzania, remained as dreams. Julius Nyerere, for instance, was instrumental in the formation of the Organization of African Unity (OAU), now African Union (AU), whose aim was to promote unity among African countries in the hope that the solidarity would spur economic development and help promote cooperation at an international level. The hopes and confidence of this Union are enormous, but how much has been achieved

---

4. Stan Chu Ilo, "Contemporary African Cultural Values: A Challenge to Traditional Christianity," *African Ecclesiastical Review* 49, no. 3–4 (Dec. 2007): 198.

remains questionable.[5] It is unfortunate that much of what the AU deals with is resolving politically instigated conflicts and disputes.

Even at regional levels, incessant efforts have been made to create political relations, but without much success. The East African Unity, for example, was intended to create a framework for economic prosperity, but it ended up in total disarray. Numerous peace treaties have been signed between different groups, but without much to show for them, mainly because "ethnic groups lack a collective ethnic agenda that can be flagged as consequential for the political economy of the polity."[6] Each group of people that shares common cultural values seeks to fulfill its individual interests facilitated within the group. Considering that most African cultures are defined along tribal lines, it may be argued that the diverse cultural groups are tribal.

To be effective in the contemporary African context, the church needs to develop a biblical theology that is relevant to the holistic construct of the society. Christian faith must be translated and contextualized in ways that deal with the problems that speak to the intricacies of such cultural diversity within the community in all aspects. In order for the church to triumph in its mission, it needs to fully and continuously define its theological basis of sociopolitical involvement. A clear understanding and articulation of theology is important in order for the church to be an effective channel through which the sociopolitical problems affecting the community can be appropriately addressed. The church needs to reflect on what the Bible says about human nature which, in essence, contributes to the shaping of culture. The church should then work toward transforming all aspects of human life, which make up human culture, to conform to God's will and purpose. The tendency of the church to condemn cultural traditions has often led Christians to dissociate themselves from active involvement in society and thus become narrow in their focus, despite their mandate to impact all of creation. The task of the church is to bring about the transformation of society, and this includes the social and cultural diversities that shape traditional African politics.

---

5. Pope John Paul II, "Pope John Paul II's Message to the OAU: To His Excellency Mr Ide Oumaro," *African Ecclesiastical Review* 30, no. 4 (Aug. 1988): 256.

6. Ngeta Kabiri, "Ethnic Diversity and Development in Kenya: Limitations of Ethnicity as a Category of Analysis," *Commonwealth & Comparative Politics* 52, no. 4 (n.d.): 513.

B. Communal and Tribal Affiliation

Communalism was a core tenet of traditional African society. The traditional structure of African society operated within the framework of communal responsibility where the existence of the individual was conceived with reference to the whole community; thus, "I am, because we are; and since we are, therefore I am."[7] The identity of an individual was therefore defined and shaped by his or her belonging to a given community. Detachment from the community or not belonging was tantamount to loss of identity and honor. Still today, to dissociate oneself from community is to sever the ties that define and give identity to a person. This is so because the idea of community pervades all aspects of African customs and society at all stages of life, from conception to the afterlife. Community is central to the existence and survival of African tradition and history.[8]

Tribal affiliations are a common human form of identity, since "Human beings belong to natural groups, which share common culture and language, and sometimes the myth of common ancestry, and which provide their members with a sense of common identity. These natural groups are not political entities, but they often are – and many believe they should be – the basis for the formation of one."[9] Tribal affiliations and groupings have shaped the philosophy of African existence in all aspects of life and worldview. Traditionally, Africans had very close-knit family ties. The family unit was the single most important structure that helped define an individual's identity and sense of belonging. It facilitated the crystallizing of an individual's sense of dignity, value, and self-worth. This unifying bond extended to distant relatives who together make up the clans and then the tribes.

The negative side of tribal affiliations has been seen in a number of ugly incidents in African politics. These include the 1994 genocide in Rwanda, pitting the Tutsi tribe against the Hutu; the 2007–2008 postelection violence in Kenya which, though politically instigated, was primarily tribal; the perpetual South Sudan war between the Dinka and the Nuer tribes; the Somali tribal clans conflict; South African apartheid between white and black people, with the sporadic xenophobic nationalistic uprising – to name just a few. Hard as it may be, tribal affiliations must always be separated from national affairs if

---

7. John Mbiti, *African Religions and Philosophy* (New York: Frederick A. Praeger, 1969), 108–9.

8. Friday M. Mbon, "Response to Christianity in Pre-Colonial and Colonial Africa: Some Ulterior Motives," *Mission Studies* 4, no. 1 (1987): 45.

9. Marina Ottaway, "Ethnic Politics in Africa: Change and Continuity," in *State, Conflict, and Democracy in Africa*, ed. Richard Joseph (Boulder, CO: L. Rienner, 1999), 300.

democracy is to thrive in African politics. As Majawa states, holding onto tribal affiliations in the political sphere is "detrimental to democracy because tribal loyalties tend to influence the presidential and parliamentary elections, job promotions, and appointment to various offices," creating a situation where injustice thrives.[10]

One of the major responsibilities of leadership in traditional African societies was to maintain harmony and peace within the community. Although chiefs and tribal kings sat at the helm of tribal leadership, generally decisions were made in a communal sense. This responsibility was vested in the council of elders who were entrusted with the enormous duty of resolving disputes through a consensus that saw all parties duly heard. There is a Swahili saying *Panapo wazee hapaharibiki neno* ("Where there is a council of elders, nothing goes wrong"), apparently because truth will ultimately emerge through discussion and consensus until justice triumphs and all parties are appeased. In this kind of communal leadership and process of decision-making, there was no dichotomy between "winner" and "loser" since the objective was to bring about harmony within the community in order to foster peaceful coexistence. This is democracy! In this case, the welfare of the individual is sustained and protected within the communal boundaries, without compromising the responsibility of the individual. This is a rich cultural value that the church in Africa ought to utilize by engaging itself in and helping shape all aspects of society.

This communal aspect characterized leadership and the political structure of traditional Africa in general. However, modernity and postmodernity have disrupted the core values of African communities. These primarily Western influences have contributed to "the collapse of the traditional structures of identity formation in most African societies, and the absence of equivalent replacements has contributed to the crisis of identity among the youth."[11] This is where the church should take a lead in being the alternative community that provides solutions for modern African society. In this respect, the church should encourage a more diversified social structure that gives guidance on how the community should act and live together, in spite of all their social, cultural, traditional, or theological differences, as members of one body.

---

10. Clement Majawa, "The Church's Role in Defining Genuine Democracy in Africa," in *African Theology Today*, ed. Emmanuel Katongole (Scranton, PA: University of Scranton Press, 2002), 102.

11. Prosper Mushy, "Terrorism in Africa: The Response of Theology," *African Ecclesiastical Review* 57, no. 1–2 (June 2015): 7–8.

Just as one gathers many pieces of wood or charcoal in order to make a fire, so it should be for the life and spiritual growth of individual believers. The same applies to the traditional African view of community as the structure within which an individual finds identity. This should serve as one of the most appropriate frameworks to guide the church in Africa to develop a relevant sociopolitical theology.

Without neglecting the importance of an individual's need for salvation, the church needs to develop a theology that goes beyond an exclusive emphasis on personal ethics. When an individual comes to faith by believing in Christ, he or she becomes a member of the community of believers, the church. We see this in the life of Jesus, who called his disciples on an individual basis to become, as a group, his followers. These individuals became, collectively, a body, a community through which Christ was to manifest himself to the world. In the second half of the first century the believers' individual collective communalism, seen in Acts 2:41–47, became one of the distinctive marks of the early church whereby all the believers shared everything communally! The early forms of evangelicalism, in contrast, laid great emphasis on personal salvation, coupled with Western individualism. This may have prompted Richard Niebuhr to say of evangelicalism that "it could not emancipate itself from the conviction – more true in its own time than in ours – that the human unit is the individual. It is unable therefore to deal with social crisis, with national disease, and the misery of human groups."[12]

Such a theology must be geared to establishing good relationships without neglecting proper doctrine. As an agent through which God seeks to extend his kingdom, the church should realize that a vision of the kingdom of God cannot accept the injustices, unrighteousness, and hatred along tribal lines that continue to prevail in Africa today. For Africans, "relationships are the essence of their Christian faith and experience. They live the Gospel in relationships. Injustice, family and community tensions, and even international issues, are processed within the redemptive framework of the church, the new community in which the love of God has tremendously enriched the traditional African experience of the person in community."[13] The church's sociopolitical theology should be grounded on the biblical revelation of God, with all his attributes and characteristics brought to the fore.

---

12. H. Richard Niebuhr, *The Kingdom of God in America* (New York: Harper, 1937), 162.

13. David W. Shenk, *Justice, Reconciliation and Peace in Africa* (Nairobi: Uzima, 1983), xii.

C. The Place of Women

Women played a significant role in traditional African society. Indeed it can be said that in Africa, women are the hub of society. Motherhood was a cardinal duty that earned the African woman a very high status in society. "The power of . . . womanhood (particularly, but not solely, as motherhood or potential motherhood) has always been of the essence in African societies. It permeated all aspects of life: from the religious, the socio-political to the economic."[14] Women occupied a significant place in society as "most African communities have a culture that provides for the creation of a women's platform from which to influence the community and stimulate change."[15] The involvement of women in sociopolitical life in Africa goes back to the precolonial period when "many women in sub-Saharan Africa engaged in local politics and community activities."[16] The African corporate kinship society ensured that women were included in political participation such that they could "rise to political leadership positions."[17] The various nuances of the saying "Charity begins at home" among many African communities have the connotation of the home being the cradle of society: the home is a central place where African values, morals, and mores are inculcated. Women were entrusted with the cardinal task and duty of being homemakers, in which task they earned the respect of the entire community.

Motherhood was a cherished role as it signified the perpetuation of society and especially the inculcation of morals and values that held the family unit and the entire community intact. We must underscore the centrality of women in the home. In most African communities, the home belonged to the woman (wife or mother), although the man (husband or father) laid claim to the house. The pride of the man and the family as a whole was the woman (mother). A successful man owed his success to the woman (wife), and thus it may be said that the man was the head, but the woman was the controller. Even in

---

14. Laurenti Magesa, "Differences That Bind the Liberation of Women in Africa," *African Ecclesiastical Review* 35, no. 1 (Feb. 1993): 49–50.

15. Fulata Lusungu Moyo, "'Is Africa Ready for a Female President?' A Feminist Theological Search into the Role of Vera Chirwa as Politician and Human Rights Activist within the Prophetic Ministry of the Livingstonia Synod of Church of Central Africa Presbyterian (CCAP) in Malawi, 1959–2004," in *Changing Relations between Churches in Europe and Africa: The Internationalization of Christianity and Politics in the 20th Century*, ed. Katharina Kunter and Jens Holger Schjørring (Wiesbaden: Harrassowitz, 2008), 201.

16. Kathleen M. Fallon, *Democracy and the Rise of Women's Movements in Sub-Saharan Africa* (Baltimore, MD: Johns Hopkins University Press, 2008), 18.

17. Gisela G. Geisler, *Women and the Remaking of Politics in Southern Africa: Negotiating Autonomy, Incorporation, and Representation* (Uppsala: Nordiska Afrikainstitutet, 2004), 19.

decision-making, women were the drivers, and "although women may not have necessarily wielded more power than men, women clearly were, and many continue to be, actively involved in social, economic, and political issues."[18] Women fed the family, and although the men may have provided the food, it was the responsibility of the mothers to ensure that all members of the family were fed and nurtured. Women toiled and labored in small-scale farms or in small enterprises like businesses and self-help projects, with the sole purpose of providing for their families.[19] A good and cherished woman was one who held her family together. In this respect, the dream of any African woman was to get married, make a home, and have children. Singleness for women was abhorred, while barrenness was considered to be unfortunate, and in some cases abnormal or even a curse, such that every effort was made, including traditional healing practices, to deal with this anomaly. Some communities have provisions for adoption of children as a custom during marriage.

Nevertheless, "African women have been treated rather like so many worthless stones in the cultures of Africa, and doubly so when the continent was subjugated by slavery, colonialism and neo-colonialism."[20] Discrimination against women in Africa on the basis of their gender has emanated from erroneous cultural beliefs that they are inferior to men. The assumed biological fragility of women was perceived to be a measure of physical weakness and hence inferiority. As Magesa notes:

> It was, unfortunately, assumed by African traditional culture that many considerations applicable to men as proper to human beings could not be applied in every respect to women. So, for example, in many ethnic groups a woman could not own property; she could not claim her own children for custody, either in wedlock or out of it. Children were deemed to belong to the biological father (or even in matrilineal and matrilocal ethnic groups, to the maternal uncle; a man). In this also lies the fundamental cultural reason why, for instance, African parents for a long time denied their female offspring formal education.[21]

---

18. Fallon, *Rise of Women's Movements*, 5.

19. Dorothy Louise Hodgson, *Being Maasai, Becoming Indigenous: Postcolonial Politics in a Neoliberal World* (Bloomington, IN: Indiana University Press, 2011), 184.

20. Laurenti Magesa, "Christology, African Women and Ministry," *African Ecclesiastical Review* 38, no. 2 (April 1996): 79.

21. Magesa, "Differences That Bind," 49.

Women have been actively involved in sociopolitical activities, having a significant influence and impact on the transformation of their individual communities and countries. Using different avenues, they have made their voices heard and had their interests addressed, particularly in the wake of the democratization process in the last two decades. There are many examples of female participation in politics throughout sub-Saharan Africa. In Ghana, women were involved in the struggle for anti-colonialism and were recognized by Kwameh Nkrumah, who reserved them ten seats in parliament.[22] In post-independent Ghana, women have stepped up pressure on the government to address their concerns. In 2003, women in the Central African Republic demanded to participate in the transitional government and were given more seats in the National Transitional Council. In Zimbabwe, women "fought in the liberation war as combatants," and although few were assimilated into political leadership after independence, many professional women have joined formal politics in the last few years.[23] In Kenya, women have been actively involved in the democratization process, particularly since the 2002 national elections. Their involvement in the drafting of the national constitution opened up female representation in positions in all civic and government sectors with the enactment of a third gender-rule constitutional requirement. In the 2003 presidential election year, women in Guinea, through protests, forced the government to reduce the price of basic commodities. In 1999 women in Namibia created a manifesto that saw more women participate in elections, increasing their numbers in the national assembly from 19 percent to 27 percent.[24]

Numerically, there are more women in both society and the church. In Malawi, for instance, "while women are the majority when it comes to membership and regular church attendance, men who occupy positions of bishops, moderators, general secretaries and other equally powerful positions when it comes to decision making are the ones whose interests are safeguarded (they are the status quo whose interests are preserved)."[25] Even with the changes that have taken place with the "emancipation" of women and the incessant efforts made toward affirmative action in the last few decades, "women in Africa are still struggling for equal treatment, whether to access health care, education, the labor market or political rights. Yet women make vital contributions in

---

22. Geisler, *Women and the Remaking of Politics*, 24.
23. Geisler, 24.
24. Fallon, *Rise of Women's Movements*, 3.
25. Fulata Lusungu Moyo, "Is Africa Ready for a Female President?," 211.

society and they use the little windows of opportunity to advocate for equality and for the future of other women."[26] There are many documented cases of African women who have made significant contributions in society, such as Leymah Gbowee, "a Liberian activist who helped bring her country out of a brutal civil war and one of the 2011 Nobel Peace Prize winners";[27] Winnie Mandela in South Africa; Wangari Maathai in Kenya; Vear Chirwa in Malawi; and a host of others who have been actively involved in political ventures, such as Martha Karua and Charity Ngilu in Kenya, and, significantly, Madam Ellen Johnson Sirleaf, "the 24th President of Liberia and the first elected female Head of State in Africa."[28] The role and place of women in society is a significant issue that the church needs to address in its articulation of theology. This is especially so because of the ill-treatment and prejudice that women have endured while yet being the majority members of the church. The question of women leadership particularly in the church is crucial, even as the call for affirmative action continues to reverberate across the continent.

D. Land and Inheritance

Central to political structures is land; however, "European and African conceptions of the essential relationship between people and the land were fundamentally different . . . Africans were concerned to use land, not to hold it."[29] As a statement attributed to a Nigerian chief says: "I conceive that land belongs to a vast family of which many are dead, few are living and countless members are still unborn."[30] This indicates that ownership of land was communal, coupled with a strong system of communalism of "moral ethnicity" based upon the extended family, lineage, and clan system of the unborn, the living, and the living dead. It should be noted here that in most African communities, "men saw themselves linked to the land through membership in social groups. They were more concerned to maintain themselves in good

---

26. Musimbi Kanyoro, "Not without Struggle: Changing Roles of African Women in the 21st Century," in Kunter and Schjørring, *Changing Relations,* 217.

27. Chris Herlinger, "Three Women Activists Take Peace Prizes," *The Christian Century* 128, no. 22 (1 Nov. 2011): 14.

28. UNESCO, "Ellen Johnson Sirleaf," n.d., https://en.unesco.org/sites/default/files/bio_ellen_johnson_sirleaf_eng_ok.pdf.

29. L. H. Gann and Peter Duignan, eds., *Profiles of Change: African Society and Colonial Rule,* Vol. 3 of *Colonialism in Africa, 1870–1960* (Cambridge: Cambridge University Press, 1969), 198–99.

30. Gann and Duignan, *Profiles of Change,* 203.

standing in society than to obtain rights in land as such."[31] Among the Luo tribe of Kenya, for instance, land was a key component of social life, for "even as Luo husbands competed with their fathers in law and other suitors over women's loyalties, they also had to compete with neighbours and relatives for control over land."[32] Land is primary to the life and sustenance of the community, as C. W. Hobley, a former senior provincial commissioner in Kenya, observes: "it has been said with truth that the basis of all African society is the land which each tribe occupies."[33] This is also attested in Jomo Kenyatta's *Facing Mount Kenya*, where he argues that land "is the key to the people's life; it secures for them that peaceful tillage which supplies their material needs and enables them to perform their magic and traditional ceremonies in undisturbed serenity."[34] Richard Cox affirms the same point: "Land . . . is the most important factor in the social, political and religious life of the tribe [Kikuyu]."[35] Another writer states, "All African tribes were either agriculturalists or pastoral people, herding their own cattle, cultivating their own small-holdings, helping one another in certain communal work, such as hut building."[36] The attachment to the land and its significance in African life must therefore be a key component of the church's theology.

Throughout the continent, Africans have depended on land for their livelihood, and therefore "African societies were land-rich societies."[37] Land ownership and inheritance was a vital aspect of African patrilineal tradition and individual communities had land-management structures and polity. In most African countries, land was communally owned; the sense of individual ownership is a new phenomenon that came with the Western capitalist mindset. In precolonial Uganda, for example, land "was by and large communally owned and its use and control were guided by custom, which had protected women's

---

31. Gann and Duignan, 200.

32. Derek R. Peterson, "Revivalism and Dissent in Colonial East Africa," in *The East African Revival: Histories and Legacies*, ed. Kevin Ward and Emma Wild-Wood (Farnham: Ashgate, 2011), 111.

33. Charles William Hobley and James George Frazer, *Bantu Beliefs and Magic* (London: Witherby, 1938), 36.

34. Jomo Kenyatta, *Facing Mount Kenya: The Tribal Life of the Gikuyu* (London: Secker & Warburg, 1953), xxi.

35. Richard Cox, *Kenyatta's Country* (London: Hutchinson, 1965), 18.

36. Adelphoi, *His Kingdom in Kenya* (London: Hodder & Stoughton, 1953), 39.

37. Madipoane J. Masenya and Hulisani Ramantswana, "*Lupfumo Lu Mavuni* (Wealth Is in the Land): In Search of the Promised Land (cf. Ex 3–4) in the Post-Colonial, Post-Apartheid South Africa," *Journal of Theology for Southern Africa* 151 (March 2015): 102.

land use rights."[38] Needless to say, in most African settings, land ownership and inheritance favored one gender, and "although many African women worked hard towards the produce of the fields (land), they had little or no say towards the produce. Even after the deaths of their spouses, the inheritance rights favoured their sons if they had any, or their deceased husbands' relatives (cf. in particular in the case of levirate marriages). In such settings, land heritage was passed on from father to son."[39] The death of the head of the family was always dreaded, though, since, as the saying goes, "When the head of the family dies, that family breaks up."

Part of the reason why colonialism was abhorred has to do with the issue of land and inheritance, as Africans were dispossessed. Thomas Spear makes this point in observing how white people manipulated customary law to aid their settlement, and cites Elizabeth Colson who analyses the glaring contradictions evident in the white settlers' enactment of their individual tenure of land while Africans had communal ownership.[40] In a sense, "this allowed colonial governments to alienate African land en bloc at the behest of the chief while also proclaiming African backwardness and restricting Africans from individual enterprise. It was, [Colson] notes, a masterful means of facilitating and justifying exploitation at the same time."[41]

The accession to and use of land was a central component of traditional African polity that colonialism sought to utilize in its favor, to the detriment of African social cohesion. This is because "colonial authorities were making new economic demands on Africans to sacrifice their land to settlers, work away from home and produce new crops, all of which dramatically affected the local lineage politics by which individuals gained access to resources and economic security through strategic alliances with patrons and one another."[42] The centrality of land and inheritance among Africans has indeed been a key contributor to the major upheavals that have faced the continent over the centuries. This is true of the struggle for independence in colonial Africa as

---

38. Sheila Kawamara-Mishambi and Irene Ovonji-Odida, "The 'Lost Clause': The Campaign to Advance Women's Property Rights in the Uganda 1998 Land Act," in *No Shortcuts to Power: African Women in Politics and Policy Making*, ed. Anne Marie Goetz and Shireen Hassim (London: Zed Books, 2003), 165.

39. Masenya and Ramantswana, "*Lupfumo Lu Mavuni*," 103.

40. See Elizabeth Colson, "The Impact of the Colonial Period on the Definition of Land Rights," in *Colonialism in Africa*, ed. Victor Turner (Cambridge: Cambridge University Press, 1971), 193–215.

41. Thomas Spear, "Neo-Traditionalism and the Limits of Invention in British Colonial Africa," *The Journal of African History* 44, no. 1 (2003): 13.

42. Spear, "Neo-Traditionalism," 4.

well as of apartheid South Africa. In Kenya, for instance, Kenyatta became a threat to the colonial government because "he was general secretary of the Kikuyu Central Association, a party which aimed to get back the 'stolen lands' from the settlers, and was strongly anti-European."[43] Most post-independent governments enacted legislation that has sought to review land-ownership policies with a view to making amends for the discriminatory colonial laws that denied certain members of society, particularly women, land rights of ownership.[44] This is a positive step that the church needs to utilize in its articulation of a theology that seeks to give hope and uplift the lowly and oppressed of society. Land is integral to human sustenance, especially as it is a gift from God. Land is therefore not just a physical territory for human habitation but the very essence of human existence brought about in creation. The importance of land and inheritance is seen in that they were key to the call of Abraham, to whom God promised a land for his inheritance and that of his descendants. If the call of Abraham, which involved land, was through him to bless all nations that identify with his blessing, then we need to take seriously the value of land and inheritance. Land also has an eschatological dimension as it is the inheritance that Christ promises the "meek" in Matthew 5:5: "Blessed are the meek, for they will inherit the earth." These nuances are important for a sociopolitical theology of the church, which will be developed below.

E. Property and Wealth

The issue of property and wealth is tied to the above discussion on land and inheritance, since for Africans land was the essence of their existence. As noted above, land ownership has traditionally favored the male figure in the primarily patriarchal African societies. In traditional Africa, ownership of land offered economic security, not just for individuals, but for entire families, and clans. Tied to property was the concept of wealth, whereby a wealthy person was more respected and honored in society. A man's wealth was viewed in terms of how much land he owned, and the number of his livestock, wives, and children – particularly male children, for the perpetuation of his name. Africans cherished having many children; as Psalm 127:3–5 says,

---

43. Cox, *Kenyatta's Country*, 18.

44. Susan Jacobs, "Zimbabwe: State, Class, and Gendered Models of Land Resettlement," in *Women and the State in Africa*, ed. Jane L. Parpart and Kathleen A. Staudt (Boulder, CO: Rienner, 1989).

Children are a heritage from the LORD,
   offspring a reward from him.
Like arrows in the hands of a warrior
   are children born in one's youth.
Blessed is the man
   whose quiver is full of them.
They will not be put to shame
   when they contend with their enemies in the gate.

Africans valued the continued survival of their kin to carry on their name; thus the more children one had, the merrier. In this sense, then, property and wealth were not individualized but communal affairs. There was a case of one renowned chief in Kenya who had ten wives whom he numbered one to ten, and so many children he could hardly identify them. It is said that when he interacted with his children, they would identify themselves by the number given to their mother.

In view of the diminishing arable land and the population explosion in virtually all African countries, change in the value and nature of property and wealth is inevitable. This situation calls for a broad transformation of mindset regarding wealth, property, and distribution among members of the community. This is a complex issue that has historically been a major cause of bloodshed. The majority of the population in Africa live on small areas of their ancestral land, while a few rich people have acquired huge parcels, mainly through unjust and unscrupulous means. Indeed "Africa's immense resources are in direct contrast to the misery of its poor. The situation becomes even more scandalous if consideration is given to the wealth amassed in the hands of a privileged few."[45] This has created numerous problems within society, and governments have established frameworks and policies to address the issue. It must be said that many well-to-do members of society have used deceptive and unethical practices to acquire land fraudulently. More disheartening is the fact that the church has also been involved in acquiring land and property irregularly. This is attested in a report by the commission established by Kenyan president Mwai Kibaki to look into how public property ended up in the hands of individuals and organizations:

Churches and foreign embassies as well as politicians and civil servants are named in the Ndung'u report as having received and

---

45. Bernadette Ndunguru, "The Role of Women in Peacebuilding and Reconciliation in the AMECEA Countries," *African Ecclesiastical Review* 51, no. 3 (Sep. 2009): 282.

sold public land. They include many of the mainstream churches like the Catholics and Anglicans as well as smaller religious groups . . . Churches and foreign missions are also alleged to have taken part in the irregular acquisitions. The churches mainly grabbed public utility plots and school playgrounds. Some received the land as an inducement or reward for mobilizing political support for Kanu. "In many instances, the religious institutions obtained public land without paying money for it," the report states. "At times they obtained large tracts of public land for very little money." . . . The moral decadence epitomized by the grabbing of public land did not spare religious institutions of all faiths. Among the churches listed in the report are the Catholic, Anglican, Africa Inland Church, Presbyterian Church of East Africa and the Seventh Day Adventist. Others are Baptist, Full Gospel of Kenya, AIPCA, Redeemed Gospel, Holy Trinity, and Pentecostal Assemblies of God.[46]

This is a serious allegation that may require further reflection and consideration in order to establish the role and responsibility of the church. In view of the commonality of experiences across many African countries, it is not farfetched to argue that each country will be able to identify cases in its own context where the church has been implicated in such malpractices.

Land is central and essential to Africans just as it was for the Israelites in the Old Testament. The sustenance of the African is linked, as it was for the Israelites, to property and land ownership. Property and land, like all other components of creation that foster existence, are understood to be gifts from God. Christopher Wright says of Israel that "family-plus-land units had a basic role and importance in Israel's understanding of their relationship with Yahweh. When therefore economic changes and human greed later combined to attack and destroy large numbers of such small family landholdings, certain prophets were moved to denounce this, not merely on the grounds of social justice, but because it represented an attack upon one of the basic socio-economic pillars on which Israel's relationship with Yahweh rested – the family and its land."[47] Property and wealth are important for human enjoyment of life, although not as ends in themselves or means to riches; rather they must be appropriated with

---

46. David Mugonyi, "Churches and MPs Named in Land Deals," *Daily Nation* online, 8 October 2004.

47. Christopher J. H. Wright, *God's People in God's Land: Family, Land, and Property in the Old Testament* (Grand Rapids, MI: Eerdmans, 1990), 65.

God in view as the provider. Indeed the promise of property and wealth is tied to the cost of discipleship in Mark 10:29–30: "'Truly I tell you,' Jesus replied, 'no one who has left home or brothers or sisters or mother or father or children or fields for me and the gospel will fail to receive a hundred times as much in this present age: homes, brothers, sisters, mothers, children and fields – along with, persecutions – and in the age to come eternal life.'" Likewise, Matthew 16:26 says: "What good will it be for someone to gain the whole world, yet forfeit their soul? Or what can anyone give in exchange for their soul?" These are important biblical admonitions requiring theological consideration by the church in Africa that we shall allude to later.

This survey of the characteristics of traditional African politics has provided significant insights for our understanding of the challenges to, and opportunities for, African political theology. The unsurpassable value and wealth of African traditions are positive for a relevant theology. The all-inclusive, holistic view of life that was characteristic of African traditional life includes God as the source and sustainer of life. This is the beginning point for dealing with the threat that these characteristics have posed for maintaining unity and the realization of African aspirations. Sociopolitical problems do not emerge from incidental situations, but from human will and purpose spurred on by a desire to control and subjugate in total disregard of God's command to "love your neighbor as you love yourself."

4

Contemporary Issues in African Politics

Numerous issues characterize politics in Africa today. The terms and concepts that we find used in relation to politics in Africa need to be understood against the backdrop of world history as they carry the imprint of ancient philosophies and vast empires associated with global human civilization. In this respect, our discussion of selected contemporary issues in African politics takes cognizance of the significance of the impact of European hegemony in transforming the African political organizations and bringing in new forms that blended with preexistent sociopolitical structures.

Africa has undergone many stages of political experience, as we have noted above, and understanding these is critical to having an insight in the intricacies of African politics today. Beside the inherent structures that were born and bred in the heart of the continent, many others were imported and conveniently assimilated to form the political quagmire that constitutes contemporary African politics. We therefore need to consider the impact of the nuances of the traditional politics as well as of the imported politics as they have contributed to the politics that we find in the continent today. The imported nuances are made up of a conglomeration of diverse European hegemonies ranging from British, Dutch, French, German, Portuguese, and Spanish, with their different interests, as they gambled and subjugated the continent. The impact of these forces on the continent is a textbook case of a political society which is "a framework of ordered relationships within which we are enabled to live together and to satisfy our communal wants and needs. A political society, in short, is a meaningful human *enterprise*. It is not merely an event, something that happens. It is an intentional human creation, devised and directed to accomplish important practical goals."[1] The colonial masters were intentional and focused in creating, for themselves, a haven in which they benefited immensely. They facilitated the formulation of laws and legislation that advantaged them over the local people, even though they utilized some traditional African norms that helped them position their polity. These included, for instance, the adoption and use of chiefs in governance so as to legitimate colonial rule. If indeed "the fundamental function of the law is to prevent the natural unfairness of society from becoming intolerable,"[2] then the colonial regimes were ostensibly guilty of negation of the intent of law in the first place. The chief became the epitome of power and authority, and most chiefs would later be associated with political leadership. It is in this sense that we see that "the historical legacies of colonialism . . . are deeply colonial products."[3] These structures have fragmented society in a major way, creating a minority of rich and powerful overloads while the majority of citizens wallow in poverty. Politically instigated conflicts arise from the desire to dominate political leadership by clinging to power through "non-compliance with democratic governance as understood by international norms."[4] Incumbents refuse to cede power even after outright defeat in national elections. Those who lose elections fail to accept defeat and incite their ardent supporters to create disturbances that often result in violence. This has been so rife in African politics that "democratically elected governments have been the exception rather than the rule in Africa."[5]

The American presidential elections of 2020, where the incumbent, Donald Trump, lost to Joe Biden, demonstrates that this is not just an African problem.

---

1. Thomas A. Spragens, *Understanding Political Theory* (New York: St. Martin's Press, 1976), 2.

2. Arthur Selwyn Miller, *Politics, Democracy, and the Supreme Court: Essays on the Frontier of Constitutional Theory* (Westport, CT: Greenwood Press, 1985), 284.

3. Dorothy Louise Hodgson, *Being Maasai, and Becoming Indigenous: Postcolonial Politics in a Neoliberal World* (Bloomington, IN: Indiana University Press, 2011), 9. She posits the positionings and repositionings as "the state as the dominant organizing principle for governance, law, economics, and social welfare; the nation as a modernist ideal embraced and pursued by postcolonial African leaders; citizenship as the privileged mode of belonging; ethnicity as a primary form of collective identification and mobilization; property as the legally sanctioned framework through which to understand, access, and use resources such as land; development (and, by implication, productivity and profit) as the self-legitimating goal of African leaders; and modernity as the aspiration of both leaders and people."

4. Rialize Ferreira, "Irregular Warfare in African Conflicts," *Scientia Militaria: South African Journal of Military Studies* 38, no. 1 (2010): 46.

5. Ferreira, "Irregular Warfare," citing Filatova's *Democracy versus the State: The African Dilemma in Consolidation of Democracy in Africa – A View from the South*.

Donald Trump, the sitting president, refused to accept defeat and claimed that he won the elections. He called upon those who voted for him to reject the results, and on 6 January 2021, his supporters stormed the US capitol in Washington in an attempt to stop congress from confirming Joe Biden as the winner. Not only did Trump fail to concede defeat, but he refused to recognize Biden as the winner and further, he snubbed the inauguration ceremony. This is ironic for a country that prides itself as the epitome of political freedom and democracy.

Although several factors contribute to political strife in Africa, "the underlying historical causes for conflict can be attributed to domestic grievances or circumstances that may prompt irregular warfare."[6] Citing Botha, Ferreira notes the following domestic grievances: "Closed political systems where democratic transition has failed; Weak and failed African states; Control over territories associated with border control; Ethnic motivations where heterogeneous groups . . . clash over superiority and self-determination; Conflict over natural resources; Religion used as a political tool and Economic circumstances."[7] These situations may not be replicated everywhere, but human greed and desire for political power are often major drives that trigger strife. In this section we will discuss three contemporary issues – democracy, power, and poverty – that characterize African politics across the continent.

A. Democracy

The term "democracy" has different definitions and interpretations, particularly as it relates to Africa, due to the complexity of the continent's historical experiences. As noted by Staffan Lindberg, "studies of elections, democratization, and transition tend to avoid debating normative democratic theory."[8] The concept of democracy needs to be understood beyond the primarily Western discourse on the form of government to include a "general philosophy of human and political life: people's state of mind, their socio-economic growth and any form of recognized or legitimate government."[9] The viability of a people's political outlook that upholds equity and justice for all, including their processes of legitimating governance, should not be dismissed

---

6. Ferreira, 46.

7. Ferreira, 46–47.

8. Staffan Lindberg, *Democracy and Elections in Africa* (Baltimore, MD: Johns Hopkins University Press, 2006), 28.

9. Clement Majawa, "The Church's Role in Defining Genuine Democracy in Africa," in *African Theology Today*, ed. Emmanuel Katongole (Scranton, PA: University of Scranton Press, 2002), 53.

as undemocratic. As Lindberg aptly puts it: the "use of democracy as a viable attribute of political systems should include an empirically oriented definition of representative liberal democracy that is general enough to apply to a variety of contexts but specific enough to discriminate against clearly nondemocratic political systems and to facilitate an unambiguous operationalization."[10] In most African countries, for example, elections are viewed "as a core institution of representative democracy" where the "democratic-ness" of elections is measured "by the degree to which they display certain democratic features." In this case, then, democracy is seen "as an attribute of the political system" rather than as an object in itself.[11]

As with many other Western aspects introduced in Africa, the Western concept and principles of democracy are still foreign to many Africans. As Mugambi points out, "If *democracy* is defined as 'government of the people, for the people, by the people themselves,'" then practices of democracy in Africa that focus on "multi-party politics and regular parliamentary elections do not, on their own, produce 'democracy.'"[12] If we are to understand democracy as a system of government in which those who rule are chosen or elected by the people as their representatives, then the mode, processes, and outcome of elections cannot be dictated by a single universal norm. There is no single prescriptive or descriptive pattern or design that can be said to be the standard for democracy globally. The West, for instance, cannot dictate the form of democracy, or even expect other, non-Western contexts to replicate Western forms of democratic structures and policies of governance. Each context must define its own forms, patterns, norms, and structures that govern its polity and processes and that are relevant and appropriate to its individual situation as embedded in its established legal framework. It is against such legal and constitutional policies and practices that conformity, or the lack of it, is determined and upheld or condemned. This becomes the standard and measure of legitimation for any legally established government. In this sense, then, democracy should be contextualized to reflect African realities, for it is only then that it "will be meaningful if it is intrinsically different from political categories of the European countries. Just as the Western politics followed the

---

10. Lindberg, *Democracy and Elections*, 29.

11. Lindberg, 23.

12. J. N. K. Mugambi, "African Churches in Social Transformation," in *Democracy and Development: The Role of Churches*, ed. J. N. K. Mugambi (Nairobi: All Africa Council of Churches, 1997), 3. This definition is borrowed from the American Constitution, which is an indication of the extent to which the whole concept of democracy is Western, and primarily American, oriented.

European pattern of thought, African democracy should respect and follow [an] African philosophy and world-view."[13] Needless to say, the issue of democracy is vital since it is at the heart of the sociopolitical cohesiveness of the community.

The shape of most traditional African governments and the leadership style in African societies was, in general, "democratic" in the very sense of the word, although not in Western legal terms. Most traditional African forms of government followed specific rules, regulations, and norms that established cohesion and order within the community. The Maasais, for example, have had a sociopolitical structure that clearly defines their identity as distinct from outsiders based on language and diet. They further "divide themselves into a number of groups based on differences of tradition and locality."[14] The various groupings in this social structure are organized according to different clans and sub-clans that are determined by age group. These were formed through various stages of initiation ceremonies which gave specific responsibilities to each group to which an individual belonged. For the Maasai,

> The uniting factor is the mutual dependence upon a common source of water and grass. Among the men there will be a network of obligations and responsibilities. It is participation in this network that gives a man the right to grass and water. This is very much a participatory democracy. The elders, meeting in this unit, organize work parties, invite evangelists or seek government help. The man who does not meet his obligations to the group cannot expect to receive his share of the natural resources. These obligations include ceremonial responsibilities as well as contributions of labor and shared food.[15]

Two structures that elucidate the polity of the Maasai are *enkang* and *olmarei*.

> In the *enkang* each man is expected to contribute to mutual defence, the labor of herding and ceremonial obligations. Women help each other obtain firewood and water. Childcare is communal and the young children eat and sleep within the *enkang*. Hospitality is provided for visitors by the *enkang*. The final unit in this organization is *olmarei*. This consists of a married

---

13. J. Ndlobvu, *Democracy in Africa: A Copy of European Political Philosophy* (London: St Paul's, 1996), 53.

14. Gordon R. Mullenix and John Mpaayei, "Matonyok: A Case Study of the Interaction of Evangelism and Community Development among the Keekonyokie Maasai of Kenya," *Missiology* 12, no. 3 (1984): 328.

15. Mullenix and Mpaayei, "Matonyok," 328–29.

man, his wives and unmarried children. The head of the *olmarei* has authority over his wives and children. They look to him for protection and expect him to make all significant decisions. They have little freedom to make individual decisions that have not been sanctioned by him.[16]

These social structures have been critical in governing the life and harmonious existence of the community, and any deviations are met with penalties and strong resistance.

Since the traditional worldview still persists in modern African societies, for many African countries the ideals of democracy in political leadership are yet to be fully internalized and are constantly undermined. This is almost always manifested during national general elections when the incumbents manipulate the system in their favor and those who "lose" fail to accept the outcome of the results as free and fair. In this sense, the spirit of fair play is extinguished. "Democracy has certain universal ideals that cannot be dispensed with if it is to have any meaning. These include representation, freedom, equality, justice, consultation, accountability, rule of law, and civil liberty. Democracy implies that form of government in which the poorer class, which is almost always numerous, is allowed free and equal participation in all political processes."[17] In practice, however, these democratic aspects should be actualized in respect to the context and cultural norms of the people so that they can bear the full realization of what democracy entails without tearing apart the fabric of social cohesiveness. If, for instance, a given people decide who the leader will be by proxy and not by ballot, then that should not be seen as a less democratic election process.

The Western concept of democracy is a fairly recent development in African politics. For most countries in Africa agitation for the democratization of politics and society came in the mid 1980s and early 1990s. This was coupled with the concept of modernity with its myriad nuances that saw numerous generational responses in Africa. Chabal observes: "Political scientists operate very largely on the assumption that modernization is unidirectional and results in due course in a variant of Westernisation. This view holds as true that development brings about the transformation of 'traditional' society, in which

---

16. Mullenix and Mpaayei, 329.

17. Cyril Imo, "Evangelicals, Muslims and Democracy: With Particular Reference to the Declaration of Sharia in Northern Nigeria," in *Evangelical Christianity and Democracy in Africa*, ed. Terrence O. Ranger (Oxford: Oxford University Press, 2008), 40. Cyril includes a significant discussion of the Nigerian situation of confrontation between Christians and Muslims in the north.

communal factors predominate, into a society of individuals pursuing their own self-interests and behaving politically as discrete citizens."[18] This is akin to "the modernization tradition [which] envisioned that the newly independent African countries eventually would forge a common national identity in place of the multiplicity of ethnic identities."[19] The ethnic affinity that an individual had in the traditional African community was now being assumed by the state, yet the ethnic ties had not yet been nationalized. Consequently, national interests became ethnicized, with the individual's identity being linked to the state along tribal lines. The call for patriotism essentially signified the support of one's kith and kin who rose to the position of leadership. Loyalty to the tribe or local leaders rather than to the nation has consistently been the trend for most African countries. The individuality of a person is in a sense defined, as in traditional Africa, in the context of identity with ethnic affiliation rather than with the interests of the nation or state. For this reason, political players often seek ethnic endorsement to gain mileage in their individual political pursuits under the guise of safeguarding the interests of the community. In essence, then, the democratic process becomes a conduit to attaining political power and authority to serve especially tribal affiliates who were instrumental in propelling one to power. It is in this vein that the voting process is mainly carried out along ethnic lines, with each individual identifying not so much with the policies of the aspirant as with what the ethnic group identifies as their collective agenda. Anyone who fails to conform to the wishes of the ethnic community to which he or she belongs is termed a traitor and more often than not ostracized or, in extreme cases, excommunicated, with his or her property destroyed. In most cases, political leaders refer to the public in their local public addresses as "my people," which is illustrative of ethnic affinity. Such attachments to ethnic identity may explain the multiple incidents of ethnic violence in which the interests of the community/tribe overshadow individual or even national interests. In a sense, then, the freedom of the individual is intertwined with ethnic interests, not only in political matters but also in day-to-day social affiliations. The challenge of the democratization of society in Africa is a major issue that cannot be left to the political elite alone.

---

18. Patrick Chabal, *Culture Troubles: Politics and the Interpretation of Meaning* (Chicago: University of Chicago Press, 2006), 98.

19. Stephen N. Ndegwa, "Citizenship and Ethnicity: An Examination of Two Transition Moments in Kenyan Politics," *American Political Science Review* 91, no. 3 (Sep. 1997): 603. "A similar liberal conception of citizenship was central to the democracy movement in Africa in the late 1980s and early 1990s. African democrats demanded that the illiberal, authoritarian states that had replaced the initial democracies return sovereignty and rights to the individual citizen."

The participation of religious groups in the democratization process of their nations is also evident in a number of African countries. The role of evangelical ministers in Nigeria through the umbrella of the Christian Association of Nigeria (CAN) is a classic example of how the church in Africa has made an effort to be involved in the democratization process within its context. Nevertheless, there are internal differences between the various denominations and differences of opinion regarding how far the church should be involved in such political engagement. A similar situation is reflected in the Kenyan context where the National Council of Churches of Kenya (NCCK) has, on occasion, condemned less democratic practices within the government, albeit with variant perspectives from member churches. Some of the most vibrant churches have, on many occasions, supported the government and its policies. An example is Bishop Kitonga, the founder of the Redeemed Gospel Churches of Kenya, who, in the wake of the multi-party democracy debate of 1991, was quoted by the *Kenya Times* on 2 February 1991 saying that "in heaven it is just like Kenya has been for many years. There is only one party, and God never makes mistakes . . . President Moi has been appointed by God to lead this country, and Kenyans should be grateful for the peace prevailing."[20] This statement carries theological sentiments which link God with the human political structures. The endorsement of Moi through an unwarranted theological stance is indicative of the lack of proper theological reflection and the potential danger of identifying with an autocratic regime. We shall engage with this aspect later in this book. In the case of Zambia, three main ecclesial bodies – the Christian Council of Zambia (CCZ), the Evangelical Fellowship of Zambia (EFZ), and the Catholic Church's Zambia Episcopal Conference (ZEC) – manifest a church–state relationship. It is noteworthy that "while these three organizations have strong theological distinctives, they have tended to put their differences aside when it comes to church–state issues."[21]

The underlying cause for the robust activity of CAN in political engagement is, however, reactional, as it is a response to Islamic militancy and the introduction of sharia law in northern Nigeria. It is commendable, though, that CAN "organized conferences, workshops, symposia, and seminars that emphasized the need for committed Christians, regardless of

---

20. Quoted in John Karanja, "Evangelical Attitudes toward Democracy in Kenya," in *Evangelical Christianity and Democracy in Africa*, ed. Terence O. Ranger (Oxford: Oxford University Press, 2008), 84.

21. Isaac Phiri, "Why African Churches Preach Politics: The Case of Zambia," *Journal of Church and State* 41, no. 2 (Spring 1999): 326.

denominational affiliation, to change their attitude toward politics."[22] Imo quotes Bishop Onaiyakan, the Roman Catholic archbishop of Abuja, to illustrate the importance of such a stance: "We can no longer avoid the question of the relationship between our Christian faith and politics. We must evolve a suitable popular theology of political engagement . . . never again should good Christians run away from politics as a dirty job to be left for crooks and rogues. Political leadership as a form of Christian stewardship whose reward is great in heaven must now become a main feature of our Christian teaching and exhortation to the faithful."[23]

It must be pointed out that participation in the democratization process is not just for Christian religious groups. Other religious groups are part of the community and they too have been involved in airing their concerns on matters of political governance. This notwithstanding, religious coexistence in most African states, particularly between Muslims and Christians, has largely been characterized by intrigue and strife in a quest for dominance and in the effort to gain converts. In Nigeria, for instance, there have been clashes between Christianity and Islam since their inception, although the struggles have intensified for both religious and political reasons. Imo observes: "When Christianity spread, Muslims clashed with Christians. For a long time this confrontation was a silent one, not taking openly political, still less violent, forms. Most evangelicals in northern Nigeria took a pious, apolitical stance and were obliged to coexist with Islam even while competing with it for converts."[24]

This religious striving for religio-political domination has been compounded by the upsurge in religious extremism in the last few decades, particularly with the Islamic insurgence of ISIS and Al-Qaeda, with its offshoots of Al-Shabaab and Boko Haram in Africa. These groups have bred terrorism that has destroyed many lives and maimed thousands of innocent civilians, and, especially in Nigeria and the East Africa region, has brought about untold poverty for many families in Africa. This is yet another challenge for the church. It is imperative, therefore, that the church in Africa designs an appropriate theology "for combating the onslaught of terror from within the circles of religion."[25] As Abuom puts it, "the church must be contextual because it is still held in high esteem and still sufficiently independent to redefine the

---

22. Imo, "Evangelicals, Muslims and Democracy," 59.

23. Imo, 59–60.

24. Imo, 37.

25. Prosper Mushy, "Terrorism in Africa: The Response of Theology," *African Ecclesiastical Review* 57, no. 1–2 (June 2015): 4.

rules that govern African societies."[26] This should, however, be the case for the church to be involved since the ideals of democracy are essentially entrenched in the gospel message that the church must not only declare but also live and abide by as a lifestyle.

> All political or social phenomena have functions . . . Such dysfunctional – some would say aberrational – matters as violence, betrayal, corruption, secrecy, and propaganda all serve definite, identifiable functions, "notably that of facilitating the adaptation of a system or regime to changing conditions occurring either in the system or in the social structure, or in the outside environment." . . . Judicial decisions are political epiphenomena, and the supreme court is an instrument of politics, both in its lawmaking proclivities and in the fact that it is a target of interest groups. The court's function is to produce decisions that are not only system-maintaining but also system-developing. "A political function," says Friedrich, "is the correspondence between a political process or institution and the needs or requirements of a political order." Any political order requires not only stability but also a process of orderly change.[27]

B. Power

The issue of power in African politics is critical and yet as complex as that of politics itself. The exercise of power in politics relates to the appropriate (legitimate) use or misappropriation (misuse/abuse or illegitimate) of the laws provided in the constitution which govern political rule. Power is an aspect of the rule of law and is therefore constitutional. The exercise of power in political leadership is thus a justifiable provision of the law. The law establishes the various institutions of governance, the role each plays, and the manner in which the exercise of power is judged to conform to the provision of the law as stipulated in the constitution. Thus we can say that "the rule of law denotes a cluster of concepts."[28]

---

26. Agnes C. Abuom, "The Church's Involvement in the Democratisation Process in Kenya," in *Peacemaking and Democratisation in Africa: Theoretical Perspectives and Church Initiatives*, ed. Hizkias Assefa and George Wachira (Nairobi: East Africa Educational Publishers, 1996), 114.

27. Arthur Selwyn Miller, *Politics, Democracy, and the Supreme Court: Essays on the Frontier of Constitutional Theory* (Westport, CT: Greenwood Press, 1985), 288.

28. Shannon C. Stimson, "Constitutionalism and the Rule of Law," in *The Oxford Handbook of Political Theory*, ed. John S. Dryzek, Bonnie Honig, and Anne Phillips (Oxford: Oxford University Press, 2006), 317.

While our discussion relates to the African context, it is worth pointing out that the African political structures and systems that we highlighted earlier have been significantly influenced by traditions in history that predate modern African politics. Central to the power exercised by politicians and political regimes is the place of the military, which is a core component of national rule and stability. In Africa, as in other nations all over the world, "military power is a symbol of national prestige which no self-respecting state can do without."[29] The display of military power and might has been a tradition during national day celebrations. As a practice, the president, whether a member of the military or a civilian, is always the commander in chief of all the armed forces. This is critical because, for any political regime to endure and be stable, support from the military is indispensable. Consequently, most political leaders have endeared themselves to the armed forces, not just for security purposes, but also for protection of their personal interests. Top-ranking military commanders are often closely allied to the president, usually along ethnic lines. In cases where a fallout between the political leadership and the military occurs, there is often unrest which results in a military-instigated coup d'état or a full-fledged military takeover of national rule. This has been experienced in a number of mostly west and central African countries, such as Burkina Faso, Burundi, Central African Republic, Chad, Democratic Republic of Congo, Gambia, Ethiopia, Ghana, Guinea and Guinea-Bissau, Liberia, Niger, Nigeria, Sierra Leone, Rwanda, and Uganda. Burkina Faso experienced a series of military regime changes fairly recently when on 30 October 2014 Lt Colonel Isaac Zida overthrew President Blaise Compaoré, became the head of state, and appointed Michel Kafando as president. Kafando appointed Zida prime minister. A year later, on 17 September 2015, Gilbert Diendéré led the presidential guard to overthrow President Michel Kafando, but the coup lasted for just one week and Kafando was reinstated. In some West African countries, such as Ghana and Nigeria, military leaders have been known to exhibit an unshakable commitment to issues of national development in support of the ruling authorities.[30] Military leaders who are accustomed to commanding power have been known to lead "liberation" from the dictatorial regimes of their countries, assume power, relinquish their military positions or service, and compete for political leadership as civilians.

In order to sustain their military might, countries spend heavily on the acquisition of military equipment – mainly powerful, modern, and sophisticated

---

29. Omo Omoruyi, "The Nature of Military Power in the Politics of West Africa and Its Implications for Christian Faith," *Ogbomoso Journal of Theology* 4 (Dec. 1989): 39.

30. Omoruyi, "Nature of Military Power," 39.

armored vehicles and artillery.[31] Due to poor control, corruption, and greed for power, these arms have found their way on to the black market and have become the source of instability and untold suffering for millions in many African countries torn by civil war. A salient challenge that has undermined the peace and security of most African states is armed violence and its attendant dynamics. Armed conflict and crime in most African countries is the cause of negative development, poor governance, and inconsistent service delivery. Armed violence and the resulting community insecurity have had a devastating impact on the African political reality. We should note, however, that this insecurity is not experienced only in war-torn countries. The upsurge of terrorism, which is a global menace, especially propelled in the last two decades through Islamic religious militant groups such as Al-Qaida, Al-Shabaab, Boko Haram, and the Taliban, has escalated this problem.

African warlords and autocratic politicians are known to cling to power quite often in total disregard of the rule of law and the constitutional mandates of their countries. Manipulation of the government machinery to circumvent policy has been witnessed in a number of countries where political dictatorship has been entrenched as a system, such as Zimbabwe and most recently Rwanda, where the presidential term was extended by a referendum sanctioned by the same parliament that had passed the regulation of term limit. Quite often, the electoral process favors the incumbent to suppress any form of opposition that threatens to depose him or her from the seat of power, as has been witnessed in Zimbabwe, Burundi, and Uganda in the recent past. The desire to remain in power in order to safeguard one's interests at the expense of the national good often affects socioeconomic development, stagnates the growth of the country, and impoverishes citizens. This is a key concern for the theology of the church. Because of its significance in the mission of the church, we shall preempt the discussion on politics and the Bible by engaging briefly here with how the church ought to deal with this problem, and the understanding of power envisaged by Christ in the Great Commission.

The evangelistic mission of the church is based on the Great Commission in Matthew 28:19–20, where Jesus says: "Therefore go and make disciples of all nations, baptizing them in the name of the Father and of the Son and of the Holy Spirit, and teaching them to obey everything I have commanded you. And surely I am with you always, to the very end of the age." A proper analysis of this passage within its immediate context, considering the opening adverb "therefore," demands that we understand it in light of the preceding

---

31. Omoruyi, 39.

statement in verse 18, where Jesus comes to his disciples and says: "All authority in heaven and on earth has been given to me." This indicates that Jesus, who is king, has been given all power and authority by his Father over all heavenly and earthly, visible and invisible, realms of existence. We shall carry out a brief analysis of this statement in our discussion of New Testament political thought, but here we observe that the verse carries with it "the same conviction that is expressed in several of the NT Christological hymns, namely, that through the resurrection, Jesus is exalted and made Lord of the cosmos. In other words, God has handed to him all authority."[32] While Jesus has always been king, even before the creation of the world, this statement signifies a new beginning in which, by his resurrection and subjugation of the power of death, he through his church lays claim to all creation and brings it under submission to his authority. This process begins with individual members of the church, with their acknowledgment and appropriation of faith that leads to transformation from sin to salvation and subsequent obedience to Christ in word and deed. It is on the basis of Christ's power and authority, then, that his disciples are to go about the business of proclaiming the gospel of God's kingdom.

The authority that Christ talks of in this passage is also referred to by Paul in Ephesians 1:19–23, which points back to the resurrection and the fact that Christ's authority is "far above all rule and authority, power and dominion . . . not only in the present age but also in the one to come." Paul uses similar terms with reference to Christ's authority over all others in Colossians 1:16 and 2:9–15. The main force behind the opposing authorities that must be brought under subjection to Christ is Satan himself, who is the "supernatural opponent of God." For Paul and his audience, the referent of these authorities may have been "(a) political, in the widest sense, persons or bodies, those people or bodies who control other people and bodies; (b) supernatural beings who exercise or attempt to exercise control over one another and over the created world including humanity."[33]

Biblical scholars continue to debate the referent of the hostile powers and authorities in Ephesians and a number of other New Testament passages like Colossians, and how to explain them in modern terms. Although suggestions have been made to explain these powers in terms of "political, social and economic forces, or as power of tradition, ethical custom, race, or psychological

---

32. W. D. Davies and Dale C. Allison, *A Critical and Exegetical Commentary on the Gospel According to Saint Matthew* (Edinburgh: T&T Clark, 1997), 683.

33. Ernest Best, *A Critical and Exegetical Commentary on Ephesians* (Edinburgh: T&T Clark, 1998), 176.

psychoses or forces like sex within us which we cannot control," it is clear that for Paul and his readers "the powers are supernatural and cannot be reduced to, and explained in, natural terms."[34] This indicates that there is a strong interrelationship and interaction between the spiritual forces and the physical, to the extent that denying the hand of the supernatural in a natural aspect may be detrimental to and a denial of reality.

In light of the above, we can deduce that the mission of the church grows out of the power and authority vested in Christ. The sociopolitical theology of the church must thus begin with the recognition of the authority and power that Christ gives – authority over all creation, all powers, all realms. Since the authority with which Jesus commands his disciples to go means that he is ruler over all, there is no realm over which Christ does not claim ownership and control. For this reason, the church must develop a theology of power, not just for evangelistic purposes or simply for the spiritual dimension which entails combating evil spirits, but an authority over all principalities and powers in all aspects and realms of creation. This includes physical entities such as human sociopolitical authorities.

The authority of Christ over all principalities and powers is a clear demonstration of God's sovereignty, portraying his lordship over all aspects of creation. For this reason, "no human structure can now lie outside the sphere of his authority or remain indifferent to his purposes. Now all things are challenged by the righteousness that has appeared in his ministry and has been confirmed by his death and resurrection. The cross and the resurrection not only marked the victory over the powers of evil (Col. 2:15), but also represented the invasion of the power of salvation in history, on the earth."[35] By having this kind of understanding and so defining its theology, the church will be able to affirm its position and activity in the world. This will aid the church in stepping up its involvement in society, not just for spiritual purposes, but also to help bring about justice and righteousness in the sociopolitical arena.

Similarly, the church's theology of power must also include the authority that Christ has given his church over the world. The command given to the disciples to "go and make disciples of all nations" entails their participation in Christ's work of transformation of individuals of all nations, tribes, and languages. The nations and political powers comprise human leaders and subjects, sinners for whom Christ died and whom he desires to be won for his kingdom. As Abraham Kuyper writes,

---

34. Best, *Ephesians*, 178–79.

35. William A. Dyrness, *Let the Earth Rejoice: A Biblical Theology of Holistic Mission* (Westchester, IL: Crossway, 1983), 188.

the *human* element – here *the people* – may not be considered as the principal thing, so that God is only dragged in to help this people in the hour of need; but on the contrary that God, in His majesty, must flame before the eyes of every nation, and that all nations together are to be reckoned before Him as a drop in a bucket and as the small dust of the balances. From the ends of the earth God cites all nations and peoples before His high judgment seat. For God created the nations. They exist for Him. They are His own. And therefore all these nations, and in them humanity, must exist for His glory and consequently after his ordinances, in order that in their well-being, when they walk after His ordinances, His divine wisdom may shine forth.[36]

This implies that the voice of the church in Africa must be heard as a call for all to recognize that all authority, including political authority and power, derives from Christ, not for individual or personal interests, but to serve the intent and purpose of the Creator from whom all creation derives. It is also crucial to underscore the fact that the authority that Christ commands derives not from any earthly source but from God alone, and as such it is essentially different from any earthly human power or authority, just as Christ affirmed "my kingdom is not of this world." Thus, all levels of human power and authority must of essence be subservient to his authority. Any form of authority that seeks to elevate itself, including authoritarianism or dictatorship, rather than serving the purposes of God is, as in the case of the Babylonian king Nebuchadnezzar, in defiance of God and subject to divine judgment.

C. Poverty

Poverty is a global phenomenon whose levels are relative to the affluence of a given social context. Poverty is pervasive in Africa, permeating all arenas of life, whether social, political, economic, or religious. Studies on poverty from different contexts but in relation to Africa have alluded to its multidimensional nature. Olatunji distinguishes between absolute poverty and relative poverty.[37] The living conditions of the majority of African populations is deplorable. Millions are unable to meet their basic human needs of clothing, food, and shelter, let alone access to health care facilities, decent education, water – the

---

36. Abraham Kuyper, *Lectures on Calvinism* (Grand Rapids, MI: Eerdmans, 1931), 81.

37. Olatunji A. Oyeshile, "Poverty and Democratic Governance in Africa," *Ogbomoso Journal of Theology* 14, no. 1 (2009): 40.

list is endless. The most affected are urban poor living in urban informal settlements "with a toxic environment, uncollected garbage, bad smells, blocked sewers and contaminated drinking water. The populations lack health care, quality education and security."[38] It would be an understatement to say that in spite of the bounty of natural resources "Africa is a suffering continent . . . poverty is Africa's greatest problem, as seen in many aspects of African life. The poverty in this land is many-sided. It is economic, social, political and religious. It is also material, physical, spiritual, moral and intellectual."[39] The existence of poverty in Africa confirms the words of Jesus in Mark 14:7 – "The poor you will always have with you, and you can help them any time you want" – pointing to the reality "that there will never be a state of affairs in this world where there is a society in which there will be no poor people."[40] The centrality of poverty and the poor in the Bible cannot be underestimated. The term "poor" alone appears about 135 times in the Old Testament and 42 times in the New Testament, indicating the importance of this issue and the concern the Bible has for those so identified. The context in which poverty occurs is important for our consideration. Poverty is also one of the foundational aspects of liberation theology that we shall discuss later. Those who bear the brunt of poverty are the most vulnerable populations, especially women and children. Musimbi Kanyoro notes that "As the poor, women lack power and influence, and they are extremely vulnerable to sickness, violence and disasters . . . It is usually women who have to deal with the daily survival issues, keeping the house clean, feeding families and nursing the sores of children's skin."[41]

The following graphic observation made by Chris Thomas about poverty in Ghana is typical of most if not all African countries:

> Ghana, in common with many underdeveloped countries, is a land of contrasts between modern Western Civilization, and traditional African Society. These contrasts all stem from a more pervasive division between the rich and the poor. The Politicians ride about in their Mercedes Benz, the peasants walk for miles in the hot

---

38. Musimbi Kanyoro, "Not without Struggle: Changing Roles of African Women in the 21st Century," in *Changing Relations between Churches in Europe and Africa: The Internationalization of Christianity and Politics in the 20th Century*, ed. Katharina Kunter and Jens Holger Schjørring (Wiesbaden: Harrassowitz, 2008), 218–19.

39. Emiola Nihinlola, "Poverty and a Theology of Human Development in Africa," *Ogbomoso Journal of Theology* 14, no. 1 (2009): 162.

40. J. Chris Thomas, "Poverty and Capitalism in West Africa: A Christian Perspective," *Ogbomoso Journal of Theology* 14, no. 1 (2009): 51.

41. Kanyoro, "Not without Struggle," 218–19.

sun; bourgeois Ghanaians and Europeans buy expensive imports in large Department stores, the peasants buy their shilling tins of fish and milk in the colourful but insanitary open air markets; the children of the rich are sent to . . . famous and established Universities; while the children of many poor villages are not even taught to read and write.[42]

This depiction is just the tip of the iceberg of the experience of millions within poverty-stricken populations. Numerous reasons have been suggested for the increase of poverty in Africa. While theological considerations attribute poverty to sin and its effect on human structures as well as nature, there is reason to adduce both natural cosmic forces (nonhuman actors) on nature or the environment and human actors, in their various forms, as contributing factors. Olatunji alludes to this, saying that the "causes of poverty range from natural factors such as climate, geography and history, to man-made factors such as bad or deficient governance . . . [that] may exhibit the . . . entrenched corruption, lack of respect for human rights, weak institutions and inefficient bureaucracies, lack of social cohesion and political will to undertake reforms."[43]

Poverty in Africa, like all the other aspects that shape African reality, cannot be detached from its historical past. The precolonial political structures with their African cultural values were compounded by the complex political and economic structures of colonialism that left the continent not only exploited but also vulnerable.[44] David Hoekema indicates that the colonial regimes did not adequately prepare their subjects for "effective independence and self-government" which were key to the maintenance of economic sustainability. This was a result of "internal factors" which were instrumental in shaping governance structures. The activists who spearheaded the cry for liberation emerged from their "forest hideouts and urban safe houses" and assumed political leadership, where they found new comfort zones in "parliament buildings and state houses" where "they settled in all too quickly and granted themselves too many of the benefits and prerogatives that their predecessors in the colonial regime had enjoyed, necessitating both high taxes and regular 'contributions' from those who stood to gain from their official acts. Corruption and nepotism were already common features of colonial administrations, but

---

42. Thomas, "Poverty and Capitalism," 49.

43. Oyeshile, "Poverty and Democratic Governance," 40.

44. David A. Hoekema, "African Politics and Moral Vision," *Soundings: An Interdisciplinary Journal* 96, no. 2 (2013): 128.

the newly independent African office holders raised them to a high art."[45] The international monetary demands of world economies have also been major contributors to the deepening of poverty in Africa, particularly the World Bank and International Monetary Fund's enslaving systems of foreign aid for sustainable development. Hoekema says significantly: "Demands from international banks and development organizations to enact 'structural reforms' led to spiraling poverty, diminished state capacity, and massive wealth transfers to domestic and international investors in many African nations. Because African export economies are heavily dependent on agricultural products and minerals, the collapse of world markets in many such commodities devastated national budgets across the continent."[46] Most African governments, when they come to power, inherit debts that the former regimes incurred from bilateral as well as unilateral agreements with the lending economies. The terms and conditions laid down for governments to benefit from such "aid" are stringent, yet the need is so severe that the end result is mortgaging the country. This stretches the debt liability to future generations – hence the unending cycle of poverty in Africa.

Poverty is a pertinent contemporary issue at the very core of African existence and thus it is one that the church must seek to address. The political theology of the church in Africa must respond to the human contributors to poverty, which include corruption,[47] which has brought many peasant farmers to their knees, lack and denial of basic social and civil services, injustice in the distribution of resources, such as land and property ownership, favoritism, nepotism, lack of disbursement of legal justice by the judiciary, as well as bribery in government offices, all due to bad political governance. With all these hindrances to human development being perpetrated by those entrusted with the responsibility of being custodians of justice within the sociopolitical structures, the church in Africa cannot be indifferent; and it ought not to just speak against these issues, but confront them decisively and fearlessly. Along with the other issues we have discussed, there is a need for proper theological approaches that will not only highlight the evils wrought by such problems in African politics, but also provide solutions to the pervasiveness of negative politics in the continent.

---

45. Hoekema, "African Politics," 129.

46. Hoekema, 128.

47. Andrew Mullei, *The Link between Corruption and Poverty: Lessons from Kenya Case Studies* (Nairobi: Africa Centre for Economic Growth, 2000). This book demonstrates how "corruption contributes to poverty through a multitude of channels" (30). It also highlights the various aspects of corruption.

Part Two

Theological Approaches
to Politics

The preceding discussion that has surveyed the problem in African political engagement is critical for laying down the theological approaches to politics that we shall discuss below. The contemporary situation and experiences have been greatly influenced by the past, to the extent that our responses cannot be detached from historical realities. Similarly, the future is also contained in the present; therefore our actions today will play a significant role in shaping the future of African politics. The discourse of our predecessors, though oral, the various sociopolitical and institutional organizations and structures they formulated, coupled with the associations they established, formed the pillars on which the current sociopolitical and religious life in Africa stands. Since "people of a certain era often feel affinity with those of a prior one,"[1] we shall relate most of the theological political thinking of contemporary society to its antecedents.

The precolonial structures that characterized traditional African politics were instrumental in the manner in which Africans reacted to the Western influx. These structures also provided a basis for the Western colonial and

---

1. Michah Gottlieb, *Faith and Freedom: Moses Mendelssohn's Theological-Political Thought* (New York: Oxford University Press, 2011), 2.

missionary structures that dominated Africa in the eighteenth and nineteenth centuries and which gave rise to major global societal stratification and the self-consciousness of individual worth and value. Major developments in human capabilities and capacity have led to exploits of human potential, creating a global unification of sociopolitical expressions. Since humanity lives in a cosmic village that is multiracial, multiethnic, and multinational, the endemic problem related to such a societal blend must be understood from the diversity of its components. Similarly, any ensuing solutions need to take cognizance of the same structures with a view to exploiting all possible avenues for creating a society that is characterized by such values as will enhance human potential for good and the enduring survival of the cohesive and harmonious coexistence of all.

This section will look at the contours that have shaped African political theological thought, beginning with the missionary movement that is responsible for many of the contemporary strands of Christian theology in Africa. The quest for the Christianization of Africa through the spread of the gospel by missionaries contributed to the development of evangelicalism, a Western theological construct with a specific focus on the reading, interpretation, and application of the biblical text. In reaction to this Western dominance and Christian stance, black theology, or liberation theology, emerged with different strands that contributed to the sociopolitical and religious experience of Africans. We shall also look at various African theologians and their quest for an authentic African theology, who have played a key role in contributing to the shaping of African theology.

We are not oblivious to the fact that most Christians in Africa have no theological or biblical foundation to guide their involvement in politics. They have not been prepared to think biblically about what to do when personal, group, and national interests clash, nor have they thought deeply about what is involved in living in states characterized by religious pluralism. As a contribution to this situation we shall focus on the Bible and politics, highlighting specific areas from the Old Testament as well as the New Testament, before concluding with practical responses to specific issues that are pertinent to the political scene in Africa.

5

Political Theological Thought

L ooking at politics in Africa as a continent, we need to take cognizance of the presuppositions that have shaped and continue to shape not only the thinking patterns but also the religious expressions of our existence. The missionary factor is an inescapable entity that has had a significant impact on the manner in which Africans view the world and their practices in their day-to-day lives. The impact that Christianity has had on Africa, especially in relation to how it was communicated and continues to be propagated, is a significant aspect that needs to be looked at. As has been observed, Africans have a holistic understanding of life in that the various components are intertwined. As a result, religion permeates all facets of life in society, and thus the secular–sacred divide is foreign to the African worldview. Each aspect of life is therefore critical for the well-being of the whole.

Considering that our theology emerges from our daily interactions and experiences in life, we shall endeavor to interrogate selected structures that are key to theological thought in African politics. These include missionary thought which, as we have pointed out above, was instrumental in establishing Christianity in Africa. Examining the actions and responses of missionaries in their involvement in African sociopolitical and religious life, and the manner in which they communicated the gospel, will help us understand the kind of theological framework that shaped their thinking. This is important because their theological mindset was foundational in shaping the outlook of the African church in general. While taking cognizance of the immense and significant input and contribution of missionaries of the Catholic Church to the sociopolitical and theological development of Africa, our focus will be on the Protestant missionary enterprise and, specifically, those of an evangelical persuasion. The theological perspective of evangelicalism was the essence of missionary endeavors in the proclamation of the gospel. We shall therefore discuss the political thought of evangelicalism so as to unravel missionary beliefs and practices. We shall argue that there was no single missionary perspective, as some mission agencies enjoyed government support, while others were critical of colonial sociopolitical practices.

One other development within the African political scene whose theological thought is worthy of our consideration is liberation. The African liberation movement was informed by the struggle of the North American minority black African Americans for liberation from the long history of dehumanizing slavery, racism, and ill-treatment by the majority white-dominated American system of democratic governance whose law and practice was highly segregational and discriminatory. Unfortunately, this situation has barely changed in practice in contemporary North American sociopolitical experience, in spite of multiple amendments to the laws and constitutional provisions. Over the years, African Americans such as Eric Garner, Javier Ambler, Manuel Ellis, Elijah McClain, and, most recently, George Floyd have lost their lives at the hands of brutal law enforcement officers. Associated with these deaths is the catchphrase "I can't breathe" which has been "used in worldwide protest against police brutality in the United States and against the lack of police accountability due to qualified immunity."[1] Such cases are, however, outside the scope of our discussion.

Dubbed "black theology," the liberation movement became instrumental in the fiery preaching ministries of black African theologians. Our discussion of the theological thought of this movement is critical for us to understand the political theology of the African church, mainly in South Africa, at the height of the apartheid supremacy of the minority white people against the majority black South Africans. A comparison of the two contexts – North America and South Africa – reveals some interesting nuances that may be worth considering at length in another study. It is ironic that in each case, when black people were the victims of oppression, the white perpetrators of the oppression were at the same time the very custodians and key proponents of Christianity – including sending missionaries across the globe – whose core tenet that they preached is self-giving love, justice, and righteousness. This raises yet another key issue: that of hermeneutics and the manner in which the Bible is read, interpreted, and applied in context. Our discussion of the theological thought that characterized liberation theology will elucidate why the Scripture was read in a particular way and its application resulted in actions that would trigger

---

1. "I Can't Breathe," Wikipedia, accessed 16 July 2020, https://en.wikipedia.org/wiki/I_can%27t_breathe.

bitter and tragic confrontations between the apartheid government and the black masses.

A. Missionary Thought

Missionary theological thought emerged partly from the prevailing sociopolitical atmosphere in which the missionaries operated as well as from the theology espoused by their sending mission boards back home. The nature of the relationship and partnership that the various missions had with the locals and colonial governments in their individual contexts was, on many occasions, instrumental in the establishment of Christianity and the teachings that emanated from missionary reading and interpretation of Scripture shaped by their theology. In a number of cases, the missionaries had a cordial relationship with the state, which facilitated their activities and gave them a head start in their pioneer mission work. In Uganda, for instance, "the religious and political interconnection in the history of Bugandan Christianity goes back to the very first missionaries to the country. On the arrival at the Buganda court on June 30, 1877, the first two Protestant missionaries presented to the Kabaka, not only a letter from the Church Missionary Society, but also one from the British Foreign Office. This association between their Christianity and the British political power inevitably remained in the King's mind and of his advisors."[2]

An endorsement of a church–state working relationship is seen in the words of E. P. C. Girourd who, in 1910, called for a harmonious relationship between the government and the various missionary societies. His statement is worth quoting at length:

> It is essential for the prosperity of the East African Protectorate and more particularly for the welfare of the natives that the government and the various missionary societies working in the native reserves should endeavor to work harmoniously in the great task before them of raising the African races to a higher level . . . Succeeding generations are in our hands, and it is for us, the government and the missionary, to mould the people as best we can with the educative means at our disposal. As these means are limited, it is wisest to commence with the education of the sons of chiefs and principal elders, and prepare them for

---

2. Raymond Moloney, "Religion, Politics and the Uganda Martyrs," *African Ecclesiastical Review* 29, no. 1 (Feb. 1987): 8.

the duties they will in course of time be called upon to perform. The education of these boys will be undertaken by the Missionary Societies with the assistance of the Government . . . It is my earnest wish that the natives not be allowed, or be taught, to think that the Government and the Missionaries are not one and all working for their common good; and this can only be brought about by mutual support and at the same time by striving to preserve and not to destroy the African nationalism.[3]

The various mission stations that were established necessitated acquiring land as well as the legal authorization to build. Miller notes that the pioneer missionaries received favors from both the government and the local authorities every time they picked a site to put up a station.[4] There seemed to be a form of interdependence between missionary societies and the Crown throughout the entire colonial period, which "is not surprising when one views their common cultural heritage and the inevitability of overlap in certain areas of common goals and endeavor."[5] Gration notes how H. R. Tate, who was District Commissioner of then Kyambu (Kiambu), speaking at a United Missionary Conference in Nairobi on 7–11 June 1909 regarding the role of missionaries, said:

> We look to them to strengthen the moral force of this country, to give a true ideal to its development; to counteract the destructive forces which inevitably follow the opening up and developments of new regions in Africa; and to deepen the unity which should hold this country together . . . I believe in the work of the missions . . . and I regard them in the true sense as an imperial force composed of faithful and trustworthy sons and daughters of the Empire.[6]

Similar sentiments are echoed by Anderson, who says that under the leadership of Charles Hurlburt, the missionaries, most of whom came from the United

---

3. Brian G. McIntosh, "The Scottish Mission in Kenya, 1891–1923" (University of Edinburgh, 1969), 481–82, quoted in John A. Gration, *The Relationship of the Africa Inland Mission and Its National Church in Kenya between 1895 and 1971* (New York: New York University Press, 1974), 48–49.

4. Catherine Miller, *Peter Cameron Scott: The Unlocked Door* (London: Parry Jackman Ltd., 1955), 36–38, discusses how Scott received multiple consents in his favor.

5. Gration, *Africa Inland Mission*, 47.

6. H. R. Tate, "Report of the United Missionary Conference, June 7–11, 1909" (Nairobi, 1909), 56, quoted in Gration, 50. He further notes that "at the same 1909 Missionary Conference a resolution was unanimously adopted affirming that 'in the work of uplifting native races Christian missions and a Christian Government are mutually dependent'" (51).

States, "managed to relate well to each of the colonial powers they met."[7] Right from the beginning of their missionary activities, "the white missionaries in East Africa were supported by the authority of the Colonial Government."[8] In essence, then, although most of the missions did not have a clearly stated theology of involvement in political matters, such close proximity to and relationship with the colonial state is indicative of the support they gave to, as well as received from, the government. To a larger extent, the missions earned the endorsement of the regime, which readily accepted them, granted them safety, aided their acquisition of land, and helped locate them in prime areas that made it easy for them to accomplish their purpose. To this extent, then, they had a political practice.

The Kenyan political scene, which was affected significantly by the events of both World War I and World War II, resulted in Africans' concerted efforts at "self-determination" and an urge for liberation from colonial domination. Harry Thuku[9] was one of the African leaders who sought to challenge the "political, economic and industrial conditions, and a labor system that compelled many of the native Africans, women and children, as well as men, to leave their homes and go out to work for European settlers."[10] The indigenous people were compelled to work on the settlers' farms, neglecting their own, thereby resulting in scanty harvests. This practice was resented, but numerous efforts to challenge it were met with hostility from the colonial government. Thuku emerged as a spokesperson for the rights of Africans in this regard, and many young and progressive Africans allied with him. For a while he gained success by getting some changes made. This brought him popularity among the Africans. His visits to the reserves attracted large crowds who applauded him as a son of God, with others declaring him to be God, including converts to Christianity who unequivocally joined his movement.

Since there arose, among the Africans, a spirit of optimism and independence as the leaders of this movement demanded that "the government and all other 'foreigners' depart and turn the country over to them, orders

---

7. Richard J. D. Anderson, *We Felt Like Grasshoppers: The Story of Africa Inland Mission* (Nottingham: Crossway, 1994), 43. He says: "Indeed, the pioneers often found a warm welcome from officials . . . God undoubtedly prepared the way in answer to prayer. Also, remoteness made a European glad to meet any other white people and to assist them in their struggle against disease and a multitude of other problems which all foreigners shared."

8. Bolaji Idowu, "The Predicament of the Church in Africa," in *Christianity in Tropical Africa*, ed. C. G. Baëta, 1st ed. (London: Routledge, 1968), 424.

9. Fred H. McKenrick, "The Thuku Movement in East Africa," *Inland Africa* 11, no. 6 (June 1927): 1.

10. McKenrick, "Thuku Movement," 1.

were issued for his arrest and he was apprehended in Nairobi, March 15, 1922."
His arrest created an uproar that the government quelled by indiscriminately
shooting at a protesting unarmed crowd, leaving at least twenty young men and
women dead.[11] These events added fuel to his movement for the independence
of Africans among his followers across the country. The reaction of missionaries
to this event was instrumental in defining their perspectives and interests –
as, indeed, were other interactions the missionaries had with the locals. They
argued that this struggle for African emancipation was a hindrance to the
spread of the gospel and an impediment to the development of the church
because of the inconveniences it created for the missionaries in terms of their
movement. This may have been a valid concern. The problem, though, was the
notion that it was a "stumbling block and a snare of the devil to hundreds if not
thousands of the members of the infant church in Kenya," and the resulting
call for prayers for "all who have to do with the work" so that "this snare
may be broken and his little ones delivered."[12] This response indicates that the
missionaries were interested only in their own welfare and projects, with no
concern whatsoever for the experiences and suffering that the Africans were
enduring at the hands of the colonialists.

While it might seem that missionaries were neutral in their political
involvement, their continued support of the colonial government indicates that
they were partisan, and biased against the struggle for political emancipation.
One mission's field director was quoted expressing appreciation for the
government's attitude toward missionaries during the days of war: "You have
granted us every reasonable facility for carrying on our work. You have allowed
our missionaries to return to Kenya from Home, and to go Home from Kenya,
so far [as] you have considered such movement safe. While we feel that our
particular duty at the present time is to remain at our usual work, we express
our sympathy with you in your task of driving invaders from the country, and
we desire to be helpful to you."[13] The words of Henry Campbell also illustrate
this point: "The people are ruled justly in East Africa. If missionaries were to be
asked to express an opinion, probably an overwhelming majority among them
would speak in highest terms of British dealings with primitive peoples, and

---

11. McKenrick, 2–3.

12. McKenrick, 3.

13. Kenneth Richardson, *Garden of Miracles* (London: Victory, 1968), 73, quoted in
Gration, *Africa Inland Mission*, 70. This statement clearly demonstrates that the missionaries
took a political position in support of the colonial government.

state that their rule had been kind and fair."[14] Numerous letters and sentiments associated with the missionaries as they carried out their normal mission work give us clues as to the kind of theological mindset that characterized their work. A demonization of local peoples by the missionaries may point to a misrepresentation of the biblical teaching of all human beings as created in the image of God, which we will allude to in our discussion of the Bible and politics.

These thoughts may be associated with the events taking place on the global scene during World War II that had a great impact on the political arena, renewing the focus of the evangelical movement worldwide. A number of movements, directing their attention to evangelism and discipleship and mainly targeting young people, rose up in the USA and spread their missions abroad. At the same time, renewal in academic scholarship brought about the founding of evangelical theological schools. These developments made an impact only on the way missionaries broadened their mission to young people, focusing more on evangelism, discipleship, and youth camps, such as Youth for Christ and Word of Life.

During the African struggle for independence in Kenya, missionaries were actively involved in the government's program of rehabilitation of Mau Mau detainees by providing chaplains who worked in prison camps. The colonial government recognized such good efforts through which the indigenous people were taught "how to behave toward parents and those in authority like chiefs and the government."[15] Due to their good relationship with the government, mission groups such as Africa Inland Mission were granted time to air Christian programs in the Kikuyu language on the government radio station in Kenya. Timothy Kamau, one of the pioneer African broadcasters, relates: "After fighting the Mau Mau for a while with guns, the government realized that guns would stop the outward manifestations of Mau Mau, but that the roots from which the action sprang could only be destroyed by the word of God. They realized that 'the weapons of our warfare are not carnal, but mighty through God to the pulling down of strongholds.' So they asked the Christian churches to give their message over the radio."[16] Since the mission continued to support and cooperate with the government, it was also allowed

---

14. Henry D. Campbell, "Editorial," *Inland Africa* 14, no. 5 (May 1930): 9.

15. Tom G. Askwith, *Kenya's Progress* (Nairobi: East African Literature Bureau, 1958), 82, quoted in Gration, *Africa Inland Mission*, 71. Gration notes that AIM was "deeply involved through missionaries as well as African Church leaders who were set apart for this ministry."

16. Timothy Kamau, "Testimony of Timothy Kamau Radio Work in East Africa," ed. Robert Davis, *Inland Africa* 46, no. 4 (August 1962): 7.

to use other social projects that it had established as avenues of evangelism. The editorial of *Inland Africa* in November 1927 alludes to this relationship: "the government has set a standard which we must follow since they have given us the privilege of primary education in the whole district. This is what we want, of course, as we then have the opportunity to give the people the Gospel before they become hardened or get too much of civilization!"[17] The missionaries regarded civilization as detrimental to African people because it would not only enlighten them but would also trigger a wake-up call for them to demand their right to freedom from colonial domination. Despite the mission having been in Kenya for over thirty years, the attitude of the missionaries toward Africans remained the same. Raymond Stauffacher, writing on "The Soul of an African," said:

> Several times people have come to me and asked: "Do those savage Africans really have souls? Aren't they only a little above animals in their mental capacity and their ability to comprehend or understand?" It is quite true that the native African in his dirt and filth, clothed with a little piece of cow-hide, smeared with red clay, and with a hard, cold gleam in his eye, may at first sight seem to be nothing but an animal. But he has lived in sin for generations and generations. The witch doctors have filled him with a devilish fear of their charms, and his whole life is filled with a terror and dread such as only Satan himself can inspire. His heart is full of sin, he grew up in sin; so is it any wonder that his whole being should be saturated in sin and awful darkness? . . . That savage African in his grease and filth, animal though he may seem to be, has inside of him a tiny germ of a soul.[18]

In view of the mutual relationship that existed in Kenya between the mission and the government, it is evident that the mission attempted to maintain, at least in part, a traditional evangelical view of the government, as a divinely ordained institution which required the obedience of those under its authority in accordance with scriptural teaching, especially in Romans 13. The problem, however, was that their approach was not wholly in accord with Scripture, since it neglected, among other things, Jesus and the prophets' call for justice and righteousness. This cordial relationship that the church had with the government provided an opportunity for the church to reach out to

---

17. "Specimens of the Lord's Work," editorial, *Inland Africa* 11, no. 11 (1927): 10.

18. Raymond Stauffacher, "The Soul of an African," *Inland Africa* 13, no. 5 (1929): 10.

thousands of local people with the gospel message. The challenge, though, was that due to the government's control of the social channels, it was difficult for the church to critique the government and its ills.

Through this cooperation with the state, the missions were able to establish schools and hospitals which helped the African people come to terms with the reality of the Western influx and its influence on the traditional African way of life. On the other hand, the missionaries and the colonial government alike were able to achieve their objective of penetrating and controlling the Africans through Western concepts, ideals, and lifestyles. The missionaries used Christianity as one of their tools to propagate their Western values primarily because Christianity and Western civilization have always been juxtaposed. In light of this, Africans did not make any distinction between the missionary and the colonialist, since both seemed to have the same objective of dividing and controlling in order to entrench themselves and occupy African land. The colonial government's strategy was to confine the politics of each tribal group independently of the others for ease of control. B. A. Ogot affirms that the missions supported this government policy of confining African politics to tribal channels.[19] This kind of missionary support of government continued up to the time when Kenya gained independence,[20] and was also carried on after independence. On the relationship between the missions and the colonial state, Andrew F. Walls says:

> The missions, irrespective of their national origin, became part of the colonial state. It could not be otherwise. When power manifestly lay with whites, there was little point in distinguishing one set of white people and another. In fact, the missions had an important place in the colonial state, for they provided a high proportion of the educational and medical infrastructure. The missions were thus major agents in producing in Africa the organs

19. B. A. Ogot and J. A. Kieran, eds., *Zamani: A Survey of East African History* (Nairobi: Longmans, 1968), 280.

20. Several letters confirm this cordial relationship between the government and missions: "no mission has supported Government as faithfully as the Africa Inland Mission" (Letter of Elwood Davis to Henry Campbell, 25 November 1929, quoted in Gration, *Africa Inland Mission*, 54). Later Davis, speaking for the mission, affirmed: "We have stood faithful to Government through all the years and have been against the K.C.A. [Kikuyu Central Association] in their fight against the Government" (Letter of Elwood Davis to Henry Campbell, 25 November 1931, quoted in Gration, 54). During the Mau Mau revolt, as Africans stepped up their struggle for freedom from colonial rule, mission adherents formed a volunteer security force that was "recognized by the Government and given identification insignia" (Wellesley Devitt, "The Courage of Kikuyu Christians," *Inland Africa* 37, no. 5 [1953]: 12–13).

of the modern state, with literacy, technology and technologically based communications.[21]

Our observation so far has indicated that missionaries cooperated closely with the colonial political regime so as to pursue and advance their cause and mission endeavors. Although the missionaries came from contexts where church and state were not only separated but also worked independently of each other, such a separation did not seem to operate in the African context. The African does not compartmentalize the various spheres of existence, as does the Westerner. Both the state and the church as "public institutions" are viewed with an air of sanctity and respect due to their role in the life of the community. Such African attitudes toward these "institutions" in general makes the separation difficult if not impossible. Every aspect of life is perceived in relation to the whole, and without the whole, the individual aspect loses its place and value. It is interesting to observe that the missionaries did not question the African "holistic" practice. This may indicate that the separation of religion and politics is, therefore, impossible, and indeed a contradiction in terms in the African context (if not in other contexts). As Lynn Buzzard puts it:

> The image of separation of church and state distorts proper policy . . . by encouraging, by its very language, a "separation" of life into different spheres. It invites us to think that life can be divided into the sacred and the secular. It has been used to separate not simply the institutions of church and state, but to encourage and advocate the separation of religion, society, and the separation of moral viewpoints and culture. Thus the separation motif becomes a sword which cuts asunder the body politic, rooting out and separating public life from its moral and spiritual roots. Such a separation of life into that kind of rigid compartmentalization is both impossible and undesirable.[22]

Such a perspective is also held by Stephen Carter in his book *God's Name in Vain*, where he argues that it is wrong to raise the separation of church and

---

21. Andrew F. Walls, "Africa in History: Retrospect and Prospect," *Journal of African Christian Thought* 1, no. 1 (June 1998): 9.

22. Lynn R. Buzzard, "Separation of Church, State, and Religious Liberty," in *Citizen Christians: The Rights and Responsibilities of Dual Citizenship*, ed. Richard D. Lard and Louis A. Moore (Nashville: Broadman & Holman, 1994), 38. Buzzard contends that "the whole question of moral and spiritual values in the role of religion is not just a question of the freedom of the church to do its thing. The question is what kind of culture and what kind of society are we going to have in which to rear our children. The issue is the character of our very culture" (45).

state as a bar to religion in politics. Christians must engage with the culture in order to bring about the transformation required of it. The call to witness is not limited to a particular sphere but is an engagement with all dimensions of human existence, which includes their environment.[23]

At this stage of its life the church was yet to develop, for the African context, a concrete theology that would clearly define its role in political issues, because the mission was still foreign to the way of life, cultural values, and beliefs of the Africans. At the same time, missionaries needed all help possible in order to get established; here the colonial government was useful. Lawson Propst, a pioneer missionary among the Nandi tribe of Kenya, points to the help received from the District Commissioner: "You can see how much this means in a place like this and among a people like this, to have a government man who is willing to do so much as this to get the work started."[24] Since the missionaries had no explicit theology of the state, they certainly were not able to perceive what the African philosophy of the state was. Apparently, the "effective" theology of the Africans was too complex for the missionaries to comprehend since they had not as yet established procedures to penetrate the kernel of African philosophy and value systems. The missionaries, shaped by their Western theological mindset, were focused only on the task of preaching the gospel message in order to convert the Africans; they had not taken the time to penetrate the social-cultural values of African existence. One of the errors the first missionaries made in converting Africans was using the Western cultural grid and value system as the measuring gauge for Africans. They were geared toward evangelizing for their own purposes and within the framework of their own perceptions. The words of Johnston demonstrate this:

> We do need a much better acquaintance with the language in order
> to make them understand God's wonderful gift, but most of all
> we need such an enduement of power from on high that whether
> our words are clear or blundering, many or few, there shall be a
> conviction of sin and a real desire to turn from it . . . We also need
> to have our own conception of sin made more acute so that "sin
> may seem exceedingly sinful," that we may be more earnest in

---

23. Stephen L. Carter, *God's Name in Vain: The Wrongs and Rights of Religion in Politics* (New York: Basic, 2000), 194.

24. Lawson Propst, "Letter to Charles Hurlburt," 8 October 1916, quoted in Gration, *Africa Inland Mission*, 55. He writes: "He [the Commissioner] ordered the chiefs to have the people dig a path from our place to the top of the escarpment, toward Kibegori, and told them to come to us and make it where we laid it out."

warning them from its consequences – and in pointing out "the Lamb of God which taketh away the sin of the world."[25]

The missionary thought on politics, then, indicates that social activities such as schools, hospitals, children's homes, feeding programs, and any other aspects that enhanced human development, were indeed tools of evangelism. They were a means by which the mission's vision of evangelism was achieved, but not in and of themselves tasks of the mission. It is important to note, though, that in other global contexts there were missionaries who did not identify with the colonial governments in any way and who were opposed to the atrocities and ills done. David Hollinger posits that, "Among 20th-century whites, missionary-connected men and women were some of the most determined and influential critics of white supremacy."[26]

B. Evangelicalism

The task of defining "evangelicalism" is made complex by the multiple variations the term has acquired over the centuries. Mark Noll provides an extensive analysis of the complexity of this definition in the second chapter of his book *American Evangelical Christianity: An Introduction*, whose details go beyond the scope of our discussion.[27] Suffice it to say that the term "evangelical" is derived from the Greek word for "gospel" or "good news." It is used to describe God's plan of salvation through Christ's redemptive act. In evangelical thought, the gospel message is the proclamation of the saving work of Christ through his death and resurrection, with a call for individuals to personally trust him for forgiveness of sin, leading to assurance of eternal life. The term "evangelicals" is therefore used with reference to churches who see their primary task as the proclamation of the gospel and whose focus of belief and practice is to uphold the "prominence of the Bible and . . . Christ as the means of salvation."[28] These doctrines were also the cornerstone of the sixteenth-century Protestant Reformation. The definition of "evangelicalism," therefore, issues from the

---

25. C. F. Johnston, "Report on the Work of Africa Inland Mission" (Kangundo, 21 July 1901), 4.

26. David A. Hollinger, "Christian Missionaries against Colonialism: In Their Time Overseas They Developed an Appreciation of Other Religions and Cultures," *Wall Street Journal* (October 19, 2017), https://www.wsj.com/articles/christian-missionaries-against-colonialism-1508455448.

27. Mark Noll, *American Evangelical Christianity: An Introduction* (Malden, MA: Blackwell, 2001), 13.

28. Noll, *American Evangelical Christianity*, 13.

doctrine and practices that characterize the theology of those churches that are generally affiliated with the Protestant movement.

The multiple social and political structures that the church has encountered throughout the centuries have resulted in an evangelicalism that exhibits diversity, flexibility, and adaptability. This renders the definition of evangelicalism much more fluid. But as Noll observes: "The most common use of the word today . . . stems from the renewal movements of the eighteenth century and from practitioners of revival in the nineteenth and twentieth centuries, especially as personified by such noteworthy preachers as Charles Grandison Finney, D. L. Moody, and Billy Graham."[29] The term "evangelical" can, therefore, be defined as the descriptive term for the heirs of the Anglo-American religious revivals who exhibit a pattern of consistency in their doctrinal convictions and practices.

"American evangelicalism,"[30] with its different perspectives on the debate of church and state, has been instrumental in shaping the theological thought of mission churches in Africa. The term "evangelical" is used to refer to those groups whose emphasis in their teaching is on the proclamation of the good news of salvation, the central authority of Scripture, and the need for personal conversion. The use of this term, which is primary to American Christianity, has evolved, giving rise to multiple theological traditions and emphases in the beliefs and the task of the church in fulfilling its mission in the world. Between the 1870s and 1920s, the evangelical movement experienced vast changes that saw it split into two wings. "On the one hand were theological liberals who, in order to maintain better credibility in the modern age, were willing to modify some central evangelical doctrines, such as the reliability of the Bible or the necessity of salvation only through the atoning sacrifice of Christ. On the other hand were conservatives who continued to believe the traditionally essential evangelical doctrines. By the 1920s a militant wing of conservatives emerged and took the name fundamentalist."[31]

It is worth pointing out here that to make a distinction between evangelical and nonevangelical churches in Africa as a whole is impractical. As Bishop Zablon Nthamburi puts it: "In Africa, to divide churches between evangelical and nonevangelical is a false division," because the gospel is at the core of the

---

29. Noll, 12.

30. Jerry S. Herbert, ed., *Evangelical Politics: Three Approaches* (Washington DC: Christian College Coalition, 1993), 2.

31. George Marsden, *Understanding Fundamentalism and Evangelicalism* (Grand Rapids, MI: Eerdmans, 1991), 3.

mission of all the churches.[32] In making distinctions between the emphases given by various churches, the term "evangelical" can be used only with reference to those churches which are more concerned with spiritual welfare than with other aspects of the human person. This group comprises mainly the missionary established churches, Pentecostal churches, and African indigenous churches. In Kenya, for instance, this category tends to be more conciliar and shuns identification with the National Council of Churches of Kenya (NCCK) because the latter is more ecumenical and more focused on addressing sociopolitical issues. It is lamentable that this "evangelical" category of churches has not made significant attempts either to engage in or to produce literature addressing sociopolitical issues. Scholarly contribution on theological issues can be found only in journals, especially *Africa Journal of Evangelical Theology (AJET).*[33] The other category of churches is the "historic churches" which are concerned with the whole welfare of the individual. These churches are generally nonconciliar. In this category are the Anglican Church and the Catholic Church. There are, however, some individual theologians in the former category who have been actively involved in social and political issues, even against the traditions of their denominations, such as Rev. Timothy Njoya of the Presbyterian Church.

As their primary task, evangelicals lay much emphasis on "the preaching of the Gospel, in the interest of individual regeneration by the supernatural grace of God."[34] Evangelical sermons are generally "replete with graphic descriptions of the torments of hell and the perils of unbelief or . . . the consequences of a false sense of security among those who merely practice religion in its outward forms and never know the experience of conversion."[35] In this respect, then, evangelicalism can be described as "a position that appeals to the New Testament as the final authority for Christians, that calls for radical discipleship under the lordship of Jesus Christ, that offers a radical critique of the social

---

32. Zablon Nthamburi, interview by author, 14 June 2002. He notes that "evangelical" is a very fluid term that does not apply in the African church setting in the way it is used in the West.

33. As stated in its purpose statement on the back pages of its volumes, "*AJET* is published twice a year by Scott Theological College, a chartered private university in Kenya, in order to provide theological educators and students with evangelical articles and book reviews related to theology and ministry in Africa."

34. Carl Ferdinand Howard Henry, *The Uneasy Conscience of Modern Fundamentalism* (Grand Rapids, MI: Eerdmans, 1947), 88.

35. Randall Herbert Balmer, *Blessed Assurance: A History of Evangelicalism in America* (Boston: Beacon, 2000), 28.

order, and calls the world to repentance and new life in the kingdom of God."[36] The evangelicals are, therefore, inclined toward a particularly spiritual emphasis in their mission to the world, with the objective of communicating the good news of the kingdom for the purpose of an individual's spiritual salvation. The ensuing political reading of the Scripture for evangelicalism is the kingdom of God, which is the target and end of evangelism. Subjects of the kingdom are thus in the world but not of the world. The affairs and concerns of the world are to be spurned since they are of no eternal value for the believer. The task of the church is to bring about the transformation of people in this fallen kingdom through Christ's sacrificial death on the cross. The kingdoms of this world are characterized by evil and are in conflict with the work of God, and these the church must preach against with a view to overcoming them. Essentially, then, there is a "two kingdom" theological stance which drives evangelicalism to shun the affairs of worldly kingdoms. For this reason, an emphasis on political matters has not been a component of the mission of evangelicalism as a whole, and may be the reason behind the lack of a clearly defined theology of state and political involvement.

C. Liberation Theology

Liberation theology emanated from the works of Gustavo Gutiérrez addressing the Latin American context of poverty in the 1960s and 1970s.[37] However, Magesa notes that liberation theology is not just a Latin American construct, but global and "fundamentally biblical and theologically valid: it has to do with the freedom of the people of God and its practical realization in society."[38] Liberation theology is also associated with the contributions of the social gospel propagated by Walter Rauschenbusch, as well as with the Christian realism ideas of Reinhold Niebuhr which "set the basic agenda for the treatment of social concerns . . . for many decades in the twentieth century."[39] Political liberation movements in Africa, as pointed out earlier, were triggered by calls for political emancipation from colonial domination in the mid twentieth

---

36. C. Norma Kraus, ed., *Evangelicalism and Anabaptism* (Eugene, OR: Wipf & Stock, 2001), 8.

37. Gustavo Gutiérrez, *A Theology of Liberation* (New York: Orbis, 1973), xi.

38. Laurenti Magesa, "Instruction on the 'Theology of Liberation': A Comment," *African Ecclesiastical Review* 27, no. 1 (Feb. 1985): 4. Consequently he argues that "liberation is a fundamental task of the Church."

39. Richard J. Mouw, "Political Theology," in *Dictionary of Christianity in America*, ed. Daniel G. Reid (Downers Grove, IL: InterVarsity Press, 1990), 915.

century. This culminated in "either peaceful or violent national struggles for independence from colonial rule." In the late 1960s and 1970s, following the independence of most countries, "politics rose to a level of prominence and predominance."[40] Most of the pioneer nationalists who spearheaded liberation in their countries and assumed political leadership would later become the key perpetrators of prejudice, which was a betrayal of the spirit of liberation and emancipation, as brought out in our discussion of postcolonialism.[41]

The spread of liberation theology from Latin America to other contexts such as Africa was instrumental as it addressed sociopolitical, economic, racial, and other forms of injustice. This implies that there are different liberation theologies. North American black theology reacted to racism against black African Americans and was spearheaded by James Cone.[42] The black liberation theology of South Africa spoke to the apartheid political system of white people against black people. Some of the key proponents of this movement were Archbishop Desmond Tutu, Jean-Marc Ela, Allan Boesak, and many others who participated in the struggle for the liberation of South Africa, such as Albert Luthuli. There is also feminist theology, which advocates for the liberation of women.

The motivating factor in liberation theology is the call for justice and freedom for those who are under the shackles of oppression in any aspect that limits human freedom. This is a theology that addresses the liberation of the poor and marginalized by identifying with them and being a solution to their plight. Liberation theology thus becomes an integral component of the existence of the church. The church cannot be passive in its quest for liberation but must suffer as it identifies with the suffering of society. Tutu brings this out clearly: "A Church which takes sides and makes options for the poor and the oppressed and the voiceless must needs suffer and perhaps die, for unless it dies it will remain alone. A Church that does not suffer cannot be the Church of Jesus Christ."[43]

The church must also be at the forefront in recognizing the martyrs who have given up their lives for the liberation of the oppressed. In the South

---

40. Laurenti Magesa, "Politics and Theology in Africa," *African Ecclesiastical Review* 31, no. 3 (1989): 151.

41. Senyo Adjibolosoo, "Ethnicity and the Development of National Consciousness: A Human Factor Analysis," in *Critical Perspectives in Politics and Socio-Economic Development in Ghana*, ed. Wisdom J. Tettey, Korbla P. Puplampu, and Bruce J. Berman (Leiden: Brill, 2003), 116.

42. James Cone, *God of the Oppressed* (Maryknoll, NY: Orbis, 1997).

43. Desmond M. Tutu, "Barmen and Apartheid," *Journal of Theology for Southern Africa* 47 (June 1984): 77.

African situation, the church has not been at the forefront in commemorating their martyrs. In this context, Khumalo explains, "The term 'martyr' in Greek means 'witness', referring to those who are witnesses of their faith. Therefore, the Christian martyr is not so much someone who has suffered and has died for Christ, as someone who has witnessed Christ in his life until the end."[44] Albert Luthuli displayed what being a Christian witness entails as he identified with the struggle for the liberation of South Africa:

> With a full sense of responsibility . . . under the auspices of the African National Congress (Natal), I have joined my people in the new spirit that revolts openly and boldly against injustice and expresses itself in a determined and non-violent manner. Because of my association with the African National Congress in this new spirit which has found an effective and legitimate way of expressing the Non-Violent Passive Resistance Campaign, I was given a two-week limit ultimatum by the Secretary of Native Affairs calling upon me to choose between the Luthuli of the Groutville Mission Reserve. He alleged that my association with Congress in its Non-Violent Passive Resistance Campaign was an act of disloyalty to the state. I did not, and do not, agree with this view. Viewing non-violent passive resistance as a non-revolutionary and, therefore, a most legitimate and humane political pressure technique for a people denied all effective forms of constitutional striving, I saw no real conflict in my dual leadership of my people: leader of this tribe as chief and political leader in Congress.[45]

His actions were driven by his beliefs and convictions about the role and responsibility of leadership. He said of his civic duty that

> a chief is primarily a servant of his people. He is the voice of his people. He is the voice of his people in local affairs. Unlike a Native Commissioner, he is part and parcel of the Tribe, and not a local agent of the government. Within the bounds of loyalty it is conceivable that he may vote and press the claims of his people even if they should be unpalatable to the government of the day. He may use all legitimate modern techniques to get these demands

---

44. Simangaliso Raymond Kumalo, "Commemoration of Martyrs of the Struggle as Contested Terrain in a Democratic South Africa: The Case of Inkosi Albert Luthuli," *Journal of Theology for Southern Africa* 135 (Nov. 2009): 43.

45. Albert John Luthuli, "The Road to Freedom Is Via the Cross," *Journal of Theology for Southern Africa* 130 (March 2008): 113.

satisfied. It is inconceivable how chiefs could effectively serve the wider and common interest of their own tribe without cooperation with other leaders of the people, both the natural leaders (chiefs) and leaders elected democratically by the people themselves.[46]

Liberation theology derives its essence from Scripture, where we see God involved in the liberation of people and communities from oppressive political regimes and powers. The Old Testament account of the exodus is the classic depiction on which liberation theology is founded. In the New Testament, the liberation motif is clearly demonstrated by Jesus when he states his messianic mandate as that prophesied in Isaiah 61 regarding the fulfilment of his work by the power of the Holy Spirit to "proclaim good news to the poor . . . to proclaim freedom for the prisoners and recovery of sight for the blind, to set the oppressed free, to proclaim the year of the Lord's favor" (Luke 4:17–21). His parables and miracles (teaching and healing) demonstrate that he came to liberate people from all forms of slavery and oppression. This was in fulfilment of the Old Testament prophecies which looked forward to the Messiah who would come and liberate his people, but it is especially reminiscent of the account of the exodus in which God delivered his people by liberating them from Egyptian bondage through the hand of his servant Moses. This becomes the biblical springboard for the theology of liberation for the church. It is also a pointer to the eschatological anticipation of liberation in the culmination of God's redemptive act through Christ by the power of the Holy Spirit, in which he will free the redeemed from the oppression of sin and its effects – tears, death, sorrow, crying, and pain (Rev 21:4). Liberation theology is thus a key approach to political theology, especially in the context of Africa, where various political regimes have been major forces of oppression and subjugation of citizens.

It is vital for us to note that liberation theology is not just understood as a concern for a sociopolitical and sometimes radical reading of the Bible, but that there is a key component of biblical teaching concerned with liberation. The liberation motif should be entrenched in the understanding of the mission of the church as involvement in the lives of communities that are undergoing all manner of oppression by their governments. Those deprived of basic human rights should find a refuge in the life of the church. Essentially, liberation theology is a practical demonstration rather than merely a theoretical or podium talk; it is active, personal involvement in the lives of people. It is

---

46. Luthuli, "Road to Freedom," 113–14.

not activism, and it should not be confused with the various civil activists or human rights organizations whose motive is to condemn governments when they are in conflict with certain requirements set by international organizations that are mainly sponsored by powerful forces with possible ulterior motives. We observe here that the African theology of liberation is born out of the African experience of different cultural contexts and situations while taking seriously "the Bible as the written word of God which has an important message for the African people. The ultimate purpose of this theology is to make the gospel and Christianity meaningful in the life and thought of African people. In order to be liberating, such theology must articulate and reflect on the concrete situation in Africa in which religious experience is perpetuated. It must evolve from the lives of the people themselves."[47] Liberation theology draws from the incarnational motif of Christ becoming human and identifying with our human frailty, Christians are called to be like him, as Paul says in Philippians 2:5–11. The call of liberation theology should therefore not be a matter of speaking against the evils of oppression, important as this may be, but of identifying with the oppressed in every aspect of life. The life of a liberator is not just inspirational but sacrificial – a practical demonstration of the transformative power of the liberating gospel of Jesus Christ which is the embodiment of agape love. Can you think of theologians in your own contexts who can truly be identified as liberationists? What distinguishes their lives, and in what ways do they inspire you in identifying with the course of Christ?

D. African Theologians

Many African theologians have been and are associated with the thought of political theology and in particular have been involved in addressing the political situations of their countries. A number of these have been mentioned in the foregoing discussion. Because of the scope and diversity of political contexts in Africa it is not feasible to highlight theologians from all regions who have addressed their specific contexts. There are those who may not have been directly involved in political engagement but whose theology has contributed significantly to the kind of politics that has shaped their individual contexts. Many pastors have spoken out in their sermons against the challenges faced by society and as such have contributed to the voice of the church in speaking about sociopolitical issues. Bishop Henry Okullu of the Anglican Church,

---

47. Zablon Nthamburi, *The African Church at the Crossroads: A Strategy for Indigenization* (Nairobi: Uzima, 1991), 4.

whom we will discuss below, made a significant contribution to the situation of the church in Kenya during the rule of Moi. He stands out, in his sermons and writings, as a voice against the one-party rule. Along with Rev Timothy Njoya of the Presbyterian Church, Okullu was vocal and always gave illustrations that equated Moi's regime with tyranny and dictatorship. The criticisms of these vocal theologians elicited strong condemnation from the ruling party, but they were significant in setting "the scene for a prolonged political battle that finally resulted in the reintroduction of a multiparty system of government."[48] Bishop Lawi Imathiu of the Methodist Church in Kenya and Bishop Alexander Muge of the Anglican Church were also staunch critics of the misdeeds of the Kenyan government, although they favored the single-party rule. They "argued that the multiparty system would merely fragment Kenya along ethnic lines. But both bishops acknowledged the need for powerful constitutional checks and balances to limit the power of the president and the ruling party."[49]

These theologians represent the diversity of evangelical theological views on democratic developments in Kenya, demonstrating the lack of a political theology of the church. If all theologians speak from different and sometimes contradictory perspectives, the church is left in limbo, not having a proper guide for understanding its role and responsibility. Our discussion of African theologians here will seek to look at the theology of African theologians and the implications of their theology for politics in Africa. Considering that there are many different political contexts in Africa, the examples to which we shall give attention will act as samples representative of the whole. Our intent is not to prescribe the shape of political theology that theologians should have, but rather to point out the diversity and seek to highlight helpful approaches and principles relevant for African Christians.

Some of the most active theologians in engaging their individual governments are South Africans to whom we have already alluded. Albert Luthuli is a classic example of a theologian who entered into civil service as a chief of his people. His theological stance was motivated by his belief that, as a minister of the gospel and as a chief, he was a servant of the people, and he was driven by the conviction that a nonconfrontational passive approach "is the only non-revolutionary, legitimate, and humane way that could be used by

---

48. John Karanja, "Evangelical Attitudes toward Democracy in Kenya," in *Evangelical Christianity and Democracy in Africa*, ed. Terence O. Ranger (Oxford: Oxford University Press, 2008), 83.

49. Karanja, "Evangelical Attitudes," 83–84.

people denied, as we are, effective constitutional means to further aspirations."[50] While the apartheid regime in his native country of South Africa wielded great power and dealt brutally with dissidents, Luthuli, guided by Peter's resolution to obey God rather than human beings, was convinced that "laws and conditions that tend to debase human personality – a God-given force – be they brought about by the state or other individuals, must be relentlessly opposed in the spirit of defiance."[51] His was a practical and indeed sacrificial approach that moved him from the comfort of religiosity to a personal determination to identify with his fellow suffering South Africans. He knew that such a move would mean putting his life on the line as it would bring about "ridicule, imprisonment, concentration camp, flogging, banishment, and even death. I only pray to the Almighty to strengthen my resolve so that none of these grim possibilities may deter me from striving, for the sake of the good name of our beloved country, the Union of South Africa, to make it a true democracy and a true union in form and spirit of all communities in the land."[52] Such is the spirit of resolve and resilience to stand in the gap for the oppressed.

Dr Allan Boesak, President of the World Alliance of Reformed Christians and Assessor of the Synod of the NG Sendingkerk, was another key South African theologian who condemned the apartheid system. He was strongly opposed to the new South African constitutional proposals which maintained "a legalized and institutionalized oppressive system based on the racial domination of the white minority upon the black majority. In these circumstances, the group concept means or implies group divisions, not for the purpose of promoting justice and equality, but for protecting and maintaining white privileges at the expense of black advancement."[53] Boesak was persuaded that any meaningful change must work toward the democratic participation of all South Africans in the political life of the country. The theology of Boesak was for the liberation of South Africa and the abolition of apartheid. Another South African theologian not related to the struggle for emancipation but involved in the immigration problem facing contemporary South Africa is Bishop Paul Verryn of the Central Methodist Mission (CMM). He went against the dictates of the Methodist Church in which he served in his ardent commitment to accommodate Zimbabwean immigrants in his Johannesburg church.

---

50. Luthuli, "Road to Freedom," 114.

51. Luthuli, 114.

52. Luthuli, 114–15.

53. M. C. Jozana, "Proposed South African Bill of Rights: A Prescription for Equality or Neo-Apartheid?," *American University International Law Review* 7, no. 1 (1991): 72–73.

Bishop John Henry Okullu

Besides the South African theologians, a number of Kenyan theologians have been at the forefront in addressing the evils meted out by the Kenyan government. Among these is Bishop John Henry Okullu, who stands out as one of the most outspoken Anglicans. In his book *Quest for Justice* he argues strongly that it is the prerogative of the church to be involved in sociopolitical affairs in its witness to call for "just political, economic and social objectives . . . while clearly distinguishing the roles of Church and State."[54]

The kind of involvement that Okullu is advocating here is that in which the church becomes vocal in addressing the evils that affect the society. In his autobiography, he describes the numerous sermons he gave that touched on sociopolitical issues affecting the society. He vehemently spoke against the social evils and unjust acts on the part of the state, and this led to him receiving numerous invitations to speak in other churches as well as schools. His sermons "touched on the day-to-day life of the people."[55]

As a spokesperson for the people through his pastoral leadership, Okullu notes how he made use of every opportunity to speak out on the social issues to which the society was exposed. He addresses the social imbalance in the distribution of wealth by means of which the few rich continue to greedily enrich themselves. It is his conviction that

> churches should . . . speak out against injustice wherever it is to be found . . . As has been said, "when justice does not exist among human beings, God is ignored." The churches must be prepared to take their stand against fascism, racism, oppression, undue materialism in human affairs, elitism, imperialism and neo-colonialism. It must stand against all those forces national and international, historical and contemporary, which militate against humanity's needs for self-expression and freedom with responsibility in contexts of equality, security and social justice.[56]

The manner of church involvement in social and political issues that Okullu has in mind is one where, as God's institution, the church seeks "to bring the mind of God to bear upon total human life and to contribute to the

---

54. John Henry Okullu, *Quest for Justice: An Autobiography of Bishop John Henry Okullu* (Kisumu, Kenya: Shalom, 1997), xv.

55. Okullu, *Quest for Justice*, 56.

56. Okullu, xvi.

building of value systems upon which a sound human society may be built."[57] His argument is that the church's role is to appeal to the hearts and consciences of the people due to its divine right to correct, admonish, and censure. Such a role gives the church the authority to address pertinent issues within the society with a view to bringing about social justice for all. As he aptly puts it, "it is no interference for the church to warn the state that unrighteousness on public matters will bring calamity to the people."[58] It is, however, imperative that the church remains sufficiently independent of political and socioeconomic systems in order for it to retain its objectivity at any given time.

One of the contributions to the kind of sorry state discussed by Okullu is the type of Christianity that the Western missionary movement planted in Africa. This faith was not able to penetrate deeply into the hearts and lives of Africans due to the missionaries' total disregard of rich traditional African values. Okullu suggests that the church should reevaluate its theology so that it can be relevant in addressing both the physical and spiritual needs that affect people within their own contexts. He underscores the need for the church to heed the wake-up call and assume its position as the "nation's conscience" on moral issues. He makes reference to a number of statements by key African politicians who see the church as society's watchdog. Among these is Dr Zechariah Onyonka, the then minister for Information and Broadcasting in Kenya, who said, "There are lapses in the minds and hearts of society, and the churches must not abdicate their responsibility of realigning our feelings and actions. A nation without a conscience is like a buoy bouncing in the waves." Speaking long before he became president of Kenya, Mr Mwai Kibaki, addressing church leaders, said: "A modern church is expected to be outspoken because other groups in society must be cautious. We must have at least some organization which speaks up for the right of man regardless of what happens tomorrow . . . an active organization which speaks of our problems which we face today. I cannot think of any other organization better placed than a church to play that role."[59] This role requires an existing relationship between church and state in which the two distinct institutions recognize and respect each other.

This relationship is critical in order for the church to play its role in society. As Abuom puts it, "the church's role in the struggle for democracy must be considered in the context of the church–state relationship, especially in light

57. John Henry Okullu, *Church and Politics in East Africa* (Nairobi: Uzima, 1974), 16.

58. Okullu, *Church and Politics*, 16.

59. Onyonka quoted in Okullu, 10.

of the fact that, in Kenya, the church and state have had very cordial relations, especially in the area of development programmes."[60] In this relationship, Okullu argues that "there is both a strong theological foundation and a desire dictated by our present situation for a friendly relationship between Church and State."[61] While underscoring the importance of the church in addressing sociopolitical matters, Okullu discusses the differences between church and state in their origin and purpose. Noting that both institutions are "divinely and independently appointed by God," he argues that they can, however, work together "harmoniously."[62] Their roles are, nevertheless, distinguishable in that the state should pay heed to the moral injunctions of the church.

Okullu critiques African governments that do whatever it takes "to ensure the continued existence of those in power and anything done in fulfilling this aim is deemed to be legitimate. Kill as many people as you wish as long as it helps you preserve the African state!"[63] Regarding the Kenyan context, Okullu observes that "those in authority have always stifled dissent and denied the people the freedom of expression in the name of state security."[64] This is the context of injustice and corruption that Okullu ardently condemns. He urges the church in Kenya to speak out against all forms of injustice, social evils, corruption, and any other means of oppression, since the church is the only forum through which justice can be demanded of the government.

Okullu suggests that the church should not only criticize and point out the evils in society, but also "provide answers to the ideals of a democratic and just society."[65] He cites his personal experience as one who spoke against political degradation and the martyrdoms of leading clergymen such as Janani Luwum in Uganda and Alexander Muge in Kenya. He condemned the assassination of key political critics of the government, such as Tom Mboya and J. M. Kariuki, as well as the torture and imprisonment without trial of outspoken citizens who were demanding sociopolitical change by the oppressive government. For Okullu, the church should not abrogate its role as the prophetic voice of society.

---

60. Agnes C. Abuom, "The Church's Involvement in the Democratisation Process in Kenya," in *Peacemaking and Democratisation in Africa: Theoretical Perspectives and Church Initiatives*, ed. Hizkias Assefa and George Wachira (Nairobi: East Africa Educational Publishers, 1996), 95.

61. Okullu, *Church and Politics*, 19.

62. John Henry Okullu, *Church and State in Nation Building and Human Development* (Nairobi: Uzima, 2003), 17–18.

63. Okullu, *Quest for Justice*, 111.

64. Okullu, 111.

65. Okullu, 112.

The points that Okullu raises are significant resources for the church to draw from in developing a biblical and culturally authentic sociopolitical theology. The church must be proactive in laying down appropriate structures through which it can challenge the shortcomings of the ruling authorities. At the same time, it should provide guidelines for how Christians can actively participate in society within their individual contexts. Like Okullu, clergy and other religious leaders ought to speak out against all forms of injustice and oppressive tendencies of the state. They must also develop a theology that will guide the church in what it should or should not do in getting involved in these matters.

Bishop Gideon Gichuhi Githiga

Another key contribution is made by Bishop Gideon Gichuhi Githiga, who discusses the relationship between church and state in Kenya since independence. The gist of his argument is that "the Church in Kenya has acted as a defender of its members and the citizens against the extremism of the State."[66] He looks at social and political life in Kenya from an African perspective in which he emphasizes, given "the inseparability of religion and politics in African life, [the] centrality of the Christian Church in bringing about political change and in defending the people against political extremism, in particular through its testimony, its emerging theology and growing unity."[67]

He analyzes the issues that both the Protestant and the Roman Catholic Churches have deemed to be critical in the life of the community. The churches spoke through their leaders or through the National Christian Council of Kenya. One of the issues the church leaders raised in unison was the oath-taking that followed the assassination of Tom Mboya.[68] The oath-taking was a tribal issue as its object was "to swear to keep the Government of Kenya within the House of Mumbi [the mythical Kikuyu Eve]."[69] This issue was significant as it was the first time in the history of the church that the different denominations spoke out unanimously against the government. There were, however, tribal undertones. "In their statements that sounded uniform, the churches signed

---

66. Gideon Gichuhi Githiga, *The Church as the Bulwark against Authoritarianism: Development of Church and State Relations in Kenya with Particular Reference to the Years after Political Independence 1963–1992* (Oxford: Regnum, 2001), xiv.

67. Githiga, *Church as the Bulwark*, xv.

68. Githiga, 53.

69. Githiga, 53.

covenants or their reaffirmations of their loyalty to Kenyatta's government but clearly stated that their first loyalty was to God and that worldly authority was derived from him. They then condemned the secret oathing which was not acceptable to God."[70] One of the strongest resolutions by Africa Inland Church was the threat to, if necessary, "hold a public demonstration in Nairobi or any other place in Kenya to declare our supreme loyalty to the Lord Jesus Christ and to protest against enforced taking of secret oaths."[71] Other sociopolitical issues that the church strongly reacted to during Kenyatta's era were tribalism, corruption, and nepotism.

During the early stages of the Moi regime, the church worked much more closely with the government because of Moi's Christian commitment. His church attendance at different denominations every Sunday and financial "contributions towards church related projects won him much confidence among the church leaders."[72] He formulated the "*Nyayo* Philosophy"[73] of love, peace, and unity which the church sought to foster. This gave the church a reason to be "pleased in that the country was to be ruled through a philosophy of love, peace and unity. It joyously decided to look for a theological interpretation of the triad and attempted to give it an application to suit an ideal government."[74]

However, as the saying goes, "absolute power corrupts absolutely," since not very long after he "sat squarely" on the seat of authority, Moi "consolidated all the state's power to himself such that there was now no distinction between the executive, the legislature, the judiciary and KANU [Kenya African National Union]."[75] The developments that followed Moi's entrenchment in power drew sharp criticism from various church leaders. The national unity and economic stability that Moi had sworn to foster through love, peace, and unity lasted only for the first few years of his time in power. The same church that had helped in formulating the *Nyayo* "theology" came to the realization that it had been manipulated by the regime in order to help it maintain the status quo.[76] The major focus of the church was now aimed at pointing out the

---

70. Githiga, 54.

71. Githiga, 55.

72. Githiga, 66.

73. *Nyayo* is the Swahili word for "footsteps," which in a literal sense means the footmarks that are left on the ground after someone has walked on a dusty or muddy path. After he came to power, Moi pledged to follow in the footsteps of Kenyatta, saying that he would "never deviate from the policies of the founding father of the nation, Mzee Jomo Kenyatta."

74. Githiga, *Church as the Bulwark*, 72.

75. Githiga, 67.

76. Githiga, 80.

irregularities that the state had adopted in various matters of governance and which needed immediate attention. These issues included the abuse of the electoral system, misuse of public property, as well as misuse of power. In each case, the government resisted while the church persisted with its efforts.

In speaking against the state's abuse of power, the church has used the Bible as its source of authority. Both the Protestant and Roman Catholic "criticisms of the Kenya government are not ill-intentioned or politically motivated, but the reading of the Bible compels them to oppose some of the attitudes and actions of the state."[77] This hermeneutical stance is important as "theology in its emphasis on the liberation of the citizenry from the authoritarianism of the state does not dichotomize spiritual and political suffering, both of which find their solution in the Scriptures."[78] Such an approach is pertinent to the African "monistic"[79] worldview that ought to shape the role of the church in addressing all areas of life.

Githiga's contribution points the church back to its task of not only teaching the Bible but also acting upon its authority, thereby giving "individual church leaders authority to proclaim the Kingdom of God and to exercise their prophetic ministry."[80] This can be achieved if the church is open and ready to interact critically with the sociopolitical situation in order to understand the flaws of society. Such an understanding will help move the church toward developing an authentic "theology that can bring about a cohesive understanding of God in his relation to his people, a theology that would remove the various doctrinal and historic differences that divide it."[81] It is vital for the church to also reflect on its antecedent historical stages that have shaped and impacted its theology.

Bishop Zablon Nthamburi

Zablon Nthamburi is a Methodist clergyman who has made a significant contribution to the role of the church regarding social and political issues in

---

77. Githiga, 154.

78. Githiga, 154.

79. The term "monistic" is used here to refer to the African worldview that distinguishes, but does not separate, the spiritual and the physical/material arenas of life. The dichotomy between church and state does not feature in this kind of worldview since all physical events have spiritual implications (causes) and, therefore, there are no physical accidents that happen without a spiritual explanation.

80. Githiga, *Church as the Bulwark*, 197.

81. Githiga, 198.

Kenya. Nthamburi sees the church as an agent that brings the emancipation of the people from dehumanizing forces. God's will in his relationship to the people is to bring about their freedom.[82] Nthamburi gives two definitions of freedom. One is freedom of lordship where one is free to do whatever one wants. The other is freedom as community, of which he says, "The truth of freedom is love. Only in love does true human freedom manifest itself. You are free and feel free when you are accepted and accept others. You are really free when you open your life and share it with others . . . From this participation in life, we are freed from the limitation of our own individualism. This is the social dimension of freedom that opens up the community to a greater degree of solidarity."[83] It is on the basis of this kind of understanding that he relates Christian faith and politics by arguing that the essence of Christian participation in politics is "to make others truly free and to understand freedom in relation to the community."[84]

Acting as the conscience of society, the church has a role to play in the total welfare of the community. Of this role of the church, Majawa says that

> the Church is divinely mandated with the mission of being the Conscience of the State. As such, the Church in Africa must be viewed as a trusted partner in advancing the aspirations, liberation and development of the people. This is especially possible because the Church is not compelled by any interest of [a] political, economic, legal or social nature. Rather, as part of its religious and prophetic mission, the Church becomes the conscience, light, guide and energy which can consolidate the human community.[85]

This, however, does not mean that the church is a political institution, but rather an institution that is "so concerned with the welfare of the people both privately and corporately that it cannot avoid getting interested in what happens to them

---

82. Zablon Nthamburi, *The Pilgrimage of the African Church: Towards the Twenty-First Century* (Nairobi: Uzima, 2000), 54. By looking at the notion of freedom from both the Old and the New Testament, Nthamburi identifies different types of freedoms: "freedom of religion, freedom of conscience, freedom of thought and association, freedom of trade, and so on." He notes that in liberating us, God sent his Son who "guaranteed our freedom."

83. Nthamburi, *Pilgrimage of the African Church*, 55. This kind of definition makes the community the determining factor of the meaning of freedom. "Community becomes the root of the word freedom. Whoever is free is well-disposed, open and delightful. Those who are free indeed are able to love and give themselves to others."

84. Nthamburi, 55.

85. Clement Chinkambako Abenguni Majawa, "Church as Conscience of the State: Christian Witness in Politics for the Transformation of Africa," *African Ecclesiastical Review* 56, no. 2–3 (n.d.): 151–52.

in a given situation."[86] It is against this backdrop that Nthamburi explains his theology of politics:

> When we speak about the church's involvement in politics we do not mean that the church would actually engage itself in party politics . . . In a broader sense it means being involved in the affairs of the people and trying to find meaning in the most perplexing questions of human existence. Such questions may deal with social ills, economics, gender issues, human rights, governance or representation. In getting involved in many of these multifaceted human relations, the church recognizes that God is the creator and Lord over all human life and therefore, God is actively involved in socio-political, economic and judicial spheres of humankind.[87]

The relationship that Nthamburi identifies between politics and theology is one in which the political structure works toward the enabling of interpersonal social relationships so that people can live freely. Such freedom enables one to reach one's fullest potential. Theology for its part presents God's decisive acts as Creator and Redeemer in all the affairs of humanity. Nthamburi contends, therefore, that "God is clearly involved in our socio-political situation as we cannot shut God out from any form of human existence."[88] The role of the church in the sociopolitical issues of society is one in which the church "being the custodian of God's Word must be able to transmit the right knowledge that will liberate people and promote the common good of all so that God's love, justice and righteousness can reign over His people in the present world."[89]

Nthamburi traces the history of the relationship between church and state, noting the tension that has existed between these two institutions in every age. He indicates that the church has always received opposition from those in political power in order to silence it from pointing out the evils of the state. However, the church has continued to stand against such pressure, especially in Africa where, as he puts it, "many African leaders complained that the church would not give in when all other institutions had succumbed to the state's authority."[90] It is unfortunate that on certain occasions, the church has been used as a tool of the state and failed to address political violations

---

86. Nthamburi, *Pilgrimage of the African Church*, 57.

87. Nthamburi, 57. He says that "in order for theology to be legitimate, it must put human existence in all its aspects clearly focused *vis-à-vis* God's existence."

88. Nthamburi, 58.

89. Nthamburi, 58.

90. Nthamburi, 67.

of human rights and freedom by the state. He underscores the need for a harmonious relationship between church and state since the two institutions exist for the common good. Under no circumstances should the church fail to exercise its prophetic role of calling upon the state to obey God as it seeks to establish law and justice for all. "The church," he says, "cannot abdicate its moral responsibility to the society for to do so would be disobedience to the gospel's imperative."[91]

On the present state of Christianity in Africa, Nthamburi notes that African Christians "are aware, more than ever before, of the need to make the gospel relevant to their culture. The gospel must be incarnated in African culture in order not only to become relevant but also intentional in speaking to the condition of the African people. There is a greater awareness of the need to contextualize the gospel than there was a few years ago."[92]

He identifies the greatest challenge to the African church as religious pluralism. This, he notes, is not a new development since Christianity has always existed in the context of other religions, right from its inception in the first century.[93] The complexity of this challenge is that there are not only other religions, but also secular ideologies that Christianity has to contend with. As noted earlier, the traditional African worldview perceives life as a whole. He observes that "if Christianity is to claim the total allegiance of an African then it must address itself to the total life. In Africa the temptation to assert a dichotomy between the profane and the sacred must be resisted since the whole of existence must be subjected to the sovereignty of God."[94]

In light of this challenge of pluralism, a number of views have been given as to how the church should respond. As an institution that provides solace for all, especially for the millions of refugees in Africa who have been displaced from their homes due to war and conflict, the church must open its doors so as to be an agent of peace and comfort. As Nthamburi puts it, "we must make churches open communities where people of different cultures, ethnic backgrounds, languages, faiths and races can come together to struggle for justice, peace and reconciliation."[95] One caution that needs to be borne in mind is the danger of the church compromising its faith and doctrine through

---

91. Nthamburi, 69.

92. Nthamburi, 1.

93. Zablon Nthamburi, "The Church and the Challenge of Religious Pluralism: A Historical and Contemporary Perspective," in *Religious Pluralism in Africa: Challenge and Response*, ed. Hance A. O. Mwakabana (Geneva: Lutheran World Federation, 1996), 26.

94. Nthamburi, *Pilgrimage of the African Church*, 5.

95. Nthamburi, 72.

trying to accommodate other religions. The church should always be on its guard so as not to expose itself to a "syncretistic" compromise that makes it fail to safeguard its unique gospel message and mission to the world.[96] There is need for members of all religions to work positively toward transforming their social, economic, and political situation. This is a major challenge that the church in Africa must address because African Traditional Religion is one of the three main religions in Africa and, since it has shaped the African person through and through, is seen to be an inevitable African cultural response.[97]

In *The African Church at the Crossroads*, Zablon Nthamburi also emphasizes the need for the church to be holistic in the proclamation of the gospel. He underscores the priority of contextualizing the gospel in Africa when he says that "the church must communicate the gospel in metaphors that can be understood and appreciated by the hearers. This must be [a] holistic gospel, for in a continent in which the majority of the people are poor, oppressed, marginalized, victims of economic exploitation, racism, sexism, militarism and many other forms of oppression, the gospel of liberation is the relevant message."[98]

The gist of Nthamburi's argument is that Christianity is to be embraced as an authentic African faith whose relevance must not only be expressed and understood in African terms but must also be holistic in the sense that it addresses and incorporates all aspects of African human life and existence. Founded on the biblical axis, the theology of the church and the communication of the gospel must be made relevant to the lives and experiences of the people. In developing an effective sociopolitical theology, the church must broaden its theological premise beyond the primarily spiritual emphasis and relate it more directly to all aspects of life prevalent within the African context. This line of argument is well articulated by Nthamburi:

> African theology must not accept the facile and artificial separation between the spiritual and the material, the religious and the profane, the eternal and temporal spheres of human life. If it does so then it is reduced to a marginal role. It will be withdrawn from those areas of people's lives which affect people in their day to day affairs. To have a liberating effect, theology must be concerned about wholeness in a community. There is no area of human life

---

96. Nthamburi, "Challenge of Religious Pluralism," 28.

97. Nthamburi, 29.

98. Nthamburi, *African Church at the Crossroads*, ii.

which is outside God's kingdom, hence all areas are part of our theological discourse.[99]

The church should work toward motivating African pastors, religious leaders, and theologians to clearly articulate a viable theology that sheds preconceived notions about faith which tend to deprive Christians of the present, here-and-now blessings of life that the gospel promises (Mark 10:29–31). Without neglecting the spiritual dimension, the church must incorporate, in its theology, the sociopolitical aspect of the gospel which has so often been sacrificed at the altar of individual salvation.[100]

Looking at the focus of these theologians it is evident that the church has a crucial role to play, as an institution, in shaping all the arenas of human life. The unifying theme of these contributions is that the church needs to reevaluate and articulate its sociopolitical theology in a manner that will give proper guidance to both clergy and laity.

Each of these theologians makes an appeal to the church in Africa to reevaluate its role and involvement in sociopolitical issues. The church ought to realize that as part of the community it has a responsibility to initiate sociopolitical transformation using its theological resources. For this reason, the church should develop a theology that is not only biblical but also applicable to the African context. As Githiga puts it: "From its own experience, rooted in its tradition of EARM [East African Revival Movement], yet moving beyond it as a result of experience of Christians outside Kenya, the Kenyan church through its leaders [should develop] a prophetic ministry, grounded in the Bible . . . [in order to educate] people in political and democratic rights."[101] This is an important approach that the church should take seriously as it seeks relevance in its mission.

The contribution of these theologians is sensitization of the church of the need to be proactive in addressing the critical sociopolitical issues affecting their fellow African brothers and sisters. This is a major shortcoming of the church. Their sentiments serve as a pointer in the direction the church should go. The issues they raise affect the entire citizenship and therefore the church should regard them as critical for its agenda. This can be achieved when the church takes a more proactive role in human affairs. In Germany during

---

99. Nthamburi, 7.
100. Nthamburi, 16.
101. Githiga, *Church as the Bulwark*, 198.

the regime of Hitler, Karl Barth and the "Confessing Church" repudiated the "German Christian" church for their appropriation of German National Socialism that led to the Holocaust. While the church should not appropriate the philosophy of any political party, it should not fail to stand up to the evils of the state. This is a wake-up call for the church to develop an authentic sociopolitical theology that will be able to deal with the prevailing injustices within the community. The church does not have to retreat from involvement in political affairs for it to retain its distinctive heritage – "the scriptural Word of God and the regenerating gospel of Jesus Christ."[102] On the contrary, Scripture demands that all believers be faithful agents of God in his task of disbursing justice and righteousness to the world.

---

102. Carl Ferdinand Howard Henry, *Evangelicals in Search of Identity* (Waco: Word, 1976), 15.

6

The Bible and Politics

For Christians, the Bible is the guide that enables us to reflect on all matters of life and living, particularly issues of human relations and moral responsibilities.[1] Numerous approaches have been taken in relating politics and the Bible. Studies in biblical political thought, for instance, have engaged especially with the kingship of Yahweh over Israel and the role Israel played as a special nation among other nations of the world. It is important for us to underscore the Bible as the foundation on which human political engagement is built. It narrates events related to God's dealings with people in their different political structures and contexts. Indeed the Old Testament for the most part is addressed to God's people who were constituted as a political entity, enjoying some degree of autonomy for most of their history.[2] The history within the Old Testament is thus concerned with the shaping of the nation of Israel as a polity with rulers who were to enact policies to govern the people with justice and equity as demanded by Yahweh. This was entrenched in the law that God gave, as a covenant, to guide his people in all aspects of life. The prophets would later come, as God's mouthpieces, to impress on the people their responsibility by calling them back to covenant obedience. It is worth noting though that, "while the law and the prophets cannot be *instructions* for our political life, they can be *illustrative* for our political life: we cannot apply their teachings directly to ourselves, but from the way in which God expressed his character and purposes in the political life of Israel we may learn something of how they should be expressed in political life today."[3] The law was intended to guide their

---

1. Ronald J. Sider, "Thinking Biblically about Politics," *Criswell Theological Review* 6, no. 1 (Fall 2008): 48.

2. Richard Bauckham, "Reading the Bible Politically," in *An Eerdmans Reader in Contemporary Political Theology*, ed. William T. Cavanaugh, Jeffrey W. Bailey, and Craig Hovey (Grand Rapids, MI: Eerdmans, 2012), 31.

3. Bauckham, "Reading the Bible Politically," 33–34.

national sociopolitical and religious life which was integral and epitomized in God's plan and purposes for his people. The Jewish worldview was very clear on the centrality of the "Torah as their founding political document."[4]

A. Old Testament Political Thought

Two contrasting aspects associated with Africa are ugly political conflicts, as we have highlighted already in our discussion, and beautiful wildlife. There are serene plains replete with beauty and vast terrains adorned with diverse wildlife, which attract tourists. Across these savannas traverse the "big five" most dreaded animals in Africa: the lion, African elephant, buffalo, leopard, and rhinoceros. Of these, the lion, commonly known as the "king of the jungle," is most feared among the big cats. The towering demeanor of a male lion with its impressive mane is a sight to behold. The impeccable sight of the wild may, however, be deceptive, especially when it comes to the survival of the animals. The lion portends terror for other animals and humans alike. In one incident in Kenya, lions wandered from the national park reserve and mauled livestock in a Maasai village. In retaliation the Maasai warriors laid an ambush and killed six of these beasts and cut their tails as a sign of their prowess, since killing a lion is "the ultimate prize."[5] The Maasai tribal group is entirely dependent on livestock for their survival; thus a threat to their animals spells doom for their existence. The question is how chaos – both in the wild and in human conflict – relates to politics and the Bible, and what the biblical response to this problem is.

We turn our attention to the creation account, which is essential for understanding the sociopolitical aspects since "belief in God the creator is itself a resource for sociopolitical critique."[6] The act of creation is the foundation for a political theology that is a symbol of hope in the context of decay and

---

4. Alan Storkey, *Jesus and Politics: Confronting the Powers* (Grand Rapids, MI: Baker Academic, 2005), 28.

5. Ponciano Odongo and Lucas Barasa, "Where Lion's Tail Is the Ultimate Prize," *Daily Nation* online, 21 June 2012. "None of the carcasses of the kings and queens of the jungle killed on Wednesday had . . . their tails on Thursday. When the *Nation* got to the scene at Ilkeek-lemedungi Village, the 'victors' were holding the cats' tails, 'happier than ever before.' Among the Maasai, killing lions is like football. 'Like footballers struggling to score between the goal post, morans [Maasai warriors] strive to reach out for the tail or spear the lion first,' said Mzee Silas ole Soropay."

6. Kathryn Tanner, *The Politics of God: Christian Theologies and Social Justice* (Minneapolis: Fortress, 1992), 78.

disorder that characterizes the various human sociopolitical structures.[7] The first chapter of Genesis recounts the act of God's creation in which humanity receives the seminal mandate to rule. As we seek to analyze this account, we need to underscore that humans are created to govern and to be governed, which is an indication of what God intended for his creation regarding politics.[8] As we relate politics to the term "city" (*polis*) and see the link in the Bible between religion and politics, the first chapters in Genesis[9] are instrumental as we see God, the Creator, bringing order to the formlessness and void that characterized the earth. This organization or ordering of that which God speaks into existence is itself a political act.

Politics as the Essence of Creation

The opening phrase of Genesis 1:1, "In the beginning God created the heavens and the earth," has elicited significant debate among scholars. One concern is whether it is to be understood as a heading of the narrative or as a subordinate to the verses that follow,[10] or even as a summary of the whole account.[11] It may also denote the initial beginning of time when God in his power brings creation into existence.[12] Without delving into the intricacies of the debate, we take the verse in its absolute sense of God bringing into existence the entirety of all that he created "out of non-being, which has become the classical Jewish and Christian position."[13] This account of Genesis is significantly different from other ancient Near Eastern creation accounts, although related in terms of style.[14] In contrast to Egyptian as well as Sumerian and Akkadian sources that

---

7. H. Martinus Kuitert, *Everything Is Politics But Politics Is Not Everything: A Theological Perspective on Faith and Politics* (Grand Rapids, MI: Eerdmans, 1986), 65.

8. Alan Geyer, "Creation and Politics in Bonhoeffer's Thought," *Church and State*, August 1995, 94.

9. Michael Hoelzl and Graham Ward, eds., *Religion and Political Thought* (London: Continuum, 2006), 2.

10. Henri Blocher, *In the Beginning: The Opening Chapters of Genesis* (Leicester: Inter-Varsity Press; Downers Grove, IL: InterVarsity Press, 1984), 61.

11. John H. Walton, *The Lost World of Genesis One: Ancient Cosmology and the Origins Debate* (Downers Grove, IL: IVP Academic, 2009), 45.

12. Vern S. Poythress, "Correlations with Providence in Genesis 1," *The Westminster Theological Journal* 77, no. 1 (Spring 2015): 76.

13. Blocher, *In the Beginning*, 63.

14. Hermann Gunkel, *The Legends of Genesis: The Biblical Saga and History* (New York: Schocken, 1964), 10. He argues that Genesis 1 is based on tradition rather than on an individual's invention. In other words, "the priestly writer has generally not set down in Genesis his random discoveries, but has reshaped traditional material according to the sensibilities of his era."

document creation activities, this account of creation is distinct in that it brings about functionality and material substance that was not present previously.[15]

The "formlessness and void" (cf. Gen 1:2) can be said to be the first creation which is here called the "earth," although the earth was not created until the third day according to Genesis 1:10. This "darkness" and "the deep" bring about the pillars of the formlessness of the cosmos which suggests divine power and authority of creation. The context of formlessness points to a state of no functionality, purposeless and without production.[16] David Tsumura makes an extensive yet balanced etymological analysis of the term "formless and empty" and concludes that this phrase in Genesis 1:2 means "emptiness" in reference to the ground, which was barren and unoccupied and thus not productive.[17] The terms in the Hebrew are *tōhū*, meaning confusion, unreality, emptiness, or formlessness (of primeval earth); or nothingness, empty space, or that which is empty or unreal (of idols figuratively); or wasteland, wilderness (of solitary places); or place of chaos or vanity; while *bōhū* means emptiness, void, waste, or to be empty as characterized by darkness and the deep.

Tōhū and *bōhū* thus present the Creator with a potent ground into which he speaks form ("Let there be") from the emptiness and void, without which creation as we know it would not have been. He brings form and order, subduing the formlessness and establishing cohesion. The act of creation is thus a political act in which order and harmony are established as God declares, after each act of creation, that it is good. Consequently the Creator subdues the emptiness and void by his sovereign power through which he displays the mastery by which order should be exhibited.

Having established the earth and its inhabiting creatures, God says in Genesis 1:26, "Let us make mankind in our image, in our likeness, so that they may rule over the fish of the sea and the birds in the sky, over the livestock and all the wild animals, and over all the creatures that move along the ground." This sets the scene for the creation of *the politician*, whose role and responsibility is to manage the polity.

---

15. Walton, *Lost World*, 53.

16. Walton, 49.

17. David Toshio Tsumura, *Creation and Destruction: A Reappraisal of the Chaoskampf Theory in the Old Testament* (Winona Lake, IN: Eisenbrauns, 2005), 35.

Humans Created to Rule

Adam is exalted above all other creatures because he has a special connection with the Creator that all the other creatures do not have.[18] God says, "Let us make mankind," and, although we will not get into a discussion of what "us" implies, my view is that it refers to the plurality of God in his majestic nature.[19]

The terms "our image" and "our likeness" have elicited significant debate.[20] It should be observed that these two terms "refer to a relation between man and his creator; a 'likeness' between man and God, with no explanation given as to exactly what this likeness consists of or implies."[21] There have been a number of suggestions regarding what "image" means, such as the shared capacity of all human beings to make conscious decisions, being connected or closely linked with the intent that humans should have dominion or rule,[22] or the nature in which human beings relate to other creatures.[23] It is evident though that, distinct from all other creatures, humans have the capacity to relate, communicate verbally, and commune with the Creator as his representatives in his creation. This is a responsibility that no other creature bears as humans render service and express love in the divinely instituted relationships of marriage and families, through which they manage and govern creation in its multiple aspects.[24]

---

18. Blocher, *In the Beginning*, 83.

19. "A number of views are suggested here. (1) One of the commonest, and certainly one of the easiest, explanations is simply that the plurals are 'editorial' or 'plurals of majesty' (a variety of terms are used, but all with about the same meaning). (2) Archaeological parallels have commended to many in recent times (e.g. Delitzsch, von Rad) the explanation that we have here a reference to the 'divine council,' in Israel composed of angels rather than of fellow-gods as in paganism. (3) Many speak of a 'plural of deliberation,' underscoring the importance of this creative act." Horace D. Hummel, "The Image of God," *Concordia Journal* 10, no 3 (May 1984): 83–93. I tend to concur with James Orr that "the Creator – Elohim – is represented as taking counsel with himself (for no other is mentioned)." James Orr, *God's Image in Man and Its Defacement in Light of Modern Denials* (Eugene, OR: Wipf & Stock, 1997), 35.

20. Hummel, "Image of God," 83–93. The discussion focuses on "whether the two nouns are synonymous and parallel (cf. Eichrodt: 'In God's image, that is to say, in His likeness'), perhaps even hendiadys ('essential likeness'?), or whether two different terms are deliberately used to prevent possible misunderstanding of either one alone."

21. Gerrit Cornelis Berkouwer, *Man: The Image of God* (Grand Rapids, MI: Eerdmans, 1962), 60.

22. Christopher J. H. Wright, *The Mission of God's People: A Biblical Theology of the Church's Mission* (Grand Rapids, MI: Zondervan, 2010), 50.

23. Orr, *God's Image*, 57.

24. James Skillen, *The Good of Politics: A Biblical, Historical, and Contemporary Introduction*, Engaging Culture (Grand Rapids, MI: Baker Academic, 2014), 21.

This indicates that the key aspect related to the image of God in the creation of human beings is the rule – the exercise of divinely mandated authority over all the other creatures. This is because, like God who is sovereign, humans are constituted in a relational context where they form political entities and communities that demand order and harmony in management for cohesive and mutual coexistence. In essence then, we can argue, God creates human beings with the direct intent or purpose of endowing them (male and female) with the responsibility of ruling over all the other creatures. Essentially, God delegates his kingly authority and responsibility by endowing them with his image and thereby mandating them to exercise that authority as a cosmic function.[25] The image and likeness of God is thus tied to the human function of ruling. Consequently, the purpose of human creation is intentionally political. God creates human beings, male and female, to reflect the King in the domain of his kingship. After establishing order through the act of creation, he endows people with his "image and likeness," ushers them into the political realm that is creation, and mandates them to rule and govern.

The Political Mandate

The mandate is indicated by the Hebrew verb *radah* which denotes "treading down" by way of subjugating or "having dominion over," "prevailing against," "reigning," "ruling," or "taking over." The creation account of humanity in Genesis utilizes political language by speaking of humans as beings who exercise dominion over the earth and its inhabitants.[26] This verb occurs mainly in contexts where there is a political nuance of the ruling of a nation by a king or a nation ruling over another nation.[27] It is striking that the first mandate given to humans is to rule, and that they are linked to the Creator as bearers of his image in relation to one another. They are to exercise this rule over the fish of the sea, the birds of the air, and all forms of life on the earth. They are told to "have dominion" over these creatures, indeed over "all the earth." Undoubtedly, given that this was the purpose of the creation of humans, the relationship between God and humans is of critical importance for their existence. Human beings are created in God's image to exercise dominion over God's creation and

---

25. Nonna Verna Harrison, "Women, Human Identity, and the Image of God: Antiochene Interpretations," *Journal of Early Christian Studies* 9, no. 2 (Summer 2001): 219.

26. James Limburg, "The Responsibility of Royalty: Genesis 1–11 and the Care of the Earth," *Word & World* 11, no. 2 (Spring 1991): 124–30.

27. Limburg, "Responsibility of Royalty," 126.

to subdue this creation in the same way God subdued the void and emptiness. They are not created to dominate other human beings or become tyrannical; the *imago Dei* (image of God) enables us to exercise our authority over creation by overturning our supremacism, since our resemblance to God and our capacity to have dominion call for our imitation of God in which we are not self-seeking but constrained by our subjection to his character. As kings and not tyrants we mirror his image, but if we lord it over others, the image in us is denied and even destroyed.[28] This implies that politics has to do with the stewardship of creation by managing and ordering it; and that we are not to be dictators of others but to rule creation.

What does this mean for the ugly political conflicts in Africa? What principles can we draw from the foregoing discussion for our understanding of politics? First, God subdues the *tōhū* and *bōhū* by forming and ordering a political domain that he declares to be very good. Second, all humans are created in God's image, and as such no individual person or group of people, whether nation, race, or tribe, is superior to another. Third, God blesses human beings and mandates them to rule, take care of, and manage creation. This divine mandate encompasses the entire human sphere (religious, social, political, legal, ethical, and environmental). Humans are "stewards" of God's "very good" creation. Some creatures that move and creep on the earth may be powerful and dangerous, but humans are to subdue and rule over them. Indeed in Genesis 9:2, when the same blessing is repeated for Noah, God declares: "The fear and dread of you will fall on all the beasts of the earth, and on all the birds in the sky, on every creature that moves along the ground, and on all the fish in the sea; they are given into your hands."

The conflict and chaos that characterize contemporary politics in Africa are a negation of the creation mandate to humans to be stewards who bring peace and harmony (shalom). Politics should not be an arena characterized by corruption or a tyranny in which humans subdue their fellow humans, for that contravenes the divine intent and mandate. As Wright puts it, "human dominion over the rest of creation is to be an exercise of kingship that reflects God's own kingship. The image of God is not a license for arrogant abuse, but a pattern that commits us to humble reflection of the character of God."[29] Any

---

28. Huw Spanner, "Tyrants, Stewards – or Just Kings?," in *Animals on the Agenda: Questions about Animals for Theology and Ethics*, ed. Andrew Linzey and Dorothy Yamamoto (Urbana, IL: University of Illinois Press, 1998), 222.

29. Christopher J. H. Wright, *The Mission of God: Unlocking the Bible's Grand Narrative* (Downers Grove, IL: IVP Academic, 2006), 427.

political rule that sets out to achieve its own ends, whether for the individual or a political party, is a contradiction of God's design and intent. Proper politics, according to the "image of God" design, is not about domineering but subduing the creation.[30] Dictators and tyrants, rebel movements, and activists who thrive by precipitating chaos are objects of condemnation in no uncertain terms.

The creation principle and model given here is order (shalom) in the context of chaos (anarchy). Such a stance in politics denounces any form of violence precipitated by the desire to rule and control others. Political violence is a denial of the value of humanity. Politics should be the exercise of our created human nature in obedience to God's command. Being "a politician" is essentially the epitome of identification with God in his "image and likeness" which is the essence of humanity. Conversely, not to be "a politician" is theologically a human impossibility, for humanity is interconnected through creation with the *Master politician*. This means we all have a political role to play in our created nature as bearers of the image of God by which we are rulers and managers of the creation which we must steward. Humans are to subdue, to bring to subjection, and command all of creation, which includes the most powerful and feared of the beasts in the deep waters and wild jungles. By implication, humans are to tame the lion – the king of the jungle!

Failure and Disruption

As we have argued, the idea of politics derives from the creation account and develops through the life of God's people as he deals with them to accomplish his plans and purpose. In the successive events of creation, God functionalizes creation through his creative act. All the creatures "simply carry out their own functions in the cosmic space that they inhabit."[31] In Genesis 2:7 we have a description of how Adam was formed: "God formed a man from the dust of the ground and breathed into his nostrils the breath of life, and the man became a living being." Adam is "formed" from the ground. The term used here is *yatsar*, which is drawn from the function of potters who take particular care and attention to mold their creations.[32] This creature bears the Creator's imprint and breath:[33] God did not just form Adam, he also "breathed into

---

30. Kuitert, *Everything Is Politics*, 10–11.

31. Walton, *Lost World*, 66.

32. Herbert Carl Leupold, *Exposition of Genesis*, vol. 1 (Grand Rapids, MI: Baker, 1942), 115.

33. David W. Cotter, *Genesis*, Berit Olam: Studies in Hebrew Narrative & Poetry (Collegeville, MN: Liturgical, 2003), 29.

his nostrils the breath of life," which connotes that Adam is a living person consisting of a body and a life-giving breath.[34] There is therefore a critical relationship between the Master politician and Adam the politician, making a clear distinction between Adam and the rest of creation.

Following Adam's creation, God brings him to his *polis* where he is to exercise his rule in a well-watered domain prepared for his habitation. Indeed the ground is set for Adam's coronation. Adam is mandated to take charge of the garden, signified by the term *abad*, to "serve" or "work," with a political connotation since it is his political domain. God commands Adam regarding his duties and responsibilities in the *polis*. While well provided for, Adam receives prohibitions as a directive from the Lord (Gen 2:16–17). The verb *tsavah*, "command," occurs here for the first time in the narrative, signifying the seriousness of the consequences of Adam's choice. Here we see a covenant from God which "clearly spells out the condition for the man, namely, obedience to God's command."[35] While this is directed to Adam since the "you" is in the second person masculine singular, "when Eve appropriates it in 3:3, she uses the plural; she has apparently received the instruction by way of her husband and has accepted him as her representative in receiving the covenant."[36]

With God now having established everything, we are confronted by the mention of the first negative aspect of creation when God says, "It is not good for the man to be alone." This "emphatically negative assessment" of creation introduces the communal structure of humanity and affirms that "from the very beginning, the human being is a *Mitsein*, a being-with; human life attains its full realization only in community."[37] What comes out clearly in this is God's relational nature. First is the creation of a human being in a living relationship with God, and second, the human being's relationship with creation and other people (Gen 2:19, 21–23). The bond within human relationships is explicated by the fact of the woman being taken from the rib of Adam, which is indicative of "the relationship of the woman to her husband."[38] Adam is made from the dust of the earth and subsequently Eve is drawn from the side of man. Walton argues that the dust and the side of the man are "archetypal" rather than a

---

34. John C. L. Gibson, *Genesis* (Edinburgh: St Andrew Press; Philadelphia: Westminster Press, 1981), 103.

35. C. John Collins, *Genesis 1–4: A Linguistic, Literary, and Theological Commentary* (Phillipsburg, NJ: P&R, 2006), 113.

36. Collins, *Genesis 1–4*, 114.

37. Blocher, *In the Beginning*, 96.

38. Umberto Cassuto, *A Commentary on the Book of Genesis, Part 1* (Jerusalem: Magnes Press, 1961), 134.

"chemical composition" or "material ingredient" or even "anatomical."[39] Adam's reaction to the "helper" as "flesh of my flesh" and "bone of my bones" indicates the bond which unites the two. There is no indication of the man sanctioning precedence over the woman, but instead a sense of overwhelming wholeness. The community thus established is the structure within which humanity is to dispense the act of rule as derived from the Creator. At this stage, no form of government is preferred, but simply the fact of the exercise of rule itself.

The first act of Adam's exercise of his role as politician comes when God, having made all the creatures, "brought them to the man to see what he would name them; and whatever the man called each living creature, that was its name" (Gen 2:19). This shows that Adam was endowed not only with wisdom and knowledge but also authority. In essence, "just as this knowledge in Adam was an outstanding gift of God, so it also pleased God exceedingly and delighted Him. Therefore He commands him to make use of this knowledge by giving names to all the animals."[40]

It should be observed here that when the narrative says "to see what he would name them," this describes not an element of curiosity on the Lord's part, but an affirmation of Adam's authority over creation, since "the naming of something or someone is a token of lordship."[41] The naming is a political statement in which Adam consolidates his political authority over all living creatures, and this seemingly even in his relationship to his wife (Gen 2:22–23; 3:20). The fact that human beings were created to be politicians (rulers) is therefore clearly reflected in the seminal chapters of Genesis from which their engagement with creation and thus also the rest of their life and relationships must be understood. Human beings (male and female) are to rule over and by implication command the creatures.

When Adam is presented with an opportunity to exercise his God-given political capability to act in obedience to God, however, he fails the test. Instead of taking charge, he abdicates his role of subduing the creatures and gives in to the serpent that casts doubt on his covenantal directive from God. The serpent engages the woman in a conversation in which it outwits her by suggesting a self-seeking effect of acting against the prohibition. The serpent is a creature and thus subject to Adam's rule and dominion. This should be viewed against the backdrop of the traditional evangelical view of this passage as espoused by

---

39. Walton, *Lost World*, 71.

40. Martin Luther and Jaroslav Jan Pelikan, *Luther's Works: Lectures on Genesis Chapters 1–5*, vol. 1 (Saint Louis, MO: Concordia, 1958), 120.

41. Cassuto, *Book of Genesis*, 130.

Kent Hughes, that the snake is "a naturally shrewd creature, under the control of Satan . . . The New Testament identifies this serpent as the devil, referring back to this scene in paradise."[42]

We could argue that the human beings here – male and female – fail the seminal political test to subdue just one creature since this "story involves one of the animals in 'man's' disobedience."[43] The focus here is on Adam and his response to God's directive over creation. Indeed the serpent "was one of the wild creatures that God had made . . . [which] represents throughout this chapter the whole animal creation."[44] Rather than consolidating his realm of authority, Adam allows the serpent to disrupt the cohesiveness of his polity by introducing an element of doubt leading to disobedience to the divine command.

Adam and Eve had previously enjoyed the blessedness of God's grace and love in the provision of life and its goodness, but once they disobey God's command, their being and existence suffer greatly. Arguably, their act brings about the brokenness of the relationships which had so far harmoniously united all of creation. While the human dominion over creation is not revoked, "there is every indication that humans will exercise it badly – exploiting and damaging the creation and using it to exploit and damage other people."[45] This act of defiance disrupts the existing order and cohesiveness and portends disorder and hostility that requires humanity to toil and labor for their sustenance. The creatures over which Adam was to rule suddenly become hostile. "Humanity finds itself confronting an untamed earth, a world which responds to his efforts with thistles . . . Mankind is [also] deprived of the nourishment he required as the image of God, that is to say, the life-giving communion with divine wisdom."[46] From this time on we have to cope with Adam's innate negative nature that impedes his ability to carry out his political mandate. The existing relationships are distorted, although we see a renewal or reestablishment that is nevertheless characterized by disharmony. This is a clear negative effect on the realm in which Adam is to exercise his rule.

Henceforth, we are confronted by the disruption of the unity and goodness wrought by man's decisive choice to disobey the very tenets that held the polity intact. The pronouncements that God makes as a consequence of humanity's

---

42. R. Kent Hughes, *Genesis: Beginning and Blessing* (Wheaton, IL: Crossway, 2004), 66.
43. Gibson, *Genesis*, 125.
44. Gibson, 124.
45. Gibson, 165.
46. Blocher, *In the Beginning*, 187.

action reveal not only a just and righteous judge but also a benevolent and gracious God. The pronouncements of curse and the due consequences of the choices made change the topography of creation. "Both serpent and ground are cursed, but the humans, however heavy their punishment, are not cursed."[47] As a consequence, alienation becomes the unquestionable characteristic of the polity or society. The narrative depicts the extent to which humanity's degeneration impacts the entire creation, and the unfolding events pit them in a downward spiral of sin in their relationship mainly with the Creator but also with the rest of creation, as the inclinations of their thoughts, their purposes, and their will are "evil all the time" (Gen 6:5–8).

While our discussion has focused particularly on the role of humanity in creation, it is important to note that the rule of God predates creation since God is transcendent and not confined to the limitations of his creation. God has always been king, and as Ebenezar Adeogun observes,

> God governed his world and humankind generally were his subjects. He facilitated our world with necessary infrastructures in advance of man who would utilize them. It was after putting [into place] those provisions such as light (sun and moon), water (rain, rivers and seas), plants and animals, that he created man. It was not the other way round. That is theocracy proper, God having his creatures, Adam and Eve and their progenies, in mind and facilitating them well ahead of their coming into existence. He also gave them directives; even when man fell by sinning, he made provision for his salvation.[48]

Covenant and Renewal

The ensuing account portrays a God who is intricately involved in all human sociopolitical affairs through his redemptive acts extended to Noah through the ark. The flood was sent as a judgment because, according to Genesis 6:5, "every inclination of the thoughts of the human heart was only evil all the time." But later it is shown as the grounds for grace (Gen 8:21–22) and, although human corruption remains unchanged, God maintains an ordered world that is guaranteed to endure. After Babel, God's grace is expressed through his

---

47. Cotter, *Genesis*, 35.

48. Ebenezer Ola Olutosin Adeogun, "The Kingdom of God and Old Testament Theocracy," *Ogbomoso Journal of Theology* 12 (2007): 68.

choosing of Abraham from among his people. The call of Abraham in Genesis 12:1–3 marks the beginning of the covenantal[49] relationship with the nation that springs from Abraham. This passage is central to our understanding of God's kingship, for as Wright points out, "it moves the story forward from the preceding eleven chapters, which record God's dealings with all nations . . . into the patriarchal narratives that lead into the emergence of Israel as a distinct nation. And it is pivotal in the whole Bible because it does exactly what Paul says – it 'announces the gospel in advance.'"[50]

The gospel is indeed political as it is the good news of the kingdom, as we shall discuss later. In the outworking of his purposes through the life of Abraham, God manifests his power and authority as he establishes a heritage in his chosen people. His promise to Abraham to establish him as a great nation is reaffirmed to Isaac (Gen 26:2–4), Jacob (Gen 28:13–15; 35:11–13), and Joseph and his sons (Gen 48:1–6). Each of these patriarchs experienced ups and downs, particularly Joseph, whose story illustrates that the plots and evil intentions of humanity cannot change the purposes of God, as expressed in Genesis 50:20: "You intended to harm me, but God intended it for good to accomplish what is now being done, the saving of many lives." In the lives of Joseph, Moses, and the Israelites in Egypt, God displays what justice and righteousness entails through his mighty acts of redeeming his people and bringing them out of the land of slavery.

God's kingship in the Old Testament is seen clearly when he constitutes the nation of Israel at Sinai in Exodus 19:5–6. He affirms their uniqueness in the statement "Now if you obey me fully and keep my covenant, then out of all nations you will be my treasured possession. Although the whole earth is mine, you will be for me a kingdom of priests and a holy nation." Indeed, "the whole Sinai experience – including the giving of the law, the making of the covenant, the building of the tabernacle and even the renewal of the covenant with the following generation on the plains of Moab in Deuteronomy – is prefaced by this text."[51] The affirmation of this covenantal relationship is stipulated in the political manifesto (the law) which reflects God's sovereignty over his people, yet without abrogating their freedom as he demands their obedience. He calls them to reflect his character. Worth noting is that Israel's election was

---

49. The Hebrew term used to describe the Old Testament is *berith*, "covenant."

50. Wright, *Mission of God*, 194. He continues by saying that this text "declares the good news that, in spite of all that we have read in Genesis 1–11, it is God's ultimate purpose to bless humanity . . . And the story of how that blessing for all nations has come about occupies the rest of the Bible, with Christ as the central focus" (194–95).

51. Wright, 225.

an indication that God's love gave them the responsibility to be witnesses to other nations. The giving of the law with its rules and regulations governing the entire life of Israel was predicated on God's character. As a just and righteous God, he taught them justice and compassion for each other and how they were to treat each other, deal with strangers in their midst as well as other nations, and also how to manage the environment on which they were dependent. Such regulations as the observance of rest in its various cycles, culminating in the jubilee that gave a new lease of life to those in debt, were manifestations of the just and egalitarian society that God intended his people to exhibit both internally and externally. The observance of various sacrifices and religious festivals by the people was not efficacious because of the people's efforts, but because of the undeserved favor and mercy of God, as depicted in Micah 6:6–8; Isaiah 1:11–20; and Hosea 6:6, which was a demonstration of his covenant relationship with them.

Once they entered the land of promise, the political life of the nation of Israel underwent many changes and challenges. While the conquest was a national venture under the leadership of Joshua, once the people got settled they did not complete the removal of all the inhabitants of Canaan, so their common objective was only partially accomplished. This state of affairs exposed them as they lacked an agreed policy for the regulation of the tribes, as well as an organized way to defend themselves. The organization of their common life as well as their defense was hampered without a king. It was inevitable that they should have a leader – a king, though not in the contemporary sense, but one through whom God could rule since they were his people. Moses had instructed that they could have a proper king (Deut 17:14–20), one who would represent God and enforce the covenant. This was to be an earthly king who would dispense justice and righteousness as depicted in the anticipation of a messianic king in Psalm 72:1–18:

> Endow the king with your justice, O God,
>> the royal son with your righteousness.
> May he judge your people in righteousness,
>> your afflicted ones with justice.
>
> May the mountains bring prosperity to the people,
>> the hills the fruit of righteousness.
> May he defend the afflicted among the people
>> and save the children of the needy;
>> may he crush the oppressor.
> May he endure as long as the sun,

as long as the moon, through all generations.
May he be like rain falling on a mown field,
    like showers watering the earth.
In his days may the righteous flourish
    and prosperity abound till the moon is no more.

May he rule from sea to sea
    and from the River to the ends of the earth.
May the desert tribes bow before him
    and his enemies lick the dust.
May the kings of Tarshish and of distant shores
    bring tribute to him.
May the kings of Sheba and Seba
    present him gifts.
May all kings bow down to him
    and all nations serve him.

For he will deliver the needy who cry out,
    the afflicted who have no one to help.
He will take pity on the weak and the needy
    and save the needy from death.
He will rescue them from oppression and violence,
    for precious is their blood in his sight.

Long may he live!
    May gold from Sheba be given him.
May people ever pray for him
    and bless him all day long.
May grain abound throughout the land;
    on the tops of the hills may it sway.
May the crops flourish like Lebanon
    and thrive like the grass of the field.
May his name endure forever;
    may it continue as long as the sun.

Then all nations will be blessed through him,
    and they will call him blessed.

Praise be to the Lord God, the God of Israel,
    who alone does marvelous deeds.

The political model for Israel was not theocracy, the direct rule of God, or strictly a monarchy, but theocracy through a monarchy. The prophet was

God's mouthpiece to the king and the nation as a whole. In this arrangement, the prophet's authority came before the king's. This meant that the king would be a political leader while the prophet would enforce the covenant values. In essence, the religious beliefs and practices of the nation were intertwined with their sociopolitical life such that the divide between the religious and the nonreligious was a matter of roles and responsibilities vested in their respective offices. Obedience to the covenant stipulations became a cardinal determinant of a king's success and the nation's sociopolitical stability.

Continued disobedience not only gave rise to the division of the formerly united kingdom of Israel, but ultimately culminated in the people's dispersion in the exile and consequent collapse of Israel. The hope for the future of the kingdom lay in God's promises as depicted by the prophets. The anticipated fulfilment of the prophetic promises, mainly through the coming Messiah, would later result in a weak polity that caused Israel to wallow under the rule of foreigners in their own land.

The depiction of politics in the Old Testament is therefore of God as king working in and through Israel. It is worth noting, however, that the term "kingdom of God" does not occur in the Old Testament, although there are numerous references to God as king and to his kingly rule; to him as the maker and sustainer of all that exists (Ps 47:2); to the fact that he rules over all (Ps 103:19); that his rule is eternal, encompassing the past, present, and future (Ps 145:13); and that he is "Jacob's King" (Isa 41:21). The fact of God's kingship prior to the monarchy points to a *theocratic* political structure, even though the term "theocracy" does not appear anywhere in either the Old or the New Testament.[52] It should be understood, though, that this was intended for Israel as a covenant people through whom the purposes and the knowledge of God would extend to all the nations of the earth. Israel could not therefore claim to have a covenantal relationship with God while living in disobedience to the covenant stipulations regarding the disbursement of justice and righteousness. In this respect, therefore, the political theology of the church must take cognizance of God's dealings with his people as depicted in the Bible.

This covenant motif resonates well with African concepts and understanding. The covenant that God made with Noah and later with Abraham and renewed through subsequent generations, particularly at Sinai

---

52. Adeogun, in "Kingdom of God," says that "'theocracy' [which is a] type of administration of governance or government, is a political concept. There is no mention of the word 'theocracy' in the Bible just as there [is] no such mention of other types of governance such as aristocracy, autocracy, democracy and plutocracy. Other types such as dictatorship, anarchy, oligarchy, monarchy, diarchy, tyranny and despotism are equally not mentioned" (66–67).

and later with David, is similar to some made in African societies. There are of course differences between the Old Testament and the African setting. Similarly, the exodus covenant of allegiance to God by the nation is reflected in the oath of freedom fighters made in their allegiance to the course of the revolt. When explained from a covenant perspective, most Africans would not have difficulty understanding a God–community relationship established through a covenant or oath.

In most African contexts such as Kenya, for example, a covenant or oath once made would "[affect] the oath taker, his household, his kinsmen and his land . . . [As] the spiritual forces participated as full members in the oath, the final decision was in the last analysis not made by the human participants but by the spiritual forces."[53] Essentially then, it can be deduced that, in general, Africans know that God participates in their lives and what matters is that an oath taken binds everyone because of the religious nature Africans associate with it. According to Mbiti, "this oath places great moral and mystical obligations upon the parties concerned; and any breach of the covenant is dreaded and feared to bring about misfortunes."[54] An oath is therefore binding, and the oath-takers are obliged to keep their promises or face dire consequences wrought by the mystical powers.

The entire Old Testament can be treated and understood as a covenant or as God's oath with his people Israel.[55] Those who were in this covenant were therefore blessed, and as they obeyed they became agents of God's blessing to those who identified with their God and were thereby included as God's people. This inclusion or exclusion was confirmed by either obedience or disobedience as depicted in Deuteronomy 28. The hallmark of this covenant relationship was love for God – "Love the LORD your God with all your heart and with all your soul and with all your strength" (Deut 6:5) – manifested through obedience to the law (reflecting the covenantal provisions) which bound the parties together. Indeed the Law, the Writings, and the Prophets which depict Israel's history are all tied to this relational provision. The prophets called

---

53. Greet Kershaw, *Mau Mau from Below* (Athens, OH: Ohio University Press, 1997), 312. She continues by observing that the oath is "fundamentally a procedure by which God is invoked . . . which is true for all oaths" (319).

54. John Mbiti, *African Religions and Philosophy* (New York: Frederick A. Praeger, 1969), 212.

55. Rolf Rendtorff, in *The Covenant Formula: An Exegetical and Theological Investigation*, trans. Margaret Kohl (Edinburgh: T&T Clark, 1998), discusses the covenant formula and argues that "the formula never merely describes an existing condition, but always a process through which Yhwh becomes, or has become, Israel's God, and Israel becomes, or has become, Yhwh's people whether it be in the past, present or future" (13).

Israel back to covenant obedience, but unfortunately the people failed to keep their covenantal obligations. As Richards observes, "The prophets had taught them to see the birth of the nation at Sinai as a covenant whereby God had made Israel the Kingdom which he graced with his holiness: 'You shall be to me a Priestly Kingdom, a Holy Nation.'"[56] God, however, does not relent from pursuing them, in keeping with his promise. The proof of the people's rejection of God is seen when they demand to have a king and God tells Samuel, "Listen to all that the people are saying to you; it is not you they have rejected, but they have rejected me as their king. As they have done from the day I brought them up out of Egypt until this day, forsaking me and serving other gods, so they are doing to you" (1 Sam 8:7–8). The transition from a strong tribal confederacy, or tribal districts, to a monarchy ushered in a tension that lasted for the rest of Old Testament history.

The concept of kingship changed the Israelite mindset because their king was not like the kings of the other nations surrounding them, although they had essentially rejected him. In the united kingdom of Israel, the evils of the monarchy were manifested clearly by the kings' self-interest and disobedience to the covenant obligations. The Davidic covenant ushered in a dynastic rule that lasted until the Babylonian Empire. Seeing God as the King of Israel then becomes key for understanding the sociopolitical life of Israel both in the Old Testament and in the fulfilment of the promises that were made in reference to the coming Messiah.

B. New Testament Political Thought

The transition from the Old Testament to the New Testament politically is a history of about four hundred years during which Judea passed under the authority of foreign powers until the appointment of Herod the Great as ruler of the Jews. During this period, the Greek rule of the Ptolemies and Seleucids ensured the disintegration of the former national barriers whereby small states with their interests and ambitions crumbled. During the Seleucid dynasty, the most antagonistic king toward the Jews was Antiochus Epiphanes, who attempted to force Hellenization (the blending of Greek culture with Jewish culture) on the Jews in Palestine. Antiochus sought to exterminate Jewish identity by destroying the Jews' religion, defiling their temple by entering the Holy of Holies and offering a pig on the altar. He also prohibited temple worship, forbade circumcision on pain of death, destroyed all copies of the

---

56. H. J. Richards, "The Kingdom of God," *The Arrow* 10, no. 6 (June 1954): 378.

Scripture that he could find and slaughtered anyone found in possession of it, sold thousands of Jewish families into slavery, and resorted to every conceivable form of torture to force Jews to renounce their religion. Many Jews revolted under the leadership of Mattathias, who was zealous for the Jewish faith, in what stands out as one of the most heroic feats in Jewish history. This marked the beginning of the Maccabean Revolt spearheaded by his son Judas, who dealt a major blow by winning battle after battle despite seemingly impossible odds. The Jews reacted strongly against Hellenization and did not want to be pressured into it. They retook Jerusalem and purified the temple, lighting candles on 15 December 164 BC, which was commemorated in the feast of Hanukkah or Lights. Under the leadership of Simon, another son of Mattathias, Syria accorded the Jews political independence in 143 BC, and this lasted until 63 BC. The semi-independence of the Jews came by permission of the foreign empire. Simon was declared general, high priest, and ethnarch (the political ruler), and these offices were made hereditary. This enabled the emergence of various Jewish sociopolitical and religious groupings, such as the Pharisees, Sadducees, Zealots, and Essenes.

Even against such a background, the life of the Jews continued to be essentially communal. Although living in a multireligious cosmopolitan context, they still had a close affinity to Jerusalem as their political hub, which was linked "directly to the Hebrew associations of Jerusalem, as clothed in the language and blended with the sentiments of old Greek citizenship."[57] This is attested in Hebrews and Revelation, where the figure of a "heavenly Canaan" is replaced by the figure of a heavenly city with a heavenly franchise – a purely Hebrew notion. What this indicates is that, even with the many sociopolitical changes that shaped their lives over such a long period of time, they still retained their faith in its various forms of expression and maintained a strong identity with their ancestral origins and affiliation.

The event of the birth of Jesus at Bethlehem during the reign of Herod begins the New Testament period by triggering a political predicament, with Herod perceiving a threat to his kingship, leading to the mass killing of babies. Reeling under the Roman rule, the Jews were without political control. Discouraged and oppressed by the ruling authorities, they were longing for a redeemer-king who would release them and restore them to their former glory of political supremacy. We see therefore a people who "though they might occasionally hope to impress the governing authorities by prophetic

---

57. E. L. Hicks, "On Some Political Terms Employed in the New Testament," *The Classical Review* 1, no. 1 (March 1887): 5.

witness (Matt. 10:18), had no ordinary means of political influence. Their only conceivable (though scarcely practical) route to political power would have been that of armed revolt, an option that they seem to have rejected."[58] As we look at Jesus's life and teachings along with the worldview of his disciples, we see strong ties of continuity with Old Testament political thought, albeit with a significant departure coming especially through Jesus's teaching on the kingdom of God. The politics of Jesus have a radical dimension that reorients our perspective on God's kingdom with its attendant paradox.

Jesus and Politics

Political thought in the life and ministry of Christ should be viewed from a wider perspective than merely party or professional politics. The Gospels' presentations of Jesus show that politics was not foreign to his life and ministry. While the significance of Jesus transcends politics, it would be a misrepresentation of his task to "exclude the political dimension of his life and fate."[59] This is true especially when we consider that the kingdom of God, which was the keynote of his ministry, "embraces the whole of human life, and because he identified in love with human beings whose lives were affected by political structures and policies, his mission impinged on the political along with other dimensions of life."[60] On a number of occasions, Jesus confronted the sociopolitical misdeeds wrought by the leaders in the contemporary society. The events leading to his arrest, trial, and crucifixion were all politically instigated as he was perceived to be a threat to the prevailing sociopolitical and religious elite in their decadence that characterized all sectors of societal leadership. The teaching of Jesus was therefore, in a sense, aimed at addressing the evils in society, and specifically directed at those in authority who had been corrupted and as a result thwarted the administration of justice. Issues such as the abuse of the law, exorbitant taxation, disputes, and disparagement, along with party attitudes, subversion, and abuse of the judicial process, became the key tenets of Jesus's challenge to the political leaders of his day.

---

58. Richard Bauckham, "Reading the Bible Politically," in *An Eerdmans Reader in Contemporary Political Theology*, ed. William T. Cavanaugh, Jeffrey W. Bailey, and Craig Hovey (Grand Rapids, MI: Eerdmans, 2012), 334.

59. Richard Bauckham, *The Bible in Politics: How to Read the Bible Politically* (London: SPCK, 2011), 142.

60. Bauckham, *Bible in Politics*, 142.

Politics and the Kingdom of God

The kingdom of God was the keynote of Jesus's teaching in parables and miracles through which he addressed the sociopolitical issues of contemporary society. The signs (miracles) which accompanied his preaching of the kingdom validated the authority of his preaching and teaching (Matt 4:23–25). As depicted in the Gospels, the miracles Jesus performed were directly linked to the Old Testament prophecies of what the Messiah would do (Isa 61:1–2a; Luke 4:18–21) – which he demonstrated as a fulfillment in the hearing of his audience. Essentially it was only the messianic king who could perform the mighty acts we see in him. Thus the parables of the kingdom are to be seen in tandem with the mighty miracles that Jesus performed and which demonstrated his justice and righteousness, as envisaged in the Old Testament. Nicodemus attests to the divine origin of Jesus when he says in John 3:2, "Rabbi, we know that you are a teacher who has come from God. For no one could perform the signs you are doing if God were not with him." In this regard, it would not be far-fetched to say that in Jesus there was a continuity of the teaching of the Old Testament prophets, especially as it related to the coming of the Messiah as a sign of the arrival of the kingdom of God.

The fulfilment of the promises of God to the Jews was found in the person of Jesus who was the Christ, or Messiah. In this sense, then, the New Testament explicates the Old Testament by affirming the kingship of God in the person of the Messiah. This is so because the concept of the kingdom of God or kingdom of heaven found in the New Testament is rooted in the Old Testament. Old Testament Jewish thought laid the emphasis on the manifestation of the kingly activity which we see demonstrated by Jesus in the New Testament through his teaching in parables and miraculous acts. Jewish anticipation of the coming Messiah who was the Davidic king not only shaped their minds but was fulfilled by Christ's ministry in every respect.[61] This is well captured in the pronouncement of the good news by Christ soon after his baptism by his forerunner, John the Baptist, in calling people to repent because the kingdom of God had come (Matt 4:17; Mark 1:14–15).[62] For this reason, then, the coming of the kingdom is intertwined with the coming of the messianic king to redeem his people from their sin. The kingdom is indeed tied to the task of Christ as redeemer which "is not a question of a general timeless statement concerning

---

61. This is also discussed by Ebenezer Ola Olutosin Adeogun, "The Kingdom of God and Old Testament Theocracy," *Ogbomoso Journal of Theology* 12 (2007): 60.

62. F. David Famell, "The Kingdom of God in the New Testament," *The Master's Seminary Journal* 23, no. 2 (2012): 198.

God's power and reign, but especially of its redemptive-historical effectuation."[63] It should be noted, though, that the kingdom Jesus taught was not of this earth. This kingdom was a demonstration of God's rule and reign over all creation in all spheres of existence. It also depicted God's plan of restoration of humanity from their fallenness and separation from God occasioned by Adam's act of disobedience. This would bring about the forgiveness of sin and a radical transformation of men and women from all nations of the earth submitting themselves to the power and authority of Christ.

Teaching about the kingdom of God or the kingdom of heaven in the ministry of Jesus must therefore be linked to the Old Testament promise that anticipates the coming of a messianic, Davidic king. This link is crucial as it enables us to relate the Old Testament covenants – such as the Abrahamic covenant in Genesis 12 and 15; the Davidic in 2 Samuel 7 (cf. Ps 2 and 110); as well as the new covenant in Jeremiah 31:31–33 and Ezekiel 36:25–27 – with the activities and proclamation of the kingdom of God by Jesus, as affirmed by Nicodemus in the words quoted above. The statements in Matthew about the "kingdom of God" or the "kingdom of heaven" used must be understood in connection with these Old Testament promises of the Davidic messianic kingdom. While the nation of Israel as God's special people was featured explicitly in the Old Testament, the notion of Israel as the kingdom of God does not feature prominently. It could be argued, however, that with God being the King of Israel and making them a holy nation, they as a people did constitute the kingdom of God. The promises that God made in the Old Testament to Israel were thus understood in light of their political existence as a special nation on earth. The promised messianic king would, according to Jewish expectations, be favorably inclined toward the Jews for their survival and supremacy over all the other nations. When Jesus proclaimed the arrival of the kingdom, therefore, the Jews understood this to mean their triumph over other nations, as they regarded themselves as that kingdom since they were the people of God. However, Jesus did not fit with their anticipations and expectations, as his proclamation of the kingdom of God was radically different, and their hopes were dashed. In Acts 1:6–8, for instance, the disciples had great expectations following Jesus's resurrection, thinking that he was going to affirm their political authority over other nations when they asked, "Lord, are you at this time going to restore the kingdom to Israel?" His response, however, did not confirm their expectations: "It is not for you to know the times or

---

63. Herman N. Ridderbos, *The Coming of the Kingdom* (Philadelphia: Presbyterian & Reformed, 1975), 19.

dates the Father has set by his own authority." This helps explain why Jesus's encounters with Jewish religious leaders brought out the sociopolitical and religious ramifications of Judaism and the intrigues of messianic expectations.

The Jewish rejection of Jesus is seen as a dominant feature throughout his ministry on account of his radical approach to his task and purpose which was essential to identification with his messianic kingship.[64] One of the major issues he had with the Jews was their corruption of their faith through following oral traditions passed down in their religious systems that misrepresented their God-given law and statutes. Much of what we see in the various expressions of Judaism is a corruption of the Mosaic law through the traditions and misleading teachings and sayings of the elders and religious leaders, which became the "mantra" that shaped the life of the Jewish people (Matt 15:1–14). By challenging their religious teachings and practices, Jesus was attacking the core of their sociopolitical and religious tenets and practices. The inclusion of non-Jews in the composition of citizens of the kingdom, for instance, was in fulfilment of the Abrahamic promise that he would be a blessing to all the nations of the earth, which for the Jews was unacceptable as they regarded themselves as the only special people of God – the people of the covenant. The fulfilment of the Abrahamic promise is found in the new people of God: the church. For Judaism, though, faith and belief in God was not just a religious affair but a total way of life, since their religion was intricately intertwined with their politics.

Politics and Crucifixion

The sociopolitical and religious environment of the Jews in the first century saw the vibrant engagement of religious leaders who were concerned about the moral decadence of society. John the Baptist, the forerunner of Jesus, for instance, was constantly at loggerheads with high-ranking religious and political leaders as he called for societal reform. He spoke against the practices of the tax collectors who were prone to defrauding the people by charging beyond the required amounts, thereby enriching themselves. Similarly he admonished the soldiers who sought his counsel not to "extort money" or "accuse people falsely" but to "be content with your pay" (Luke 3:12–14). John's stance indicates that religious leaders have a responsibility to be the conscience of society and therefore give proper guidance on sociopolitical affairs. John did not shy away from these issues but was even bold enough to speak against the evils of Herod Antipas, whom he castigated particularly for

---

64. Famell, "Kingdom of God," 199.

his adultery in marrying Herodias, the wife of his brother Philip, which was unlawful. This enraged Herod Antipas, who imprisoned John (Luke 3:19–20) and ultimately ordered his beheading (Matt 14:3–12). In this regard, we can see John as a victim of a political assassination on account of his outspoken opposition to the evils (in this case, Antipas's personal interests) of the political leadership of his time. It is no wonder that his stand and confrontation of the leaders' evil deeds occasioned his death, and this is in some ways similar to what Jesus faced.

The repercussions of Christ's radical teaching and its implications for Judaism eventually led to a major sociopolitical and religious conspiracy by the religious leaders that culminated in his removal by crucifixion under Roman rule. We need to observe that the Jewish religious leaders, who by implication held the greatest socioreligious as well as political influence in Judaism, were the main instigators of the false accusations leveled against Jesus. In a strong honor–shame society, the religious leaders were not oblivious to their dwindling popularity and the threat of losing their sociopolitical and religious enclaves. As crowds followed Jesus while he performed miracles, the religious leaders were enraged and eventually plotted to eliminate him (John 11:45–53). The events leading to the crucifixion point to the cross being a political symbol, not so much because of the political innuendos that characterized his arrest, condemnation, and crucifixion, but because it was a sign of victory over the power of sin and the dominion of Satan. The Jewish religious leaders stirred up the crowds to clamor for the crucifixion of Jesus to insinuate that he was under the curse of God (Deut 21:23) and hence could not be the Messiah. In this way they hoped to gain popularity. Indeed all the structures that precipitated the trial that led to the crucifixion were corrupt. "The Sanhedrin resort[ed] to dishonest legal procedure in its trial – dishonest witnesses; illegal time, place, and processes; charges not related to wrongdoing; and abuse of the prisoner . . . this is wicked judicial procedure. Further, the relationship between the Jews and the colonial power [was] corrupt both ways."[65] Every event that preceded the crucifixion was an outright abuse of justice, demonstrating "the overwhelming sense . . . of the innocent person being taken to judicial murder."[66] In keeping with his character and disposition, Christ could not

---

65. Alan Storkey, *Jesus and Politics: Confronting the Powers* (Grand Rapids, MI: Baker Academic, 2005), 246.

66. Storkey, *Jesus and Politics*, 248.

"avoid confrontation with the structures of evil."[67] His acclamation as king in his triumphal entry of Jerusalem, riding on a donkey, was a direct affront to both the Roman political regime and the Jewish religious elite (Zech 9:9). The fact that Jesus made statements regarding his kingship identifying him with the throne of authority of God (John 10:30) clearly indicates that his trial was not merely a religious event but was essentially political.

The conversation between Christ and the religious leaders during his trial indicates that his accusers recognized his claims to deity, the very reason given for his elimination. The gravity of Christ's statement that "from now on you will see the Son of Man sitting at the right hand of the Mighty One and coming on the clouds of heaven" was met by a violent reaction from the high priest who "tore his clothes and said, 'He has spoken blasphemy! Why do we need any more witnesses? Look, now you have heard the blasphemy. What do you think?' 'He is worthy of death,' they answered. Then they spit in his face and struck him with their fists. Others slapped him and said, 'Prophesy to us, Messiah. Who hit you?'" (Matt 26:64–68). Paradoxically, their mockery of him – "Prophesy to us, Messiah" – confirmed his messianic role. The soldiers made a similar affirmation in their mockery of him when they "twisted together a crown of thorns and put it on his head. They clothed him in a purple robe and went up to him again and again, saying, 'Hail, king of the Jews!'" (John 19:2–3).

The trial of Jesus, when he appeared before Pilate and the interrogation that ensued, brings out some fundamental issues regarding the political contest of power and authority. In view of the divine authority of Jesus, it may not be far-fetched to say that "the meeting of Pilate and Jesus is perhaps the greatest political event of all time."[68] With the question of kingship is the more profound implication of authority which Christ's kingship portends not just for the Jews but for Pilate as the representative of the Roman Empire. The question that Pilate asked, "Are you the king of the Jews?," elicited confirmation from Christ: "You have said so" (Matt 27:11; cf. Luke 23:3). Paradoxically, his kingship was recognized and attested by the existing sociopolitical structures. We do not see Pilate disputing it in any way. What emerges from this encounter is the truth concerning the source of authority. On the one hand, Pilate, as governor,

---

67. David W. Shenk, *Justice, Reconciliation and Peace in Africa* (Nairobi: Uzima, 1983), 88. Shenk is spot on when he says, "Jesus was disturbingly confrontational. He pronounced woes on the religious establishment for practising pieties which had no relevance to justice. And that is why the roof came down on his head. Christ as God with us commanded righteousness and justice. His confrontational presence was deeply disturbing. It is for this reason that he was crucified."

68. Storkey, *Jesus and Politics*, 266.

was in a position of power which was vested in him by the Romans, and he was thus authorized to free or condemn people within his jurisdiction. Jesus, however, had a distinctly different understanding of the true source of power and authority. In response to Pilate's insinuation that he had authority over Jesus in that he had the power to crucify or set him free, Jesus put things in their proper perspective: Pilate would have had no power unless God had allowed him to have it (John 19:10–11). In this sense, Jesus tore into the misguided sociopolitical perspective and understanding of his contemporaries. All kingship and authority derive from God, and no one holds a position of authority outside the divine mandate. In this respect, then, human political structures must recognize and acknowledge that their authority is ordained by God; failure to do so means they are serving their self-interests in disobedience to God's intent and purposes.

Nevertheless, Pilate, although not a Jew, was cognizant of Judaism and its structures as he finally gave in to pressure from the Jews: "'Here is your king,' Pilate said to the Jews. But they shouted, 'Take him away! Take him away! Crucify him!' 'Shall I crucify your king?' Pilate asked. 'We have no king but Caesar,' the chief priests answered" (John 19:14–15). This declaration by the chief priests is reminiscent of the demand for a king by the Jews in 1 Samuel 8:19 when "the people refused to listen to Samuel. 'No!' they said. 'We want a king over us'" – when God was their king all along. Essentially it appears that the Jews were prone to denying their heritage. They did not only reject God ("they have rejected me as their king," 1 Sam 8:7) but they also rejected their Messiah (John 1:11). This was a precursor to the new people of God: of all those who received him of all nations, peoples, and tribes becoming his followers. This implies, therefore, that "the gospel, the grace of God regarding the kingdom, would now go to all nations (Matt 28:19–20; cp. Matt 13)."[69]

The cross of Christ can therefore, in light of our discussion above, be seen as a political symbol through which the King of kings was hung, manifesting the outrageous indignation of human evil. Christ's declaration to his disciples after the resurrection that "all authority in heaven and on earth has been given to me" (Matt 28:18) brings out the notion that his death was intricately political. The mandate he gives the disciples puts them on a political path of an ongoing power encounter between the kingdom of God and the forces of evil. The

---

69. Famell, "Kingdom of God," 201. He notes that "[Jesus's] rejection of them is due to their responsibility (John 19:11) for rejecting the Jewish Messiah: 'Therefore I say to you, the kingdom of God will be taken from you, and be given to a nation (εθνει) producing the fruit of it' (Matt 21:43; Rom 11:26; cp. LXX Dan 2:44)" (199).

mission of Christ is thus transferred to his disciples. The disciples of Jesus Christ as depicted in the book of Acts took over his mission as a continuation of God's dealings with humanity through the salvific ministry of the Messiah that was to be effective in the lives of all the nations, in keeping with the promises God gave to Abraham. In this respect, the church must understand that its mission to the world is a political engagement of calling people to submission to the authority of Christ as they live in obedience to God's word. The task of proclaiming the gospel is for the holistic transformation of people of all tribes, cultures, and nationalities as they take their rightful position in Christ as his ambassadors.

Politics and the Disciples' Teaching

The foregoing discussion is important in relating the disciples and the kingdom of God. The teaching of Jesus on the kingdom had political significance that shaped the teaching and ministry of his disciples. When he told the disciples that "it is not for you to know the times or dates the Father has set by his own authority [but] you will receive power when the Holy Spirit comes on you; and you will be my witnesses in Jerusalem, and in all Judea and Samaria, and to the ends of the earth" (Acts 1:7–8), this was an indication that the task of Christ was from now on to be carried out by his disciples. The mission of Christ was now the mission of his disciples who, as the church, would be actively involved in proclaiming the kingdom of God. In carrying out this task they, like their Master, would inevitably be involved in the sociopolitical and religious affairs of the society in which they lived. As an offshoot of Judaism, the followers of Christ would continue to exist in the tension that resulted from the overlap of the Jewish expectations of the kingdom and the teaching of Christ. It is important to point out here that their constitution as the church is related to, but is not equal to, the kingdom of God. Christ's references to the church in his teaching and ministry (Matt 16:18–19; 18:17) point to a constant struggle between his followers and the forces of evil, although their triumph is guaranteed! In this sense, then, there is a close relationship between the church (the new people of God) and the kingdom of God in relation to victory over the forces of evil.

The church and the kingdom are thus distinct, with the church being an instrument or agency for proclaiming the kingdom (Acts 8:12; 19:8; 20:25; 28:23, 31). The kingdom should be understood as the exercise of God's rule and reign, rulership or right to rule, and the church as the realm of God or the people under God's rule.[70] The church is, therefore, the realm over which God exercises his authority, and, at the same time, a manifestation of the kingdom, where God creates a new way of life demonstrating the ethics or quality of kingdom life, which involves righteousness and justice, as well as peace and love, the hallmarks of the fruit of the Spirit. The task[71] of the church is therefore to exhibit these characteristics of justice and righteousness that manifest the kingdom of which it is part. The church has a political responsibility which should essentially make it see itself as a political entity.[72] This perspective is essential because the church's political engagement, to a large extent, lies in its self-understanding in terms of both its existential reality and the hermeneutical mandate and duty. If the Bible is thus concerned with the political aspects of life, then political praxis is an inevitable prerogative of the church.

Much of what we see in the lives of the early disciples of Christ is an ongoing interaction with the sociopolitical world of the time. They contended with the political structures in both negative and positive ways. They faced the challenge of monotheistic allegiance to God in the context of the Greco-Roman world with its diverse religious manifestations shrouded in polytheistic and pantheistic tendencies. The disciples proclaimed the gospel of Jesus Christ within their own sociopolitical context. They made a significant impact on their communities by standing against the tyranny of the Roman political regime of the time as they defended their faith in Christ in the face of insurmountable opposition and persecution. The book of Acts narrates many instances when the apostles stood before religious as well as political authorities and boldly defended the gospel truth. They withstood the incessant pressure to denounce their faith. In Acts 4:7–20, Peter and John illustrated the power of the gospel as they were questioned regarding the authority behind their actions: "By what power or what name did you do this?" They explicitly identified Christ as the source of power behind their acts of kindness:

---

70. Stanley James Grenz, *Theology for the Community of God* (Nashville: Broadman & Holman, 1994), 617.

71. John Howard Yoder, in *The Politics of Jesus: Vicit Agnus Noster* (Grand Rapids, MI: Eerdmans, 1994), observes that "the very existence of the church is its primary task. It is in itself a proclamation of the lordship of Christ to powers from whose dominion the church has begun to be liberated. The church does not attack these powers; this Christ has done . . . By existing the church demonstrates that their rebellion has been vanquished" (150).

72. John Howard Yoder, in *The Christian Witness to the State* (Newton, KS: Faith and Life, 1964), says, "In biblical thought the church is properly a political entity, a polis" (18).

"It is by the name of Jesus Christ of Nazareth, whom you crucified but whom God raised from the dead, that this man stands before you healed. Jesus is

'the stone you builders rejected,
which has become the cornerstone.'

Salvation is found in no one else, for there is no other name under heaven given to mankind by which we must be saved."

When they saw the courage of Peter and John and realized that they were unschooled, ordinary men, they were astonished and they took note that these men had been with Jesus.

When called to desist from proclaiming the gospel, their resolve was strong: "Peter and John replied, 'Which is right in God's eyes: to listen to you, or to him? . . . As for us, we cannot help speaking about what we have seen and heard.'" When the apostles were imprisoned on account of their faith, more miraculous signs were displayed: "They arrested the apostles and put them in the public jail. But during the night an angel of the Lord opened the doors of the jail and brought them out. 'Go, stand in the temple courts,' he said, 'and tell the people all about this new life'" (Acts 5:18–20). Yet even in these circumstances, the disciples' resolve was clear: "Peter and the other apostles replied: 'We must obey God rather than human beings!'" (Acts 5:29). Their allegiance to Christ in their task of proclaiming the gospel was essentially a political stand against the earthly political powers as well as against the spiritual powers of evil and darkness. Paul alludes to this stance when he says in Ephesians 6:12: "our struggle is not against flesh and blood, but against the rulers, against the authorities, against the powers of this dark world and against the spiritual forces of evil in the heavenly realms." This indicates that the gospel is in every respect political in the sense that it seeks to disturb the evils underlying the seemingly stable and comfortable human sociopolitical structures. The gospel message is therefore intended to bring about change upon societies as well as individuals. This transformation is God's work of reconciliation and redemption affecting all aspects of human life and structures: "all shepherding, schooling, family relationships, economic institutions, and political practices."[73] There is no human being, whether "Jew or Gentile, believer or unbeliever, private person or public official, who is exempt from the moral and juridical obligation before

---

73. James Skillen, *The Good of Politics: A Biblical, Historical, and Contemporary Introduction*, Engaging Culture (Grand Rapids, MI: Baker Academic, 2014), 10.

God to submit to Christ's lordship over every aspect of his life in thought, word, and deed."[74]

The impact of the gospel entails unsettling the status quo. Those in political power and authority, however, fail to recognize that they are stewards, as the positions they hold are divine appointments. As mentioned above, this was affirmed by Jesus when he said to Pilate, "You would have no power over me if it were not given to you from above" (John 19:11), and Paul confirms this in Romans 13:1: "Let everyone be subject to the governing authorities, for there is no authority except that which God has established. The authorities that exist have been established by God." Similarly Peter exhorts believers in 1 Peter 2:13–15 to "submit yourselves for the Lord's sake to every human authority: whether to the emperor, as the supreme authority, or to governors, who are sent by him to punish those who do wrong and to commend those who do right. For it is God's will that by doing good you should silence the ignorant talk of foolish people." The political responsibility of Christians is to be subject to God and his design for the administration of his creation as he exercises his rule administered through his divinely ordained institutions. Human governments and those in positions of authority are thus custodians entrusted with the responsibility of administrating justice and righteousness for all God's creation.

The kingdom of God or the realm over which God exercises his power and authority consists of all things visible and material as well as invisible and immaterial. His reign is manifested in all realms of existence, even to those opposed to his will and purpose. It implies that Satan, fallen angels, demons, and the angelic beings, as well as humans are under the authority of God. The spiritual forces of evil and darkness and the kingdom of God are in conflict, although God's sovereign authority and power is far greater than the evil forces of Satan. Paul attests to this strife in the words quoted above from Ephesians 6:12, that "our struggle is not against flesh and blood, but against the rulers, against the authorities, against the powers of this dark world and against the spiritual forces of evil in the heavenly realms." Christian life is a political engagement where the physical realm is a visible manifestation of the invisible reality which determines the authority to which one attests allegiance. Christians around the world should demonstrate what life in the kingdom of God ought to be like amidst the fierce opposition and persecution they endure

---

74. Jay Grimstead and E. Calvin Beisner, eds., *Articles of Affirmation and Denial on the Kingdom of God: A Summary of the Biblical and Historical View* (Mountain View, CA: Coalition on Revival, 1999), 8.

on a day-to-day basis. This kingdom conflict between the forces of good and evil will continue until the final triumph of good over evil: "Then the end will come, when he hands over the kingdom to God the Father after he has destroyed all dominion, authority and power" (1 Cor 15:24). The ultimate scene, as depicted in the book of Revelation, is when Satan and his forces are defeated, which will signify the culmination of the redemptive work of Christ: "Then I heard a loud voice in heaven say, 'Now have come the salvation and the power and the kingdom of our God, and the authority of his Messiah. For the accuser of our brothers and sisters, who accuses them before our God day and night, has been hurled down'" (Rev 12:10). This triumph over evil and darkness will mark the consummation of God's kingdom which the church anticipates. In this sense, then, Christian involvement in the sociopolitical affairs of the world today is part and parcel of the plan and purposes of God which are integral to their existence. This is a cardinal component that the theology of the church must embrace so as to present a holistic view of life in Africa and for all humanity.

7

Politics and Praxis

The actualization of a biblically based sociopolitical theology calls for the church to be actively engaged by involving its members and theologians, who may include pastors and elders, in the process of developing such a theology. This praxis of political theology is necessary for the church as it endeavors to inculcate an authentic Christian presence in all spheres of African life. It is inevitable that this theology of the church will prompt Christians to be involved in sociopolitical issues while maintaining the uniqueness which the Christian calling entails. The premise of such a praxis is the fact that the church has a cardinal duty to shape the sociopolitical terrain of African politics positively because it is at the core of the society. As Katongole, citing Foucault, observes, "Every society . . . writes its own history that legitimizes its own regime of truth, its 'general politics' of truth: that is, the type of discourse which it accepts and makes function as true."[1] This is critical because when we as Christians engage in political activity, we must maintain our integrity and keep our biblical values intact. While we may frequently settle for "half-a-loaf," we must never compromise principle by engaging in unethical behavior or endorsing or fostering sin. As we rightly engage in supporting legislation, candidates and political parties, we must be clear that biblical faith is vastly larger and richer than every limited, inevitably imperfect political agenda and that commitment to the Lordship of Christ and his one body far transcends all political commitments.[2]

---

1. Emmanuel M. Katongole, "'African Renaissance' and the Challenge of Narrative Theology in Africa," in *African Theology Today*, ed. Emmanuel M. Katongole (Scranton, PA: University of Scranton Press, 2002), 212.

2. Ronald J. Sider and Diane Knippers, *Toward an Evangelical Public Policy: Political Strategies for the Health of the Nation* (Grand Rapids, MI: Baker, 2005), 367.

One of the challenges facing the church is to change its approach of dissociating itself from social and political issues so as to prepare its members to be active in demonstrating their faith in the public arena. This calls for the church to look again at the deficiencies of the theology that it inherited from the missions, which is not only inadequate but also irrelevant for addressing the pertinent sociopolitical issues that affect Africans and their way of life. The ideas and ideals of the missionaries who are credited with the formulation of the doctrines and theology of the African church did not fully capture the essence of the African worldview. Similarly, some of the Western ideas and practices which have been adopted in shaping the African sociopolitical terrain are yet to penetrate the kernel of the African context and worldview.

The church in Africa therefore bears the mantle for educating the people so that they will be aware of their civic duty and responsibility in the society as well as their spiritual, civil, political, and human rights. This will help entrench a sense of national beliefs and a code of moral behavior and values that will shape every facet of community life. The task of the church in this matter must therefore transcend the approach of being a spiritual guide in order to address every aspect that relates to the well-being of the society as a whole. There is a need for an active and decisive approach in the manner in which the participation of the church in sociopolitical matters is carried out, so as to avoid the laissez-faire attitude evident today. The church must therefore move away from its sporadic practice, by some clergy, of only pointing out evils committed by the state or state agencies. Political engagement by the church must instead take center stage so that this occasional speaking without consistent engagement on sociopolitical matters is checked. This will remove the sense of the church in Africa being asleep and speaking occasionally in its dreams only when there is a political crisis. The involvement of the church in these matters should be broad-based and not limited to the national agenda of a particular party that is geared to enhancing party politics; rather it must remain nonpartisan and seek the well-being of all citizens. The areas in which the church has an obligation to focus on praxis include, but are not limited to, the following.

A. Elections

Elections and the electioneering process are among the key aspects that contribute to the making of political states and leadership. Elections are a primary structural facet that is core to establishing proper citizen participation in the sociopolitical life of a country. Stipulating the theological and practical significance of elections should therefore be an important component of the church's theological praxis. Staffan Lindberg discusses the concepts of democracy and elections in Africa. Elections and the process of electioneering are "an institutionalized attempt to actualize the essence of democracy [which is] one of many ways of choosing leadership and disposing [of] old governments in a political system. As a core institution of representative democracy, elections are supposedly the means of deciding who should hold legislative and executive power."[3] It should be pointed out, however, that ignorance on the part of the citizens is a major obstacle to the democratic process in elections since "people come to the polls completely ignorant of what is expected of them. They, therefore, vote into office wrong candidates whose interests are power and wealth, but not serving the people who elected them. This group of leaders has no intention of establishing healthy channels of communication between them and the electorate, so they quickly forget the promises they made to the people during political campaigns."[4]

Elections are, for the most part, an engaging and strenuous exercise both for those who aspire to run for positions as well as for their ardent followers and for the citizens as a whole. In most African political structures, as elsewhere, political party systems are used to field candidates who are nominated for elections. Individual affiliation and membership of the party becomes a critical component of the electoral process as the parties tend to determine the trajectory of the political topography of any given country. Although deep ethnic divisions tend to characterize party membership and affiliations in most African countries, such as Kenya, the democratic process during elections may not necessarily be curtailed. Following the established legal or constitutional procedures and processes is key to carrying out free and fair elections in any given context. Since the church is at the heart of the community, it is vital for church leadership to entrench within its theological educational process a mechanism for educating its membership and the community as a whole regarding their responsibility in elections. This must be based on a well-informed approach that clearly understands the legal provisions of the country and the sociopolitical intricacies that define that country's political structures and practices. The church's involvement at a national level in the formulation of electoral processes and procedures is important so that its voice can be heard

---

3. Staffan Lindberg, *Democracy and Elections in Africa* (Baltimore, MD: Johns Hopkins University Press, 2006), 22–23.

4. Clement Majawa, "The Church's Role in Defining Genuine Democracy in Africa," in Katongole, *African Theology Today*, 101.

at the policy-making stage of the election process. Care must always be taken on the part of the church to demonstrate an objective, nonpartisan approach in its teaching and to allow its members to make appropriate decisions about engagement in elections. The church must be alert to the malpractices that can characterize elections, such as voter manipulation through bribery or intimidation, which often cloud elections in African states, resulting in a rejection of the outcome or nullification of the whole process, as was the case in the Kenyan 2017 presidential elections. At the same time, conflict of interest must always be avoided, where individual Christians and church leaders have personal interests in vying for political office or in helping particular individuals to positions of power.

It must be understood that elections are a process that a given polity utilizes in accordance with the requirements entrenched in the country's constitution to legally allow citizens to elect representatives to leadership positions. In this respect, then, there is no single universally established mode of elections that is devoid of human errors and machinations. It is the responsibility of the church, however, to make a decisive stand to desist from engagement in party politics that will be detrimental to its objective of inculcating unity among Christians of different political affiliations and ethnic backgrounds.

Based on the laid-down procedures, elections must be seen to be free and fair, with the rights of each eligible voter maintained. Irrespective of the outcome of the votes cast, peaceful and harmonious coexistence must be sustained. In case of disputes, legal provisions and proper channels of complaint should be followed to avoid any form of anarchy and violence. Acceptance of the outcome of the elections or petitions therein is of paramount importance for all parties involved as the opposite may result in postelection violence of the kind witnessed in many African contexts. In situations where one party dominates the elections mainly because of the tyranny of numbers, this should not be confused either with ethnic partisanship or with less-democratic authoritarianism.[5] Erdmann and Basedau point out that "we need to distinguish between dominance as a result of free and fair elections and dominance as a result of electoral manipulation and oppression. The first is democratically legitimized; the second lacks this qualification and is therefore a party system within an authoritarian context."[6] The church must therefore

---

5. Lindberg, *Democracy and Elections*, 22–23.

6. Gero Erdmann and Matthias Basedau, "An Overview of African Party Systems," in *One-Party Dominance in African Democracies*, ed. Renske Doorenspleet and Lia Nijzink (Boulder, CO: Lynne Rienner, 2013), 26.

focus on its sociopolitical responsibility as it relates to elections so that the members and citizens as a whole are well guided in how to carry out credible elections that befit a society that values the maintenance of order and peace.

B. Constitutionalism

National constitutions have become cardinal tenets guiding the structure of countries, especially in the new democracies that have emerged in the last few decades. The constitutional framework provides guidance for the ordering of a functional society and ties together the various arms of government and other entities for the sake of cohesiveness. Different African countries have gone through individual processes of constitution-making with a view to entrenching the unique features of their sociopolitical contexts. Constitutionalism is not just a legal framework of embedding prohibitions and structures in a document. With reference to the South African constitution, for instance, William Everett states that "presidents, parliamentarians and everyday citizens now seek shelter under its canopy, tended by a Constitutional Court that is also new to these ways."[7] Since "a Constitution is not an order to be obeyed but a tree where people gather to share their life,"[8] it embodies the "deep soil" of values of a people's heritage, religion, and culture. It gains legitimacy by the incorporation of the common good of all in an all-inclusive and impartial treatment of a people's life. As Everett points out,

> legitimation is mediated by powerful symbols shared by the people. Symbols mediate between the unseen soil of religious intuition, memory and hope and the visible trees of law, society and human institutions. Shared images, songs, words, places of memory and ritual actions sink into people's emotions and minds. These symbols not only galvanize emotional commitment but also organize the way we see the world, each other and our role in society. They are common reference points for resolving disagreements and organizing collective action. They are compact programs of social behavior.[9]

---

7. William Johnson Everett, "Seals and Springboks: Theological Reflections on Constitutionalism and South African Culture," *Journal of Theology for Southern Africa* 101 (July 1998): 71.

8. Everett, "Seals and Springboks," 80.

9. Everett, 72.

A constitution that caters for the entire community ought to embrace the diversity of the people's cultural structures and be open to the emerging challenges of globalization and postmodern trends. The church should be at the forefront in embracing the whole process of constitutional structure as a key component of its theology. This will involve the entire membership that makes up the community of the church, with its diverse cultural and ethnic composition. This approach will help create a sense of community that engages in open dialogue with a commitment to coexist harmoniously during and after the process of constitution-making. Each member of the community is an important part of the whole whose welfare is affirmed and sustained through "practical moral reasoning," of which Yoder says: "The alternative to arbitrary individualism is not established authority but an authority in which the individual participates and to which he or she consents. The alternative to authoritarianism is not anarchy but freedom of confession."[10] Borrowing from the wealth of traditional African communalism in decision-making on matters affecting the entire community can be of great help in this context. The African social context demonstrates a communal orientation where

> authentic decision making in Africa is through the process of consensus. This process does not permit the humiliation and depersonalization of defeat. All must win through the process of right decision. Everyone has the opportunity to speak. As the eventual decision begins to emerge, the positions of the participants gradually shift until all are unanimous. No one leaves the group feeling that his opinion has not been heard. All have been affirmed. Personhood and community have been enhanced. African group processes never vote, because when a vote is cast, someone's opinion is defeated. It is the truth which unites the group and that truth cannot be determined by the vote. It is only perceivable through discussion and consensus.[11]

Indeed, engaging the community is critical and therefore the elders must be brought to the core of constitutionalism. Traditionally, the council of elders was headed by a chief who was the most respected elder due to his proven ability for making wise decisions and enhancing the welfare of the entire community. It is for this reason that "in some traditional societies a chief or king became the apex

---

10. John Howard Yoder, *The Priestly Kingdom: Social Ethics as Gospel* (Notre Dame, IN: University of Notre Dame Press, 1984), 24–25.

11. David W. Shenk, *Justice, Reconciliation and Peace in Africa* (Nairobi: Uzima, 1983), 23.

of power. He was the link between the living dead and the living, between God and humankind. In his personhood the life and harmony of the community was assured. Any violation of his personhood was therefore also a violation of community and life itself."[12] This kind of traditional social leadership has significantly affected modern African political structures to the extent that the process of democratization based on Western concepts has created more confusion and disruption in the cohesiveness of some African states. Shenk says that most modern African states are "exceedingly uncomfortable having more than one person running for president. The national political apparatuses are sufficiently attuned to consensus that only one candidate actually runs for presidential office. Harmony is the key to life. Divisive campaigns for the key office in the land would be seriously disruptive to life and freedom. Unified leadership is the key to community harmony and life."[13]

It is in light of this structure that we see the political rule in some African countries still retaining and maintaining the traditional chiefdom mindset where the chief as the authoritative voice of the village would never be questioned under any circumstances. This position was highly cherished and desired. Those who were closely allied to the chief enjoyed benefits and privileges such as wealth and prestige. Since the colonial system did not understand this African political background and seek to prepare the African governments once independence was attained, we now see a form of African democracy which fails to be an effective governing system, especially when it is forced into Western patterns of governance. The president, like a traditional chief, seeks to hold on to power following the same traditional structures, by clustering supporters around him and giving them protection, irrespective of their corrupt and unjust deeds in the society. This implies that the democratic system of rule and its principles, which are Western-oriented, remain foreign to the African mindset in principle. The challenge facing the church in Africa as a whole is how to help governments model an alternative political structure that will incorporate all societies that make up its citizenry in the ownership and support of the constitutional provisions. Therefore, the church must be at the forefront in demonstrating how citizens should rise above regional interests coupled with negative tribal and ethnic attachments which hinder progress in actualizing the constitutional mandate of a country.

There is a need to educate the people so that they will be aware of their duty and responsibility in the society as well as their spiritual, civil, political,

---

12. Shenk, *Justice, Reconciliation and Peace*, 37.
13. Shenk, 37.

and human rights. This will help create a sense of national beliefs and a code of moral behavior and values that will shape every facet of community life. The task of the church in this matter must go beyond the traditional approach of being a spiritual guide: the church must also address every aspect that facilitates the well-being of human existence. We have pointed out that the kind of theology that ought to address issues in sociopolitical matters has not been contextualized in most African polities, meaning that the church's role and contribution are inadequate and thus ineffective.

The process of constitution-making in most African countries is mostly dogged by partisan interests, even when, as in the case of Kenya, for instance, representatives from all parts of the country were chosen and mandated to deliberate on and come up with a constitution that would be representative of all Kenyan communities. Even at the point where the final document was adopted by parliament, ratified, and promulgated, there were many contentious issues, some of which were politically engineered. The call for constitutional amendments continues to be made, and granted, in a number of African countries in order to accommodate certain interests, particularly of the incumbents and their cronies. This has been witnessed in countries such as Rwanda, Burundi, and Uganda. In cases of national referendums, the processes are normally tedious and costly as the people seek to express themselves, creating a sense of ownership by direct participation rather than an endorsement of such an important national document by proxy. This has also faced numerous problems due to lack of proper mechanisms ensuring that the interests of all are catered for. It is for this reason that the church in Africa needs to take a leading role in the constitution-making process as its political responsibility.

C. Human Rights

Another cardinal component that is essential to understanding the polity of any given sociopolitical structure, especially within the African context, is the whole question of human rights. As Gabriel Msoka states, human rights is a notion that has elicited much discussion and contention among different schools of thought.[14] While the definition of human rights is a matter of debate among scholars today, we can take the term to refer to "the rational basis for

---

14. Gabriel Andrew Msoka, "Cosmotheandrization of Human Rights: A Focus on Refugees and Internally Displaced Persons in Africa," *African Ecclesiastical Review* 49, no. 1 & 2 (2007): 63.

a justified demand"[15] regarding any aspect pertaining to human existence. In this respect, then, it is any demand being claimed by an individual and duly warranted, not as a favor or privilege, but as a basic entitlement without any bias in ethnic or racial, sociopolitical, religious, or gender parity. This is a basic entitlement of each individual which must be provided for and safeguarded by law to each citizen. Human rights are therefore basic necessities for all human beings for the enjoyment of their subsistence in society without any form of discrimination. The "Universal Declaration of Human Rights" was "adopted and proclaimed by General Assembly resolution 217 A (III) of 10 December 1948."[16] The thirty articles of the declaration give an overview encapsulating the rights of all humanity. Each citizen is entitled to enjoyment of these rights, which ought to be safeguarded by the state and other international sociopolitical actors. It is the prerogative of the state or government to ensure that there is social cohesion and order by providing the requisite security of its citizens, thereby avoiding any form of violence or conflict, such as civil war, which often results in an upsurge in victims who are abused and denied their basic human rights of freedom and enjoyment of life in its fullness. The legislation of laws, policies, and structures that promote justice and equity for all is a cardinal requisite of any government that seeks to promote the well-being of its citizens.

Current developments in the global sociocultural, economic, and political arena continue to compound the understanding and effectual application of human rights, particularly in non-Western contexts. The notion of human rights as a Western construct, along with Western hegemony, capitalism, and the impact of modernity as well as postmodernity, is a matter of ongoing concern. It must be noted that there are social changes affecting each sociopolitical context that "are intensified by the forces of global economics, global culture, and global communication."[17] Essentially, human rights will continue to be defined by individual, cultural, national, and international factors in view of the global changes prevalent in society today.

The church in Africa must continue to ensure that a conducive environment for the promotion of human rights is maintained by bringing to the attention of all players the importance of such an environment. In this respect, the

---

15. Msoka, "Cosmotheandrization of Human Rights," 63.

16. United Nations, "United Nations Universal Declaration of Human Rights 1948," 2, https://www.jus.uio.no/lm/en/pdf/un.universal.declaration.of.human.rights.1948.portrait.letter.pdf.

17. Rhoda E. Howard-Hassmann, "Culture, Human Rights, and the Politics of Resentment in the Era of Globalization," *Human Rights Review* 6, no. 1 (2004): 7.

theology of the church must not only be true to the biblical teaching but also must be practical and relevant to the African sociopolitical context by responding appropriately to the present socioeconomic and political situation. At the same time, there is a need to educate the members and the citizenship as a whole regarding the role, responsibilities, and implications of their political involvement. As citizens of their country, they need to be made aware that it is their responsibility to help shape the kind of government that will be committed to the protection of human rights for all its citizens without discrimination. The sociopolitical theology of the church must be set within a framework in which Christians will see their responsibility, in view of their calling, to be involved in national politics, as agents of the cross whose priority is the promotion of justice through righteous living and obedience to Christ. They will thus set a good example that will seek to impact and change policies at the national level that promote the protection and enhancement of human rights.

D. Governance

Governance structures in most African political systems reflect the traditional leadership structure which, as we have observed, is the traditional chiefdom mindset where the chief was the authoritative voice of the village and would never be questioned under any circumstances. Those who were closely allied to the chief enjoyed benefits and privileges. Today, the president, like a traditional chief, seeks to hold on to power following the same traditional pattern. This implies that in principle the democratic governance system and its principles, which are Western-oriented, remain foreign to the African mindset. The challenge for the church in this respect, then, is to be at the forefront in modeling a suitable governance structure for the government that will incorporate all members of the community for ownership and support of their government. The church must therefore rise above ecclesial sectarianism coupled with the tribal factor, which unfortunately is still a major determinant of African political leadership and affiliation.

For the church to dissociate itself from the governance operations of sociopolitical affairs is a refusal to bring the power of the gospel into confrontation with the ever-increasing abuse of power and corruption exemplified by the political regimes. In light of this, the church, as a part of the society, has a great role to play in the task of inculcating governance principles that derive from the citizens themselves and help avoid the imperialistic imposition of Western forms of government. The church in its theology has to cultivate ways and means of urging African political actors to institute structures that promote just and righteous governance. For this to happen, the church must leave behind its traditional view that relegates politics to the sphere of evil, and become actively involved in, among other things, the education of its members on the need to cultivate ownership and support of the sociopolitical governance of their states.

While the focus of the church generally is on evangelism and discipleship, the issue of governance in the sociopolitical arena must also be seen as part of the mission in which Christians live out exemplary lives modeling justice and righteousness. In this way the church will be influencing the society from within, thus becoming salt by identifying with and yet being distinct from the society. Moreover, the church ought to redirect the focus of its members to prayer and a search for revival and renewal so as to attract the attention of the world by giving credence to the fact that "God is alive in the history of our times."[18] This implies that any change that will counter the prevailing governance ills must first begin from within the church as Christians live out their faith by participating in the governance structures of the state. The following words of Carl Henry on how to shape an evangelical counterculture are applicable to the African church context:

> It must root in changed lives, in members whose new birth . . . is no longer the only referent wherein God became alive for them, in a neighborly interest in townspeople that makes others think that the crucified and risen Jesus may indeed still have hands and feet today. Let the restoration of the prayer meeting be the mirror of a rising evangelical counterculture, one that begins not with the self but with God, and places others, if not before one's self, at least on a par with ourselves.[19]

In order to retain its prophetic voice, the church should be at the forefront in condemning and attacking sin and evil, holistically, without any compromise, by reprimanding wrongdoers and not heaping general negative comments upon the government. This is particularly true in the African context in general where sociopolitical governance and economic problems continue to cripple the society. In response to these problems it is important for "Christians to address the effects of sin at all levels, from the international economic order, to the policies of governments . . . to the formal and informal institutions

---

18. Carl F. Henry, "The Uneasy Conscience of Modern Fundamentalism: 45 Years Later," in *Citizen Christians: The Rights and Responsibilities of Dual Citizenship*, ed. Richard D. Land and Louis A. Moore (Nashville: Broadman and Holman, 1994), 62.

19. Henry, "Uneasy Conscience," 62.

of local cultures, down to the worldviews of the poor themselves."[20] Such an involvement by the church is a good reflection of its mission and role to the world.

E. Injustice

Injustice is the act of depriving a person of something to which he or she is entitled as a right and not a privilege. Injustice occurs whether such a deprivation is deliberate or unintentional. It is apparent "when we see it functioning to diminish, disregard, dismiss, deny, denigrate and disrespect persons. It entails those things which we immediately react to with a sense of it being wrong."[21] Injustice in Africa is brought about by unjust social "structures of exploitation and domination that cause poverty."[22] Different forms of injustice are rampant in human societies and especially on the African sociopolitical scene. While cases of injustice are related to virtually all aspects of human life, politics seems to be the major cause of acts of injustice in Africa.

Africans exhibit a kind of supernaturalism that sets them apart from the West due to their holistic view of life. Trust in God for sociopolitical matters is not a foreign issue since Africans in general have complete confidence in God's justice, which has given them resilience in the face of the innumerable experiences of oppression in their history. David Shenk makes this point vividly:

> God as the Life giver and Divider of Land is also the God of peace and justice. In fact, in Gikuyu traditional theology God is pre-eminently the God of justice. His justice is revealed in the human community . . . The one true God for the Gikuyu, and for the African people generally, is and always has been above everything else, the God of socio-political justice. Africans have an amazing confidence in God as the just one. Whenever injustice seems to prevail, the Swahili say *Mungu yuko* (God is present). The implication is, be patient and persistent, God will eventually bring justice to pass. Similarly when two people have a disagreement,

---

20. Bob Goudzwaard, *Globalization and the Kingdom of God* (Grand Rapids, MI: Baker, 2001), 58–59.

21. Emma J. Justes, "Doing Pastoral Theology in a Context of Injustice: Society for Pastoral Theology Luncheon Address, June 18, 2005," *Journal of Pastoral Theology* 16, no. 1 (Spring 2006): 32.

22. Majawa, "The Church's Role," 101.

the argument can be readily dismissed by saying, "God will judge between us."[23]

The church's involvement in and formulation of a sociopolitical theology that enhances justice, even with total reliance on God, is long overdue. Such a praxis must be geared toward the establishment of good relationships that deal with aspects of injustice at all levels of society. For Africans, "relationships are the essence of their Christian faith and experience. They live the Gospel in relationships. Injustice, family and community tensions, and even international issues, are processed within the redemptive framework of the church, the new community in which the love of God has tremendously enriched the traditional African experience of the person in community."[24] The church's sociopolitical theology should be grounded on the biblical revelation of God with all his attributes and concern for human value that calls for the enactment of justice. This will be a good beginning point because for Africans in general, the perception and understanding of God comes in light of his dealings with nature. For example, most of the names for God in both African Traditional Religion and Christianity are descriptive of his works as creator and sustainer, the giver or divider of all things, as well as the just judge of all creation.

Among those who have suffered great injustice in society are refugees, especially women and children. The issue of refugees and immigration is one of the major challenges facing African politics. Numerous refugees have been migrating to more stable countries, such as South Africa and Kenya, from politically unstable countries such as Zimbabwe, Somalia, and southern Sudan, where high levels of inflation, political violence, and abject poverty have left millions of people without food or hope. While most of these immigrants have fled in search of a livelihood and better working conditions for survival, others are seeking political asylum. Such a situation is repeated in many countries around the world, particularly with the recent increase in eastern European refugees occasioned by the crisis in Syria.

The refugee issue in South Africa, for instance, has elicited a wide range of responses ranging from harassment and rejection (including xenophobic reprisals) to torture and extortion by local police, and refusal by South African legislative bodies to enact laws that define refugee status and protect the refugees' basic human rights. The church has, in general, made few positive responses, to the detriment of its own biblical mission and calling. The 2007–

---

23. Shenk, *Justice, Reconciliation and Peace*, 6.
24. Shenk, xiii.

2008 postelection violence in Kenya and the violence that ensued after the announcement of the results of the 2018 elections in the Democratic Republic of Congo are other situations that have brought about all manner of injustice. Many people have lost their lives, which is the ultimate form of injustice. As Kahiga observes: "Diverse political leaders seek to be crowned as tribal elders or gods with dogmatic, powerful and manipulative authority. Such authority is normal and meticulously obeyed even if it leads to death. Those who die in such obedience are declared martyrs of the tribe and are awarded with cultural medals of bravery [posthumously] and they remain perpetually in the memory of the living as heroes."[25] Any means by which an individual is denied or deprived of the enjoyment of his or her dignity, in its various forms, amounts to an act of injustice. This then becomes one of the cardinal vices that the church in Africa has a duty and responsibility to focus on as a core component of the proclamation of the gospel message. A political theology of the church in Africa must address injustice head-on. Tutu illustrates this from his own experience:

> We were frequently accused of mixing religion with politics, being told that we should confine our concern to the pulpit, that we should strive to save people's souls and not meddle in politics. We replied that it was almost always those who benefited from some unjust status quo who were most vociferous about the apparently heinous crime of mixing religion with politics. Indeed, I had not yet heard the down-trodden complain that I was a politician trying very hard to masquerade as an archbishop. Rather, the oppressed would have been exhorting one to be even more political. I used to say, if God did not care that people were hungry, or downtrodden, or were living in squalor and deprivation, then I would not worship such a God.[26]

The task of the church is to actively demonstrate in action the gospel message that it preaches and teaches by calling the people to put God first, and

---

25. Joseph Kahiga Kiruki, "Education for Transformation: A Focus on the Post-Election Violence in Kenya," *African Ecclesiastical Review* 51–52, no. 4–1 (Dec. 2009–March 2010): 488.

26. Desmond M. Tutu, "Dark Days: Episcopal Ministry in Times of Repression, 1976–1996," *Journal of Theology for Southern Africa* 118 (March 2004): 33. He adds that "God cared so much that God gave his son to become a human being, to take on our human nature, and so sanctified our entire existence, body and soul. This Jesus did not say to the hungry, 'Let us pray,' and then send them away hungry. No, this Jesus, this God-man, fed the hungry, healed the sick, forgave sinners, raised the dead, and proclaimed the Gospel, and declared that all of these things were of a piece, as signs of the Kingdom of His Father."

strive for societal decency by displaying personal godliness and public justice. This includes seeking, through prayer, for spiritual renewal to reach people with "the good news of God's grace" and "exude the joy of God in the climate of shameful violence, and to promote truth in the nation's executive offices, justice among judges, integrity among legislators, dignity in the media, impartiality by journalists, industry among workers, and equity by management – every such gain we register, alongside a recognition of our own limits and needs, is a service that looks toward the kingdom of God."[27]

This calls for the church to reread the Bible and relate it within the perspective of their experience. The teaching of the Bible is central in providing guidance that helps in making decisions in all matters of life and living. Issues of social justice within society must be examined and understood in full and looked at from a reading of the Bible as it sheds light on diverse experiences and the call for social justice. The Old Testament, for instance, is replete with calls for the disbursement of social justice, particularly toward the lowly in society – foreigners, orphans, and widows.[28]

One practical illustration of how the church can be proactive in dealing with issues of injustice is the life of Albert Luthuli, who embraced the struggle to deal with injustice in South Africa. He understood his calling to be one of self-sacrifice as he stood firm in his role as leader of the ANC, a role for which he was prepared to pay the price as he exhibited a spirit of trust and surrender to God's will in his life.[29]

F. Corruption

Corruption in Africa is multifaceted and complex, manifesting itself in diverse ways. Ignatius Edet cites Robert Calderisi who says, "Corruption is endemic in Africa for the same reasons as elsewhere. But it hurts the continent more than other regions, is more brazen, and accepted more readily."[30] Most African countries are now celebrating more than four to five decades of independence

---

27. Henry, "Uneasy Conscience," 60.

28. Musa W. Dube, "Rereading the Bible: Biblical Hermeneutics and Social Justice," in *African Theology Today*, ed. Emmanuel Katongole (Scranton, PA: University of Scranton Press, 2002), 65.

29. Scott Everett Couper, "'When Chief Albert Luthuli Launched "into the Deep"': A Theological Reflection on a Homiletic Resource of Political Significance," *Journal of Theology for Southern Africa* 130 (March 2008): 84.

30. Cited in Ignatius Edet, "The Church and Corruption in Africa," *African Ecclesiastical Review* 51–52, no. 4 (Dec. 2009): 625.

from colonialism. However, as John Mbaku notes, "Despite more than forty years of statism, mass poverty and deprivation remain endemic in the continent; few African countries have been able to achieve reasonable rates of economic development. Excessive regulation of private exchange, coupled with state ownership of the means of production, have encouraged, enhanced and facilitated nepotism, corruption, and significantly constrained the creation of the wealth that could have been used to confront poverty."[31]

A number of studies have been carried out in different African countries on aspects related to corruption. One such survey was carried out by Blundo and de Sardan in Benin, Niger, and Senegal[32] which surveyed the sectors of "customs and transport, justice, health, public procurements, local tax systems, development projects and anti-corruption provisions" and "revealed an astonishing convergence in terms of both informal administrative functioning and the various 'corrupt' practices – in the broadest sense – facilitated by this informal functioning."[33] The forms of corruption embedded within the political and administrative structures were found to be numerous. They included the following:

> *"Commissions" paid for illicit services*
> This form of corruption involves the payment of money by users of administrative services who provide access to illicit advantages, exemptions or discounts . . .
> *Unwarranted fees for public services*
> In this case, the official forces the user to pay for the implementation of an act associated with his office . . .
> *The "gratuity"*
> . . . is given *ex post* and appears as a spontaneous gesture on the part of the service user . . .

---

31. John Mukum Mbaku, *Bureaucratic and Political Corruption in Africa: The Public Choice Perspective* (Malabar, FL: Krieger, 2000), 4.

32. These three countries are "former colonies of French West Africa and thus share the same kind of colonial past. The influence of their colonial heritage with regard to the relationship between the administration and the populations should not be underestimated: the colonial bureaucracy was characterized by despotism and arbitrariness, a contempt for users, inordinate privilege, and the use of intermediaries, corruption and favours. These 'administrative habits' were extended and intensified after independence" (Giorgio Blundo and Jean-Pierre Olivier de Sardan, "Everyday Corruption in West Africa," in *Everyday Corruption and the State: Citizens and Public Officials in Africa*, trans. Susan Cox [Cape Town: David Philip, 2006], 71).

33. Blundo and de Sardan, "Everyday Corruption in West Africa," 69.

"String-pulling"
... favoritism at the expense of competence and efficiency ... the
   "general exchange" . . . between officials and representatives
   of the administration . . .
The levy or "toll"
. . . pure and simple extortion for service being supplied, be it
   legal or illegal . . .
The "gombo," petty "white-collar" theft and the "sideline"
. . . use of company materials and resources by workers for the
   completion of private paid work, for example the use of
   company computers by secretaries for typing academic theses
   for payment – either during or outside the official working
   hours.[34]

The impact of corruption is enormous both on the state and on individual citizens. There are the few who gain from the vice, but the majority of the population are the ones who suffer. Mbaku observes that corruption benefits a few individuals and families who hoard massive wealth, while the majority of the people are disadvantaged and deprived, creating a negative social and economic impact on development. This is because national resources are misallocated as economic incentives are distorted negatively, affecting microeconomic performance. All this is a result of the vice of corruption which "encourages civil servants to pursue perverse economic programs, which impose significant costs on the economy."[35]

Giorgio Blundo observes that virtually all who demand political change call for a war on corruption, intending to increase the popular disapproval of incumbents by mobilizing the opposition, who consist mainly of the poor, to give legitimacy to new political regimes. Once political change is realized, however, the "latter quickly forget their promises and devote themselves to selective political campaigns essentially aimed at excluding rival factions from access to the financial resources necessary to engage in democratic politics. Hence, commissions of inquiry are a common byproduct of regime change."[36]

---

34. Blundo and de Sardan, 73–78.

35. Mbaku, *Bureaucratic and Political Corruption*, 27.

36. Giorgio Blundo and Jean-Pierre Olivier de Sardan, "Corruption in Africa and the Social Sciences: A Review of the Literature," in *Everyday Corruption and the State: Citizens and Public Officials in Africa*, trans. Susan Cox (Cape Town: David Philip, 2006), 47. They cite the example of Niger, where "the military coup that brought an end to the Hamani Diori regime and installed Seyni Kountaché in power was followed by the immediate establishment of a commission of control and inquiry." In Sierra Leone, "the seizure of power in 1992 by Valentine Stasser gave

From this analysis of corruption in Africa, it may be concluded that there is no single form of political regime, be it "authoritarian or pluralist, military or civil," that has greater potential to promote and foster corruption than others. It is therefore not "plausible to establish a correlation between the stability of a regime and the forms of corruption that occur under it."[37] Corruption must therefore be understood as a vice that is embedded within fallen human nature. It is a manifestation of the inherent sinful nature whose "corrupting impulse [is] resident at the core of human personality."[38] Human political and social systems and structures therefore reflect this human impediment which is characteristic of human reflexes at all levels.

Several approaches have been taken to deal with corruption in Africa, such as establishing legal systems that define the functions of bureaucrats, checking their excesses and constraining their practices. The law often addresses itself to corrupt behavior and provides procedures for convictions. The vigilance of the general public regarding corruption and reporting to authorities for judicial prosecution procedures is also utilized, particularly through whistleblowing. The press is used as an investigative channel exposing corrupt individuals in various sectors of society.[39] These have different degrees of effectiveness, although it can be argued that one of the most effective ways of dealing with corruption is to entrench reforms within institutions so that the society as a whole can have effective and efficient mechanisms and structures for enforcing rules and regulations.[40] Such internal mechanisms for fighting corruption have been embraced in the last few decades in a number of African countries that have adopted "public integrity reforms which are associated with the 'New Public Management' approach to governance."[41] Such approaches call for commitment on the part of citizens and dedication from the leaders if corruption is to be dealt with effectively on the continent. Such social institutions as government, legal systems, family units, and businesses are pertinent divinely ordained

---

rise to the creation of three commissions of inquiry into corruption, whose purpose was to examine the origins of the assets of the presidents, vice-presidents and minister in the office from 1986 to 1992."

37. Blundo and de Sardan, "Corruption in Africa," 48.

38. Richard B. Gaffin, "Total Depravity and Business Ethics," in *Biblical Principles and Business: The Foundations*, ed. Richard C. Chewning, Christians in the Marketplace 1 (Colorado Springs, CO: NavPress, 1989), 139.

39. Mbaku, *Bureaucratic and Political Corruption*, 114.

40. Mbaku, 114.

41. Mark Robinson, *Corruption and Development* (London: Frank Cass, 1998), 133.

avenues through which society checks acts of human disobedience for the preservation of order and the provision of accountability.[42]

While the church ought to be at the forefront in the fight against corruption, this is not always the case. There are instances where the church has been indicted of abetting corruption through its association with known corrupt individuals. In the Kenyan context, for instance, the archbishop of the Anglican Church of Kenya, Jackson Ole Sapit, called for church leaders to reject large donations from corrupt individuals. Nevertheless, many selfless leaders have taken risks to fight corruption and corrupt leaders, based on their deep conviction that it is their responsibility to give leadership for the sake of the welfare of their fellow human beings. Such people persist in their fight against corruption not as an end in itself but out of the conviction that "corruption is the largest single barrier to the development of decent living for their fellow men and women across most of the world. Their misery is a cause worth fighting for, irrespective of the personal risks."[43] The church must stand out in fighting corruption decisively since it is the representative of Christ on earth. Tony Carnes highlights the role of the church in this regard:

> That enormous challenge doesn't seem to discourage this new coalition of Christians. Rock star Bono has issued a public challenge to Christians: "If the church doesn't respond to the plagues afflicting Africa, who will?" The presence of evangelicals in the fight against global poverty, many note, brings fresh talent and resources to the table, which are being noticed in high places. Advisers to British Prime Minister Tony Blair's Africa commission wrote, "From the start, ideas about development generally overlooked the role of religion . . . in Africa." However, "Africa's development in the 21st century will be shaped largely by religion."[44]

The problem of corruption and corrupt governments in Africa requires the church to be at the forefront in bringing the needed transformation that seeks to deal with human greed and desire for self-aggrandizement.

---

42. Alexander Hill, *Just Business: Christian Ethics for the Market Place* (Downers Grove, IL: IVP Academic, 2008), 19.

43. Frank Vogl, *Waging War on Corruption: Inside the Movement Fighting the Abuse of Power* (Lanham, MD: Rowman & Littlefield, 2012), 56.

44. Tony Carnes, "Can We Defeat Poverty? Unless Africa Tames Corruption, New Aid Efforts Will Fail," *Christianity Today* 49, no. 10 (Oct. 2005): 38.

G. Power

Power in African politics is more often than not associated with the negative exercise of authority by individuals who take advantage of systems and citizens, especially the poor, to ascend the echelons of control. In most cases politicians ascend to positions of power as liberators with an agenda for the well-being of citizens, but once they have attained power they crave more and establish a band of cronies to ensure their position is sustained. Most African leaders, whether in civic or political leadership or, unfortunately, in private and Christian circles, tend to hold on to their offices by all means possible in order to retain their power. Power and authority has become a cancer that is destroying institutional and organizational reputations on account of individual interests and egos. This confirms the well-known words of Sir John Dalberg-Acton: "Power tends to corrupt, and absolute power corrupts absolutely. Great men are almost always bad men."[45] While many may dismiss this statement or be cynical about it, the truth is that, once someone has tasted power, even on a very small scale and at a very low level, the desire to hold on to it by whatever means becomes uncontrollable. The greater the power, the greater the drive to retain it, and the more dangerous it becomes. This, unfortunately, can result in the elimination of friends as well as foes who oppose or block the plans and purposes of the leader. Millions of people in Africa have lost their lives as leaders have struggled to achieve power or to retain it. Power has come to be associated with a myriad of evils because of the way it is abused.

For example, Idi Amin Dada ruled Uganda from 1971 to 1979 after toppling Apollo Milton Obote amidst great jubilation on the part of many Ugandans. This celebration was, however, short-lived as Idi Amin's rule soon gained notoriety for its utter brutality and oppression. The "savior" who had achieved political power turned out to be a ruthless dictator who eliminated thousands of people. Similarly, Jean-Bédel Bokassa assumed power in the Central African Republic through a coup d'état on 1 January 1966 and remained in authority until he was overthrown in a subsequent coup on 20 September 1979. Gnassingbé Eyadema became the president of Togo in 1967 after a military coup and is known for being one of Africa's longest-serving dictators until his death in 2005.[46] Hastings Kamuzu Banda of Malawi ruled from 1963

---

45. John Emerich Edward Dalberg Acton, "Letter to Archbishop Mandell Creighton," 5 April 1887, https://history.hanover.edu/courses/excerpts/165acton.html.

46. Anne Janette Johnson and Sara Pendergast, "Gnassingbé Eyadéma Biography: 1937–2005; President of Togo," n.d., https://biography.jrank.org/pages/2747/Eyad-ma-Gnassingb.html.

to 1994. As one of Africa's greatest dictators, he made Malawi into one of the poorest countries in the world, with thousands dying of starvation. He eliminated thousands of his political opponents through torture and murder, with many others jailed without trial.[47] Charles Taylor, president of Liberia from 1997 until 2003, was described as the "tyrant of death." He was brought before the International Criminal Court (ICC), where he was convicted of acts of terrorism, murder, multiple forms of violence, and physical or mental torture, and he is currently serving a fifty-year jail term for his involvement in what the judge described as "some of the most heinous and brutal crimes recorded in human history."[48] These are just a few illustrations of the extent to which the quest for power has driven those who hunger and thirst for it and are determined to retain it at all costs, thereby becoming agents of destruction, shattering the lives of individuals and families, and devastating the national and political economies of their countries.

Power can be understood as the exercise of might or authority to gain influence through affluence and control of resources. It is intrinsic to offices that are held by individuals and controlled by specific agencies that gather intelligence and access to information for the exercise of military might and political control. Power is in and of itself good if used to render service to others. It is the abuse and misuse of power for selfish personal ends that turns power into a cancer that eats up communities. In this sense, then, "the exercise of power is legitimate if it is in accordance with existing [communal or societal rules and regulations] . . . if these rules can be justified by shared beliefs, and if there is evidenced consent to the arrangement"; but the greed for domination of others "is arguably in every practical sense subjective."[49] The same exercise of power applies in the context of the church and church leadership in general, where the church involves itself with issues affecting the community. The church is also an institution that has its own politics through the "distribution and exercise of power by various members of the Church and how internal relations of authority, decision-making and participation are exercised."[50] The struggle to attain and hold on to power can then become

---

47. "Influential Africans: Hastings Kamuzu Banda," VOA News, 31 October 2009, https://www.voanews.com/archive/influential-africans-hastings-kamuzu-banda.

48. Marlise Simons and David Goodman, "Ex-Liberian Leader Gets 50 Years for War Crimes," *New York Times*, 30 May 2012.

49. Lindberg, *Democracy and Elections*, 33.

50. Elaine Graham, "Power, Knowledge and Authority in Public Theology," *International Journal of Public Theology* 1 (2007): 44.

an evil that eats up the cohesiveness of society, thus undermining the value, intent, and purpose of communal life and the good of the whole.

When greed for power overrides the common good of service, those in positions of authority tend to extend power for themselves illegitimately. This negates the intent of power in the first place and calls for the church and individual believers to exercise their God-given mandate of being their brother or sister's keeper in speaking out and acting. Failure to do so is an abdication of our Christian calling and responsibility before God.

One of the key responsibilities of the church is to be a true steward of God through its teaching by standing up against self-seeking politicians who hoard power for themselves. The church should also uphold selfless politicians who are committed to upholding justice and righteousness – individuals who hold political office and promote human values and morality without compromising their integrity. By upholding the lordship of Christ over all powers and authorities, including political power, the church has a moral obligation to live up to this claim and hold leaders accountable.

Conclusion

The purpose of this book has been to provide a theological reflection of politics in Africa. We have seen that today's politics in Africa have evolved out of a long history laden with multiple traditional sociocultural trends and values that have shaped the continent since time immemorial, along with the influences of outsiders who came with ulterior motives and purposes. To a great extent also, many churches in Africa generally can trace their theological heritage back to the Western missionary enterprise laden with fundamentalism, which for the most part was a reaction against liberalism. This reaction made the church steer away from sociopolitical issues and emphasize spiritual matters, focusing mainly on personal conversion and faith in Christ. We have noted the manner in which the theology of the church in Africa in general has continued to retain this missionary mindset at the expense of a holistic view of an individual's transformation. Indeed the doctrinal statements adopted by the church in Africa were largely adopted from the missions that established it, albeit with some changes due to the incessant calls for the church's nationalization and Africanization. This implies that the sociopolitical theology of the church is essentially defined by a fundamental noninvolvement passivity, which means that the church fails to bear witness to the holistic call of its biblical mission. Similarly, the prophetic voice of the church seldom addresses the sociopolitical situation in a meaningful way.

In its commitment to the biblical mandate to be salt and light to the world, the church needs to review its participation in social and political matters so as not to appear to give blanket endorsement to the political status quo. In affirming biblical authority, the church should cultivate an ongoing engagement in social and political affairs. This responsibility requires the development of a biblical theology that seeks to bring about positive and holistic societal transformation. Such a theology encompasses the holistic mission of the church in its endeavor to proclaim the gospel message of God's kingdom and his reign in the African continent for the promotion of justice and righteousness in all sectors of society. The development of this theology requires the church to be cognizant of the pertinent issues and the challenges of validity and relevance for the sake of applicability, acceptance, and ownership within individual sociopolitical contexts. A theology that is viable for the African context will seek to address the needs of the people using terms and concepts that are easily identifiable and applicable in each context.

Among the concerns raised about missionary Christianity is that the missionaries never saw that their theological assumptions were often in tension with African perspectives. The missionaries failed to take time to consult with Africans, instead unilaterally prescribing what Africa needed. This echoes Mercy Oduyoye's statement: "Needs were stimulated in light of the European lifestyle. They were not needs of the people in Africa. Thus the structures created to meet these needs were European and Africans were ill at ease with them."[1]

Given such a situation, the church in Africa must rethink its mission by way of revisiting its Western-oriented theological focus in light of the changes and developments prevalent in the contemporary African context. The traditional African mindset that prevailed during the missionary era is long gone. Major developments have increased global accessibility, communication, and connectivity. Nevertheless, a diversity of factors – social, political, economic, cultural, and religious – continue to impact people's interactions and thus change their worldviews. In keeping with these changes in contemporary society, the church needs to constantly review and adjust, as necessary, its theological approach to sociopolitical issues and their diverse dynamics. This is relevant not just for the church in Africa but for the cause of Christianity in the world as a whole.

James Engel and William Dyrness, in their book *Changing the Mind of Missions*,[2] have made significant observations regarding recent changes in the world and the challenge facing Western Christian missions. The gist of their argument focuses on the distortions of the Great Commission by the West and the need to change approach with a view to returning to the biblical foundation as laid out by Christ and the apostles in the New Testament. Similarly the church in Africa needs to come to terms with the sociopolitical changes in the continent, coupled with the multiple complexities occasioned by global challenges, along with other factors such as corruption, poverty, industrial and technological underdevelopment, civil unrest, global human migration, crime, terrorism, and epidemics including the COVID-19 pandemic. These have negatively impacted life in Africa, requiring that the church proactively rethink

---

1. Mercy Amba Oduyoye, *Hearing and Knowing: Theological Reflections on Christianity in Africa* (Maryknoll, NY: Orbis, 1986), 42.

2. James F. Engle and William A. Dyrness, *Changing the Mind of Missions: Where Have We Gone Wrong?* (Downers Grove, IL: InterVarsity Press, 2000).

its theological and biblical approach. Thousands of people in the continent today are unable to afford food for their daily sustenance, and the church must be concerned with their physical as much as their spiritual needs. The church must address the needs of many more who are homeless and destitute before the eschatological doctrine of an eternal home will have any impact and relevance. The church's theology must be true to the lives of its people in the reality of their individual contexts.

Although drawing from its Western evangelical Christian heritage, the church must be decisive in formulating a contextually relevant theology that upholds scriptural authority. The call made by the Reformed evangelicals of the first generation, led by Carl Henry, as well as the second generation, for the renewal of "the evangelical mind" on sociopolitical theological views, provides a good example for the church in Africa to follow. In essence, the church should be actively involved in the sociopolitical matters of the community and seek to reevaluate its strong opposition to Christian political involvement. A sociopolitical theology does not necessarily entail Christians running for civic or political office, nor does it prohibit one from active participation in politics. The problem lies not in politics but in the individuals and the moral and ethical choices they make. One of the questions the church may have to consider is what the impact would be of Christian politicians, who are committed to upholding biblical and ethical values with moral uprightness, holding civic and political office as agents of justice and righteousness.

As it upholds the claim of Christ's lordship over all created powers and authorities in all realms of existence, the church in Africa has a moral responsibility to defend this claim by recognizing that the sociopolitical realm is subject to Christ. His claim that "All authority in heaven and on earth has been given to me" is the foundation on which Christ sends his followers to go and make disciples of all nations and to teach them "to obey everything I have commanded you." It is the responsibility of the church to teach and thereby hold all nations, powers, and authorities accountable to Christ's claim. The church, therefore, has an obligation to obey the command of its Master, and this entails addressing every aspect of human existence, including sociopolitical matters. This calls for the development of a biblically sound sociopolitical theology that addresses the issues facing individual contexts in Africa.

The influence of the church in transforming the sociopolitical scene will be achieved not by abnegation or separation but by being a witness of the gospel in its implications for the world. This implies that the church's mission will be holistic in scope, encompassing sociopolitical issues in the evangelistic and discipleship mandate. In this way, the sociopolitical theology of the church will be contextual, addressing specific local issues without creating the unwarranted secular–sacred dichotomy. Caution has to be exercised in order to guard the church against drifting away from its unique nature as Christ's ambassador by establishing checks and balances that will continually evaluate how the church's theology encompasses its holistic mission. The church must always guard itself from falling into the trap of appropriating the evils of the state, by supporting the status quo, and thus becoming assimilated with the existing sociopolitical ills. The church will therefore have to come up with a clearly defined theological stand that stipulates its role and responsibilities in sociopolitical matters while holding the ruling authorities accountable to God as they carry out their responsibilities and service to all citizens indiscriminately. It will also be necessary to establish an ongoing theological structure that will constantly reevaluate the church's sociopolitical involvement as it relates to the whole mission of the church in the world.

It is imperative also that the church develops a structure through which its civic duty of prayer will be enhanced. Throughout Scripture we see a call to pray for political leaders and nations. In Jeremiah 29:7, the prophet in his letter to the exiles exhorts them not only to seek the peace and prosperity of the city in which they are held captive, but also to pray for it. Paul, in 1 Timothy 2:1–4, urges believers to pray and intercede for kings and all those in authority in order to enhance a life of peace and quiet. This implies that the church has a responsibility to pray and intercede especially for those in positions of political authority, irrespective of their religious affiliation, since they are God's agents entrusted with the responsibility of administering justice and righteousness. Through prayer, the church will be involved in spiritual warfare against forces of evil and thereby bring the authorities to subjection under the feet of Christ. Prayer is active and dynamic, not merely passive and detached pious incantations!

It is important also that the church becomes sensitive to its African sociocultural heritage which has undoubtedly shaped the African context. A myriad of leaders and theologians have made incessant appeals regarding the need for Africans to embrace the Christian faith and make it truly their own. Since theology is never done in a vacuum but always in the context of a preexisting worldview and philosophy, the church ought to take a lead in the development of an authentic and relevant African sociopolitical theology.

The African sociopolitical scene is shaped by a diversity of unique African perspectives and features that the church must seriously consider as it seeks to contextualize the gospel message. Any theology intended to address this context must take into account the holistic African worldview that looks at all spheres of life as inseparably intertwined. Politics and religion are part of the whole and each affects the other. Like a web, all aspects of the sociopolitical and religious structures combine to form the whole without distinction. As Jim Wallis puts it, "when politics loses its vision, religion loses its faith, and culture loses its soul; life becomes confused, cheap, and endangered. Nothing less than a restoration of the shattered covenant will save us. That will require a fundamental transformation of our ways of thinking, feeling and acting. At the core of prophetic religion is transformation – a change of heart, a revolution of the spirit, a conversion of the soul that issues forth in new personal and social behavior."[3]

Sociopolitical issues, as much as they pertain to the management of the civic life of a community, must be seen in light of the people's religious customs, beliefs, and practices. The worldview or philosophy that guides the way of life, dreams, and aspirations of a people is dictated by their understanding of and connectedness with the divine. Both political and religious leaders are highly regarded in African communities, and as such their service must rise above personal interests. The two are, however, different in the sense that the former are elected by the people to represent them in legislative and governance matters, while the latter are recognized by the community to be spiritual guides appointed through the ecclesiastical structures as defined and stipulated in the Bible. For this reason, spiritual leaders command a higher authority in society and are consequently looked on as the hope of the community in cases where politicians are driven by greed for personal gain.

However, we must be quick to point out that the church has not been totally free from compromise, and some of its leaders and members have often fallen prey to deceptive unethical practices and desires. One of the most disheartening aspects regarding the church's integrity has to do with its involvement in acquiring land and property irregularly. A number of cases of corruption, as we pointed out above, have bedeviled political and religious leaders alike. This is a challenging and disturbing situation that may need further reflection and consideration that is beyond our scope here, in which the church will lay down specific procedural guidelines and principles for how to be involved in sociopolitical matters while retaining its holiness and distinctiveness. In other words, the task will revolve around the practicality of being in the world yet not of the world. As an agent of change, the church

---

3. Jim Wallis, *The Soul of Politics: Beyond "Religious Right" and "Secular Left"* (San Diego/New York/London: Harcourt, Brace and Co., 1995), 49.

is salt, light, and leaven that permeates every arena of society, without being assimilated into society's practices.

The sociopolitical theology of the church should endeavor to capitalize on the unique value of communalism that shaped traditional Africa. Not only did the community give and shape an individual's identity, but it also helped to cultivate moral responsibilities and accountability for the well-being of the whole. The problems of greed, corruption, injustice, violence, and crime have escalated primarily due to the fragmentation of community life. This is true in all human communities since "the moral requirements of relationship and community serve to correct our human tendencies toward individual selfishness and exploitation of our neighbors and the earth. Today the fundamental covenant that holds life together has been profoundly damaged."[4] An emphasis on communalism will not only help the church to address social ills within its own context, but will also be one of its main contributions to the wider Christian community ravaged by individualism and self-seeking exclusivism, reverting back to the sense of community in the early church which was characterized by the selflessness of individual believers (Acts 2:42–47).

The church can, therefore, model an alternative political structure where politicians will realize that their role as leaders is to serve the people by being faithful custodians of the national resources entrusted to them by the masses (electorate) and ultimately by God. Their accountability is, therefore, not just to the electorate but to God, from whom all power and authority derives. Politics is one of the various ways in community life facilitating governance for the sake of maintaining law and order which aids the sustenance of cohesive coexistence among the peoples and between nations. Its purpose is to facilitate proper channels through which all aspects of justice can be distributed to all without favoritism or prejudice. For this reason, the church has a moral duty, as the custodian of God's law, to act as the conscience of society that points political powers back to their moral obligations. The church and the state should therefore not be mutually exclusive, but neither should there be a marriage of convenience between them. In the African context, we cannot talk of separation between church and state, just as we cannot talk of separation between the spiritual and the secular realms. Life is viewed as one whole with various distinct components that are always interacting and complementing each other.

---

4. Wallis, *Soul of Politics*, 48.

Given this kind of sociopolitical perspective, the church in Africa should seek to develop some principles to guide its sociopolitical involvement. An example is the following summary of principles for civic responsibility in the declaration of the National Association of Evangelicals in the United States, which admonishes the church to consider developing a viable sociopolitical theology:

1.   Work to protect religious freedom and liberty of conscience.

2.   Work to nurture family life and protect children.

3.   Work to protect the sanctity of human life and to safeguard its nature.

4.   Seek justice and compassion for the poor and vulnerable.

5.   Work to protect human rights.

6.   Seek peace and work to restrain violence.

7.   Labor to protect God's creation.[5]

In order for the church to be able to address these issues adequately, it must prepare its pastors and leaders through training and theological institutions where they will not only be grounded in biblical principles but will also raise relevant questions that address concrete issues affecting the society. This will aid the church to do justice to the local social structures by identifying with the reality of each situation and providing the necessary theological perspective for an appropriate interpretation of the problems and the relevant solutions. The curriculum must include core issues that shape the African sociopolitical scene as well as the implications of the modern African cultural structure, rather than dwelling primarily on ancient African Traditional Religion whose impact on society is changing. It is through the academy that the church will be able to test the viability of its theological views as well as guard against irresponsible tendencies. The church must, therefore, be purposeful not only in developing but also in documenting its sociopolitical theology, rather than continuing to operate according to the whims of individuals or the authority of councils that have no biblical foundation for their theological views and position. The development of this theology will therefore need to include the different community players and stakeholders.

The church in Africa must continue to evaluate its role in social and political issues through theological analysis of sociopolitical realities and make

---

5. Jo Anne Lyon, "The State of the Evangelical Church," in *The State of the Evangelical Mind: Reflections on the Past, Prospects for the Future*, ed. Todd C. Ream, Jerry Pattengale, and Christopher J. Devers (Downers Grove, IL: IVP Academic, 2018), 53.

explicit biblical judgments about issues of justice, democracy, and governance; property and land ownership; poverty, unemployment, and crime; drought and famine; epidemics such as malaria and the threat of AIDS, COVID-19, and its consequent implications – to name just a few. The church must develop a theology that is focused on addressing these issues with a view to bringing about human transformation in all aspects and dimensions of life. The church's theology is a significant component in bringing about transformation, since

> theology looks at the concept of crime not only in a framework of deviant behavior and institutionalized sanctions, but also in terms of forgiveness, reconciliation and conversion. Theology analyzes the growing gap between the rich and poor not only in economic terms of social balance and social stability but also in terms of responsibility and solidarity. There is a special way to look at the world with theological eyes. These eyes can be sharpened if we put on social glasses.[6]

Involvement in sociopolitical issues will be a clear demonstration of the church's faith and obedience in following the example of Christ, who was not oblivious to the sociopolitical issues of his time while he was on earth, and who continues to be involved through his church, the body of Christ. A theology that takes seriously the teaching of Christ will take seriously the sociopolitical problems of the people.

---

6. Clemens Sedmak, *Doing Local Theology: A Guide for Artisans of a New Humanity* (Maryknoll, NY: Orbis, 2002), 105.

Bibliography

Abuom, Agnes C. "The Church's Involvement in the Democratisation Process in Kenya." In *Peacemaking and Democratisation in Africa: Theoretical Perspectives and Church Initiatives*, edited by Hizkias Assefa and George Wachira. Nairobi: East Africa Educational Publishers, 1996.

Adebayo, Rafiu Ibrahim. "The Role of Traditional Rulers in the Islamization of Osun State (Nigeria)." *Journal for Islamic Studies* 7, no. 30 (2010): 60–77.

Acton, John Emerich Edward Dalberg. "Letter to Archbishop Mandell Creighton," 5 April 1887. https://history.hanover.edu/courses/excerpts/165acton.html.

Adelphoi. *His Kingdom in Kenya*. London: Hodder & Stoughton, 1953.

Adeogun, Ebenezer Ola Olutosin. "The Kingdom of God and Old Testament Theocracy." *Ogbomoso Journal of Theology* 12 (2007): 59–86.

Adjibolosoo, Senyo. "Ethnicity and the Development of National Consciousness: A Human Factor Analysis." In *Critical Perspectives in Politics and Socio-Economic Development in Ghana*, edited by Wisdom J. Tettey, Korbla P. Puplampu, and Bruce J. Berman, 107–34. Leiden: Brill, 2003.

Africa Inland Church – Kenya. *Constitution and Regulations*. Kijabe: Kijabe Printing Press, 2002.

Allen, Chris. "Understanding African Politics." *Review of African Political Economy* 22, no. 65 (1995): 301–20.

Anderson, Richard J. D. *We Felt like Grasshoppers: The Story of Africa Inland Mission*. Nottingham: Crossway, 1994.

Aristotle. *Aristotle's Politics*. Translated by Benjamin Jowett. Oxford: Clarendon, 1967.

Aseka, Eric Masinde. *Transformational Leadership in East Africa: Politics, Ideology and Community*. Kampala: Fountain, 2005.

Balmer, Randall Herbert. *Blessed Assurance: A History of Evangelicalism in America*. Boston: Beacon, 2000.

Barnett, Donald L., and Karari Njama. *Mau Mau from Within: Autobiography and Analysis of Kenya's Peasant Revolt*. London: MacGibbon & Kee, 1966.

Bauckham, Richard. *The Bible in Politics: How to Read the Bible Politically*. London: SPCK, 2011.

———. "Reading the Bible Politically." In *An Eerdmans Reader in Contemporary Political Theology*, edited by William T. Cavanaugh, Jeffrey W. Bailey, and Craig Hovey, 29–47. Grand Rapids, MI: Eerdmans, 2012.

Bediako, Kwame. *Christianity in Africa: The Renewal of Non-Western Religion*. Edinburgh: Edinburgh University Press, 1995.

Bellamy, Richard. "The Challenge of European Union." In *The Oxford Handbook of Political Theory*, edited by John S. Dryzek, Bonnie Honig, and Anne Phillips, 245–61. Oxford: Oxford University Press, 2006.

Bennett, George. *Kenya: A Political History*. London: Oxford University Press, 1963.

Berkouwer, Gerrit Cornelis. *Man: The Image of God*. Grand Rapids, MI: Eerdmans, 1962.

Best, Ernest. *A Critical and Exegetical Commentary on Ephesians*. Edinburgh: T&T Clark, 1998.

Blakeslee, H. Virginia. "Is a Curtain Falling on Africa?" *Inland Africa* 39, no. 1 (1955): 10–12.

Blocher, Henri. *In the Beginning: The Opening Chapters of Genesis*. Leicester: Inter-Varsity Press; Downers Grove, IL: InterVarsity Press, 1984.

Blundo, Giorgio, and Jean-Pierre Olivier de Sardan. "Everyday Corruption in West Africa." In *Everyday Corruption and the State: Citizens and Public Officials in Africa*, 70–102. Translated by Susan Cox. Cape Town: David Philip, 2006.

Brown, Graham K., and Arnim Langer. "The Concept of Ethnicity: Strengths and Limitations for Quantitative Analysis." In *Ethnic Diversity and Economic Instability in Africa: Interdisciplinary Perspectives*, edited by Hiroyuki Hino, 56–90. Cambridge: Cambridge University Press, 2012.

Buijtenhuijs, Rob. *Essays on Mau Mau: Contributions to Mau Mau Historiography*. Leiden: African Studies Centre, 1982.

Buzzard, Lynn R. "Separation of Church, State, and Religious Liberty." In *Citizen Christians: The Rights and Responsibilities of Dual Citizenship*, edited by Richard D. Lard and Louis A. Moore, 32–46. Nashville: Broadman & Holman, 1994.

Campbell, Henry D. "Editorial." *Inland Africa* 14, no. 5 (May 1930): 8–10.

Carey, Walter. *Crisis in Kenya: Christian Common Sense on Mau Mau and the Colour-Bar*. London: Mowbray, 1953.

Carnes, Tony. "Can We Defeat Poverty? Unless Africa Tames Corruption, New Aid Efforts Will Fail." *Christianity Today* 49, no. 10 (Oct. 2005): 38–40.

Carter, Stephen L. *God's Name in Vain: The Wrongs and Rights of Religion in Politics*. New York: Basic, 2000.

Cassuto, Umberto. *A Commentary on the Book of Genesis, Part 1*. Jerusalem: Magnes Press, 1961.

Chabal, Patrick. "The African Crisis: Context and Interpretation." In *Postcolonial Identities in Africa*, edited by Richard Werbner and Terence Ranger. London & New Jersey: Zed Books, 1996.

———. *Culture Troubles: Politics and the Interpretation of Meaning*. Chicago: University of Chicago Press, 2006.

Chweya, Ludeki. "Reversing Rural Poverty in an African Country: A Review of the Kenyan Policy Regime." Paper presented at the Development Policy Management Forum, Nairobi, 26 October 2006.

Cochrane, James R. "Religious Pluralism in Post-Colonial Public Life." *Journal of Church and State* 42, no. 3 (Summer 2000): 443–65.

Cohen, William B. *Rulers of Empire: The French Colonial Service in Africa*. Stanford, CA: Hoover Institution Press, 1971.

Cole, Keith. *Kenya: Hanging in the Middle Way*. London: Highway, 1959.

Collins, C. John. *Genesis 1–4: A Linguistic, Literary, and Theological Commentary*. Phillipsburg, NJ: P&R, 2006.

Colson, Elizabeth. "The Impact of the Colonial Period on the Definition of Land Rights." In *Colonialism in Africa*, edited by Victor Turner, 193–215. Cambridge: Cambridge University Press, 1971.

Cone, James. *God of the Oppressed*. Maryknoll, NY: Orbis, 1997.

Copher, Charles B. "The Bible and the African Experience: The Biblical Period." *The Journal of the Interdenominational Theological Center* 39, no. 1 (2014): 57–79.

Cotter, David W. *Genesis*. Berit Olam: Studies in Hebrew Narrative & Poetry. Collegeville, MN: Liturgical, 2003.

Couper, Scott Everett. "'When Chief Albert Luthuli Launched "into the Deep"': A Theological Reflection on a Homiletic Resource of Political Significance." *Journal of Theology for Southern Africa* 130 (March 2008): 76–89.

Cox, Richard. *Kenyatta's Country*. London: Hutchinson, 1965.

Curtin, Philip D. *African History*. New York: Macmillan, 1964.

———. *Cross-Cultural Trade in World History*. Cambridge: Cambridge University Press, 1984.

Curtin, Philip D., Steven Feierman, Leonard Thomson, and Jan Vansina. *African History: From Earliest Times to Independence*. London: Longman, 1995.

Davies, W. D., and Dale C. Allison. *A Critical and Exegetical Commentary on the Gospel According to Saint Matthew*. Edinburgh: T&T Clark, 1997.

Davis, Robert. "Testimony of Timothy Kamau Radio Work in East Africa." *Inland Africa* 46, no. 4 (July 1962): 7–11.

Devitt, Wellesley. "The Courage of Kikuyu Christians." *Inland Africa* 37, no. 5 (1953): 12–13.

Dube, Musa W. "Rereading the Bible: Biblical Hermeneutics and Social Justice." In *African Theology Today*, edited by Emmanuel Katongole, 57–68. Scranton, PA: University of Scranton Press, 2002.

Dyrness, William A. *Let the Earth Rejoice: A Biblical Theology of Holistic Mission*. Westchester, IL: Crossway, 1983.

Edet, Ignatius. "The Church and Corruption in Africa." *African Ecclesiastical Review* 51–52, no. 4 (Dec. 2009): 625–55.

Engle, James F., and William A. Dyrness. *Changing the Mind of Missions: Where Have We Gone Wrong?* Downers Grove, IL: InterVarsity Press, 2000.

Erdmann, Gero, and Matthias Basedau. "An Overview of African Party Systems." In *One-Party Dominance in African Democracies*, edited by Renske Doorenspleet and Lia Nijzink. Boulder, CO: Lynne Rienner, 2013.

Everett, William Johnson. "Seals and Springboks: Theological Reflections on Constitutionalism and South African Culture." *Journal of Theology for Southern Africa* 101 (July 1998): 71–80.

Fallon, Kathleen M. *Democracy and the Rise of Women's Movements in Sub-Saharan Africa*. Baltimore, MD: Johns Hopkins University Press, 2008.

Famell, F. David. "The Kingdom of God in the New Testament." *The Master's Seminary Journal* 23, no. 2 (2012): 193–208.

Ferreira, Rialize. "Irregular Warfare in African Conflicts." *Scientia Militaria: South African Journal of Military Studies* 38, no. 1 (2010): 45–67.

Fortes, M., and E. E. Evans-Pritchard. *African Political Systems*. London: Oxford University Press, 1940.

Gaffin, Richard B. "Total Depravity and Business Ethics." In *Biblical Principles and Business: The Foundations*, edited by Richard C. Chewning, 139–54. Christians in the Marketplace 1. Colorado Springs, CO: NavPress, 1989.

Galgalo, Joseph D. *African Christianity: The Stranger Within*. Eldoret, Kenya: Zapf Chancery Africa, 2012.

Gann, L. H., and Peter Duignan, eds. *Profiles of Change: African Society and Colonial Rule*. Vol. 3 of *Colonialism in Africa, 1870–1960*. Cambridge: Cambridge University Press, 1969.

Gcabashe, Tandi. "From Luthuli to Mandela: The Struggle Goes On." *The Journal of the Interdenominational Theological Center* 16, no. 1–2 (1988–1989): 175–79.

Geisler, Gisela G. *Women and the Remaking of Politics in Southern Africa: Negotiating Autonomy, Incorporation, and Representation*. Uppsala: Nordiska Afrikainstitutet, 2004.

Gennaioli, Nicola, and Ilia Rainer. "Precolonial Centralization and Institutional Quality in Africa." Paper, 2005.

Geyer, Alan. "Creation and Politics in Bonhoeffer's Thought." *Church and State*, August 1995, 93–100.

Gibson, John C. L. *Genesis*. Edinburgh: St Andrew Press; Philadelphia: Westminster Press, 1981.

Ginio, Ruth. *French Colonialism Unmasked: The Vichy Years in French West Africa*. Lincoln, NE: University of Nebraska Press, 2006.

Githiga, Gideon Gichuhi. *The Church as the Bulwark against Authoritarianism: Development of Church and State Relations in Kenya with Particular Reference to the Years after Political Independence 1963–1992*. Oxford: Regnum, 2001.

Gottlieb, Michah. *Faith and Freedom: Moses Mendelssohn's Theological-Political Thought*. New York: Oxford University Press, 2011.

Goudzwaard, Bob. *Globalization and the Kingdom of God*. Grand Rapids, MI: Baker, 2001.

Graham, Elaine. "Power, Knowledge and Authority in Public Theology." *International Journal of Public Theology* 1 (2007): 42–62.

Gration, John A. *The Relationship of the Africa Inland Mission and Its National Church in Kenya between 1895 and 1971.* New York: New York University Press, 1974.

Gray, R. *Christianity in Independent Africa.* London: Rex Collings, 1978.

Grenz, Stanley James. *Theology for the Community of God.* Nashville: Broadman & Holman, 1994.

Grimstead, Jay, and E. Calvin Beisner, eds. *Articles of Affirmation and Denial on the Kingdom of God: A Summary of the Biblical and Historical View.* Mountain View, CA: Coalition on Revival, 1999.

Gunkel, Hermann. *The Legends of Genesis: The Biblical Saga and History.* New York: Schocken, 1964.

Gutiérrez, Gustavo. *A Theology of Liberation.* New York: Orbis, 1973.

Haar, Gerrie ter. "African Christians in Europe: A Mission in Reverse." In *Changing Relations between Churches in Europe and Africa: The Internationalization of Christianity and Politics in the 20th Century,* edited by Katharina Kunter and Jens Holger Schjørring. Wiesbaden: Harrassowitz, 2008.

Hamilton, Carolyn. *Terrific Majesty: The Power of Shaka Zulu and the Limits of Historical Invention.* Cambridge, MA: Harvard University Press, 1998.

Harrison, Nonna Verna. "Women, Human Identity, and the Image of God: Antiochene Interpretations." *Journal of Early Christian Studies* 9, no. 2 (Summer 2001): 205–49.

Healey, Joseph G., and Donald Serbertz. *Towards an African Narrative Theology.* Nairobi: Paulines Publications Africa, 1996.

Henry, Carl Ferdinand Howard. *Evangelicals in Search of Identity.* Waco: Word, 1976.

———. *The Uneasy Conscience of Modern Fundamentalism.* Grand Rapids, MI: Eerdmans, 1947.

———. "The Uneasy Conscience of Modern Fundamentalism: 45 Years Later." In *Citizen Christians: The Rights and Responsibilities of Dual Citizenship,* edited by Richard D. Land and Louis A. Moore. Nashville: Broadman & Holman, 1994.

Herbert, Jerry S., ed. *Evangelical Politics: Three Approaches.* Washington: Christian College Coalition, 1993.

Hicks, E. L. "On Some Political Terms Employed in the New Testament." *The Classical Review* 1, no. 1 (March 1887): 4–8.

Hill, Alexander. *Just Business: Christian Ethics for the Market Place.* Downers Grove, IL: IVP Academic, 2008.

Hobley, Charles William, and James George Frazer. *Bantu Beliefs and Magic.* London: Witherby, 1938.

Hochschild, Adam. *King Leopold's Ghost: A Story of Greed, Terror, and Heroism in Colonial Africa.* Boston: Houghton Mifflin, 1998.

Hodgson, Dorothy Louise. *Being Maasai, Becoming Indigenous: Postcolonial Politics in a Neoliberal World.* Bloomington, IN: Indiana University Press, 2011.

———. *The Church of Women: Gendered Encounters between Maasai and Missionaries.* Bloomington, IN: Indiana University Press, 2005.

Hoekema, David A. "African Politics and Moral Vision." *Soundings: An Interdisciplinary Journal* 96, no. 2 (2013): 121–44.

Hoelzl, Michael, and Graham Ward, eds. *Religion and Political Thought*. London: Continuum, 2006.

Hollinger, David A. "Christian Missionaries against Colonialism: In Their Time Overseas They Developed an Appreciation of Other Religions and Cultures." *Wall Street Journal*, October 19, 2017. https://www.wsj.com/articles/christian-missionaries-against-colonialism-1508455448.

Howard-Hassmann, Rhoda E. "Culture, Human Rights, and the Politics of Resentment in the Era of Globalization." *Human Rights Review* 6, no. 1 (2004): 5–26.

Hughes, R. Kent. *Genesis: Beginning and Blessing*. Wheaton, IL: Crossway, 2004.

Hummel, Horace D. "The Image of God." *Concordia Journal* 10, no. 3 (May 1984): 83–93.

Hydén, Göran. *African Politics in Comparative Perspective*. New York: Cambridge University Press, 2006.

Ibrahim, M. Zakyi. "Islam in Africa: The Impact of Dan Fodio's Reforms on the Muslim Family." *Hamdard Islamicus* 29, no. 2 (June 2006): 69–79.

"I Can't Breathe." Wikipedia. Accessed 16 July 2020. https://en.wikipedia.org/wiki/I_can%27t_breathe.

Idowu, Bolaji. "The Predicament of the Church in Africa." In *Christianity in Tropical Africa*, edited by C. G. Baëta, 417–39. 1st ed. London: Routledge, 1968.

Ilo, Stan Chu. "Contemporary African Cultural Values: A Challenge to Traditional Christianity." *African Ecclesiastical Review* 49, no. 3–4 (Dec. 2007): 184–219.

Imo, Cyril. "Evangelicals, Muslims and Democracy: With Particular Reference to the Declaration of Sharia in Northern Nigeria." In *Evangelical Christianity and Democracy in Africa*, edited by Terrence O. Ranger, 37–66. Oxford: Oxford University Press, 2008.

"Influential Africans: Hastings Kamuzu Banda." VOA News. 31 October 2009. https://www.voanews.com/archive/influential-africans-hastings-kamuzu-banda.

Jacobs, Susan. "Zimbabwe: State, Class, and Gendered Models of Land Resettlement." In *Women and the State in Africa*, edited by Jane L. Parpart and Kathleen A. Staudt. Boulder, CO: Rienner, 1989.

Jenkins, Philip. *The Next Christendom: The Coming of Global Christianity*. New York: Oxford University Press, 2002.

Johnson, Anne Janette, and Sara Pendergast. "Gnassingbé Eyadéma Biography: 1937–2005; President of Togo." N.d. https://biography.jrank.org/pages/2747/Eyad-ma-Gnassingb.html.

Johnston, C. F. "Report on the Work of Africa Inland Mission." Kangundo, 21 July 1901.

Jozana, M. C. "Proposed South African Bill of Rights: A Prescription for Equality or Neo-Apartheid?" *American University International Law Review* 7, no. 1 (1991): 45–81.

Justes, Emma J. "Doing Pastoral Theology in a Context of Injustice: Society for Pastoral Theology Luncheon Address, June 18, 2005." *Journal of Pastoral Theology* 16, no. 1 (Spring 2006): 31–43.

Kabiri, Ngeta. "Ethnic Diversity and Development in Kenya: Limitations of Ethnicity as a Category of Analysis." *Commonwealth & Comparative Politics* 52, no. 4 (n.d.): 513–34.

Kamaara, Eunice. "Towards Christian National Identity in Africa: A Historical Perspective to the Challenge of Ethnicity to the Church in Kenya." *Studies in World Christianity* 16, no. 2 (2010): 126–44.

Kanyoro, Musimbi. "Not without Struggle: Changing Roles of African Women in the 21st Century." In *Changing Relations between Churches in Europe and Africa: The Internationalization of Christianity and Politics in the 20th Century*, edited by Katharina Kunter and Jens Holger Schjørring, 217–24. Wiesbaden: Harrassowitz, 2008.

Karanja, John. "Confession and Cultural Dynamism in the Revival." In *The East African Revival: Histories and Legacies*, edited by Kevin Ward and Emma Wild-Wood, 143–52. Farnham: Ashgate, 2011.

———. "Evangelical Attitudes toward Democracy in Kenya." In *Evangelical Christianity and Democracy in Africa*, edited by Terence O. Ranger, 67–94. Oxford: Oxford University Press, 2008.

Katongole, Emmanuel M. "'African Renaissance' and the Challenge of Narrative Theology in Africa." In *African Theology Today*, edited by Emmanuel M. Katongole, 207–20. Scranton, PA: University of Scranton Press, 2002.

Kawamara Mishambi, Sheila, and Irene Ovonji-Odida. "The 'Lost Clause': The Campaign to Advance Women's Property Rights in the Uganda 1998 Land Act." In *No Shortcuts to Power: African Women in Politics and Policy Making*, edited by Anne Marie Goetz and Shireen Hassim, 160–87. London: Zed Books, 2003.

Kenyatta, Jomo. *Facing Mount Kenya: The Tribal Life of the Gikuyu*. London: Secker & Warburg, 1953.

———. *Suffering Without Bitterness: The Founding of the Kenya Nation*. Nairobi: East African Publishing, 1968.

Kenzo, Mabiala Justin-Robert. "Thinking Otherwise about Africa: Postcolonialism, Postmodernism, and the Future of African Theology." *Exchange* 31, no. 4 (2002): 323–41.

Kershaw, Greet. *Mau Mau from Below*. Athens, OH: Ohio University Press, 1997.

Kilson, M. "The Analysis of African Nationalism." *World Politics* 10, no. 3 (1958): 484–97.

Kiruki, Joseph Kahiga. "Education for Transformation: A Focus on the Post-Election Violence in Kenya." *African Ecclesiastical Review* 51–52, no. 4 & 1 (Dec. 2009–March 2010): 484–92.

Kiteme, Kamuti. "The Impact of European Education upon Africans in Kenya: 1846–1940." DEd diss., Yeshiva University, 1970.

Klein, Martin A. *Slavery and Colonial Rule in French West Africa*. Cambridge: Cambridge University Press, 1998.

Kraus, C. Norma, ed. *Evangelicalism and Anabaptism*. Eugene, OR: Wipf & Stock, 2001.

Kuitert, H. Martinus. *Everything Is Politics But Politics Is Not Everything: A Theological Perspective on Faith and Politics*. Grand Rapids, MI: Eerdmans, 1986.

Kumalo, Simangaliso Raymond. "Commemoration of Martyrs of the Struggle as Contested Terrain in a Democratic South Africa: The Case of Inkosi Albert Luthuli." *Journal of Theology for Southern Africa* 135 (Nov. 2009): 42–55.

Kuyper, Abraham. *Lectures on Calvinism*. Grand Rapids, MI: Eerdmans, 1931.

Last, Murray. *The Sokoto Caliphate*. New York: Humanities Press, 1967.

Leupold, Herbert Carl. *Exposition of Genesis*. Vol. 1. Grand Rapids, MI: Baker, 1942.

Leys, Norman. *Kenya*. London: Hogarth, 1924.

Limburg, James. "The Responsibility of Royalty: Genesis 1–11 and the Care of the Earth." *Word & World* 11, no. 2 (Spring 1991): 124–30.

Lindberg, Staffan. *Democracy and Elections in Africa*. Baltimore, MD: Johns Hopkins University Press, 2006.

Luther, Martin, and Jaroslav Jan Pelikan. *Luther's Works: Lectures on Genesis Chapters 1–5*. Vol. 1. Saint Louis, MO: Concordia, 1958.

Luthuli, Albert John. "The Road to Freedom Is Via the Cross." *Journal of Theology for Southern Africa* 130 (March 2008): 112–15.

Lyon, Jo Anne. "Churches: The State of the Evangelical Church." In *The State of the Evangelical Mind: Reflections on the Past, Prospects for the Future*, edited by Todd C. Ream, Jerry Pattengale, and Christopher J. Devers, 37–58. Downers Grove, IL: IVP Academic, 2018.

Maathai, Wangari. *The Challenge for Africa*. London: Arrow, 2010.

Magesa, Laurenti. "Christology, African Women and Ministry." *African Ecclesiastical Review* 38, no. 2 (April 1996): 66–88.

———. "Differences That Bind the Liberation of Women in Africa." *African Ecclesiastical Review* 35, no. 1 (Feb. 1993): 44–53.

———. "Instruction on the 'Theology of Liberation': A Comment." *African Ecclesiastical Review* 27, no. 1 (Feb. 1985): 3–8.

———. "Politics and Theology in Africa." *African Ecclesiastical Review* 31, no. 3 (1989): 143–60.

Majawa, Clement Chinkambako Abenguni. "Church as Conscience of the State: Christian Witness in Politics for the Transformation of Africa." *African Ecclesiastical Review* 56, no. 2–3 (n.d.): 151–81.

———. "The Church's Role in Defining Genuine Democracy in Africa." In *African Theology Today*, edited by Emmanuel Katongole, 99–120. Scranton, PA: University of Scranton Press, 2002.

Marsden, George. *Understanding Fundamentalism and Evangelicalism*. Grand Rapids, MI: Eerdmans, 1991.

Masenya, Madipoane J., and Hulisani Ramantswana. "*Lupfumo Lu Mavuni* (Wealth Is in the Land): In Search of the Promised Land (cf. Ex 3–4) in the Post-Colonial, Post-Apartheid South Africa." *Journal of Theology for Southern Africa* 151 (March 2015): 96–116.

Maxwell, Leigh. *The Ashanti Ring: Sir Garnet Wolseley's Campaigns 1870–1882*. London: Leo Cooper in association with Secker & Warburg, 1985.

Mbaku, John Mukum. *Bureaucratic and Political Corruption in Africa: The Public Choice Perspective*. Malabar, FL: Krieger, 2000.

Mbiti, John S. *African Religions & Philosophy*. New York: Frederick A. Praeger, 1969.

———. *Bible and Theology in African Christianity*. Nairobi: Oxford University Press, 1986.

Mbon, Friday M. "Response to Christianity in Pre-Colonial and Colonial Africa: Some Ulterior Motives." *Mission Studies* 4, no. 1 (1987): 42–54.

McKenrick, Fred H. "The Thuku Movement in East Africa." *Inland Africa* 11, no. 6 (June 1927): 1–3.

Miller, Arthur Selwyn. *Politics, Democracy, and the Supreme Court: Essays on the Frontier of Constitutional Theory*. Westport, CT: Greenwood Press, 1985.

Miller, Catherine. *Peter Cameron Scott: The Unlocked Door*. London: Parry Jackman Ltd., 1955.

Moloney, Raymond. "Religion, Politics and the Uganda Martyrs." *African Ecclesiastical Review* 29, no. 1 (Feb. 1987): 7–15.

Mott, Stephen Charles. *A Christian Perspective on Political Thought*. New York/Oxford: Oxford University Press, 1993.

Mouw, Richard J. "Political Theology." In *Dictionary of Christianity in America*, edited by Daniel G. Reid. Downers Grove, IL: InterVarsity Press, 1990.

Moyo, Fulata Lusungu. "'Is Africa Ready for a Female President?' A Feminist Theological Search into the Role of Vera Chirwa as Politician and Human Rights Activist within the Prophetic Ministry of the Livingstonia Synod of Church of Central Africa Presbyterian (CCAP) in Malawi, 1959–2004." In *Changing Relations between Churches in Europe and Africa: The Internationalization of Christianity and Politics in the 20th Century*, edited by Katharina Kunter and Jens Holger Schjørring. Wiesbaden: Harrassowitz, 2008.

Msoka, Gabriel Andrew. "Cosmotheandrization of Human Rights: A Focus on Refugees and Internally Displaced Persons in Africa." *African Ecclesiastical Review* 49, no. 1 & 2 (2007): 62–96.

Mugambi, Jesse Ndwiga Kanyua. "African Churches in Social Transformation." In *Democracy and Development: The Role of Churches*, edited by J. N. K. Mugambi, 1–37. Nairobi: All Africa Council of Churches, 1997.

———. *Democracy and Development in Africa: Role of the Churches*. Nairobi: All African Conference of Churches, 1997.

Mugonyi, David. "Churches and MPs Named in Land Deals." *Daily Nation* online, 8 October 2004.

Mullei, Andrew. *The Link between Corruption and Poverty: Lessons from Kenya Case Studies*. Nairobi: Africa Centre for Economic Growth, 2000.

Mullenix, Gordon R., and John Mpaayei. "Matonyok: A Case Study of the Interaction of Evangelism and Community Development among the Keekonyokie Maasai of Kenya." *Missiology* 12, no. 3 (1984): 327–37.

Mushy, Prosper. "Terrorism in Africa: The Response of Theology." *African Ecclesiastical Review* 57, no. 1–2 (June 2015): 4–23.

Ndegwa, Stephen N. "Citizenship and Ethnicity: An Examination of Two Transition Moments in Kenyan Politics." *American Political Science Review* 91, no. 3 (Sep. 1997): 599–616.

Ndlobvu, J. *Democracy in Africa: A Copy of European Political Philosophy*. London: St Paul's, 1996.

Ndunguru, Bernadette. "The Role of Women in Peacebuilding and Reconciliation in the AMECEA Countries." *African Ecclesiastical Review* 51, no. 3 (Sep. 2009): 279–87.

Ngugi wa Thiong'o. *Mother, Sing for Me: People's Theatre in Kenya*. London: Zed, 1989.

———. *Moving the Centre: The Struggle for Cultural Freedoms*. London: J. Currey; Portsmouth, NH: Heinemann, 1993.

Niebuhr, H. Richard. *The Kingdom of God in America*. New York: Harper, 1937.

Nihinlola, Emiola. "Poverty and a Theology of Human Development in Africa." *Ogbomoso Journal of Theology* 14, no. 1 (2009): 161–75.

Njogu, Kimani. *Youth and Peaceful Elections in Kenya*. Nairobi: Twaweza Communications, 2013.

Noll, Mark. *American Evangelical Christianity: An Introduction*. Malden, MA: Blackwell, 2001.

———. *The Scandal of the Evangelical Mind*. Grand Rapids, MI: Eerdmans, 1994.

Nthamburi, Zablon. *The African Church at the Crossroads: A Strategy for Indigenization*. Nairobi: Uzima, 1991.

———. "The Church and the Challenge of Religious Pluralism: A Historical and Contemporary Perspective." In *Religious Pluralism in Africa: Challenge and Response*, edited by Hance A. O. Mwakabana, 25–34. Geneva: Lutheran World Federation, 1996.

———. *The Pilgrimage of the African Church: Towards the Twenty-First Century*. Nairobi: Uzima, 2000.

Nthamburi, Zablon, ed. *From Mission to Church: A Handbook of Christianity in East Africa*. Nairobi: Uzima, 1991.

Obeng, Emmanuel Adow. "The Use of Biblical Critical Methods in Rooting the Scriptures in Africa." In *The Bible in African Christianity: Essays in Biblical Theology*, edited by H. W. Kinoti and John Mary Waliggo, 8–24. Nairobi: Acton, 1997.

Odongo, Ponciano, and Lucas Barasa. "Where Lion's Tail Is the Ultimate Prize." *Daily Nation* online, 21 June 2012.

Oduyoye, Mercy Amba. *Hearing and Knowing: Theological Reflections on Christianity in Africa*. Maryknoll, NY: Orbis, 1986.

Ogot, Bethwell Allan. "Essence of Ethnicity: An African Perspective." In *Ethnic Diversity and Economic Instability in Africa: Interdisciplinary Perspectives*, edited by Hiroyuki Hino, 91–126. Cambridge: Cambridge University Press, 2012.

Ogot, B. A., and J. A. Kieran, eds. *Zamani: A Survey of East African History*. Nairobi: Longmans, 1968.

Okullu, John Henry. *Church and Politics in East Africa*. Nairobi: Uzima, 1974.

————. *Church and State in Nation Building and Human Development*. Nairobi: Uzima, 2003.

————. *Quest for Justice: An Autobiography of Bishop John Henry Okullu*. Kisumu, Kenya: Shalom, 1997.

Omolewa, Michael. "Traditional African Modes of Education: Their Relevance in the Modern World." *International Review of Education* 53, no. 5 (Nov. 2007): 593–612.

Omoruyi, Omo. "The Nature of Military Power in the Politics of West Africa and Its Implications for Christian Faith." *Ogbomoso Journal of Theology* 4 (Dec. 1989): 38–41.

Orr, James Edwin. *Evangelical Awakenings in Africa*. Pasadena, CA: Mission to the Academic Community, 1972.

————. *God's Image in Man and Its Defacement in Light of Modern Denials*. Eugene, OR: Wipf & Stock, 1997.

Ottaway, Marina. "Ethnic Politics in Africa: Change and Continuity." In *State, Conflict, and Democracy in Africa*, edited by Richard Joseph, 299–318. Boulder, CO: L. Rienner, 1999.

Oyeshile, Olatunji A. "Poverty and Democratic Governance in Africa." *Ogbomoso Journal of Theology* 14, no. 1 (2009): 37–48.

Parratt, John. *Reinventing Christianity: African Theology Today*. Grand Rapids, MI: Eerdmans, 1995.

Petersen, Henrik Sonne. "Political Engagement of Historic Churches in Eastern Africa." *Svensk Missionstidskrift* 101, no. 1 (2013): 67–106.

Peterson, Derek R. "Revivalism and Dissent in Colonial East Africa." In *The East African Revival: Histories and Legacies*, edited by Kevin Ward and Emma Wild-Wood, 105–18. Farnham: Ashgate, 2011.

Phiri, Isaac. "Why African Churches Preach Politics: The Case of Zambia." *Journal of Church and State* 41, no. 2 (Spring 1999): 323–47.

Pope John Paul II. "Pope John Paul II's Message to the OAU: To His Excellency Mr Ide Oumaro." *African Ecclesiastical Review* 30, no. 4 (Aug. 1988): 255–56.

Posner, Daniel N. *Institutions and Ethnic Politics in Africa*. Cambridge: Cambridge University Press, 2005.

Poythress, Vern S. "Correlations with Providence in Genesis 1." *The Westminster Theological Journal* 77, no. 1 (Spring 2015): 71–99.

Rendtorff, Rolf. *The Covenant Formula: An Exegetical and Theological Investigation*. Translated by Margaret Kohl. Edinburgh: T&T Clark, 1998.

Richards, H. J. "The Kingdom of God." *The Arrow* 10, no. 6 (June 1954): 377–89.

Ridderbos, Herman N. *The Coming of the Kingdom*. Philadelphia: Presbyterian & Reformed, 1975.

Ringa, Mathias. "AIC Neutral in Succession Debate, Says Head." *East African Standard* online, 2 September 2002.

Robinson, Mark. *Corruption and Development*. London: Frank Cass, 1998.

Rosberg, Carl G., and John Nottingham. *The Myth of "Mau Mau": Nationalism in Kenya*. New York: Frederick A. Praeger, 1966.

Roy, Donald I. "Chiefs in Their Millennium Sandals: Traditional Authority in Ghana – Relevance, Challenges, and Prospects." In *Critical Perspectives in Politics and Socio-Economic Development in Ghana*, edited by Wisdom J. Tettey, Korbla P. Puplampu, and Bruce J. Berman, 241–72. Leiden: Brill, 2003.

Sampong, Kwasi Addo. "Traditional Governance and Social Transformation through the Gospel in Ghana." *Ogbomoso Journal of Theology* 17, no. 3 (2012): 117–32.

Schreiter, Robert J. *Constructing Local Theologies*. Maryknoll, NY: Orbis, 1985.

———. "Some Conditions for a Transcultural Theology: Response to Raimon Panikkar." In *Pluralism and Oppression: Theology in World Perspective*, edited by Paul F. Knitter, 23–28. Lanham, MD: University Press of America, 1991.

Sedmak, Clemens. *Doing Local Theology: A Guide for Artisans of a New Humanity*. Maryknoll, NY: Orbis, 2002.

Shenk, David W. *Justice, Reconciliation and Peace in Africa*. Nairobi: Uzima, 1983.

Sider, Ronald J. "Thinking Biblically about Politics." *Criswell Theological Review* 6, no. 1 (Fall 2008): 43–56.

Sider, Ronald J., and Diane Knippers. *Toward an Evangelical Public Policy: Political Strategies for the Health of the Nation*. Grand Rapids, MI: Baker, 2005.

Simons, Marlise, and David Goodman. "Ex-Liberian Leader Gets 50 Years for War Crimes." *New York Times*. 30 May 2012.

Skillen, James. *The Good of Politics: A Biblical, Historical, and Contemporary Introduction*. Engaging Culture. Grand Rapids, MI: Baker Academic, 2014.

Smith, James Howard. "Making Peace with the Devil: The Political Life of Devil Worship Rumors in Kenya." In *Displacing the State: Religion and Conflict in Neoliberal Africa*, edited by James Howard Smith and Rosalind I. J. Hackett, 49–81. Notre Dame, IN: University of Notre Dame Press, 2012.

Sodiq, Yushau. "Can Muslims and Christians Live Together Peacefully in Nigeria?" *The Muslim World* 99, no. 4 (Oct. 2009): 646–88.

Spanner, Huw. "Tyrants, Stewards – or Just Kings?" In *Animals on the Agenda: Questions about Animals for Theology and Ethics*, edited by Andrew Linzey and Dorothy Yamamoto, 216–24. Urbana, IL: University of Illinois Press, 1998.

Spear, Thomas. "Neo-Traditionalism and the Limits of Invention in British Colonial Africa." *The Journal of African History* 44, no. 1 (2003): 3–27.

"Specimens of the Lord's Work." Editorial. *Inland Africa* 11, no. 11 (1927): 10.

Spragens, Thomas A. *Understanding Political Theory*. New York: St. Martin's Press, 1976.

Stauffacher, Raymond. "The Soul of an African." *Inland Africa* 13, no. 5 (1929): 10–11.

Stimson, Shannon C. "Constitutionalism and the Rule of Law." In *The Oxford Handbook of Political Theory*, edited by John S. Dryzek, Bonnie Honig, and Anne Phillips, 317–32. Oxford: Oxford University Press, 2006.

Storey, Peter. "Mandela, Nelson, 1918–2013." *The Christian Century* 131, no. 1 (8 Jan. 2014): 10–11.

Storkey, Alan. *Jesus and Politics: Confronting the Powers*. Grand Rapids, MI: Baker Academic, 2005.

Strayer, Robert. *The Making of Mission Communities in East Africa: Anglicans and Africans in Colonial Kenya, 1875–1935*. London: Heinemann; Albany, NY: State University of New York Press, 1978.

Tanner, Kathryn. *The Politics of God: Christian Theologies and Social Justice*. Minneapolis: Fortress, 1992.

Thomas, J. Chris. "Poverty and Capitalism in West Africa: A Christian Perspective." *Ogbomoso Journal of Theology* 14, no. 1 (2009): 49–59.

Thomson, Alex. *An Introduction to African Politics*. London/New York: Routledge, 2000.

Tignor, Robert L. *The Colonial Transformation of Kenya: The Kamba, Kikuyu, and Maasai from 1900 to 1939*. Princeton, NJ: Princeton University Press, 1976.

Tsumura, David Toshio. *Creation and Destruction: A Reappraisal of the Chaoskampf Theory in the Old Testament*. Winona Lake, IN: Eisenbrauns, 2005.

Tutu, Desmond M. "Barmen and Apartheid." *Journal of Theology for Southern Africa* 47 (June 1984): 73–77.

———. "Dark Days: Episcopal Ministry in Times of Repression, 1976–1996." *Journal of Theology for Southern Africa* 118 (March 2004): 27–39.

UNESCO. "Ellen Johnson Sirleaf," n.d., https://en.unesco.org/sites/default/files/bio_ellen_johnson_sirleaf_eng_ok.pdf.

United Nations. "United Nations Universal Declaration of Human Rights 1948." https://www.jus.uio.no/lm/en/pdf/un.univcrsal.dcclaration.of.human.rights.1948.portrait.letter.pdf.

van der Walt, B. J. *When African and Western Cultures Meet: From Confrontation to Appreciation*. Potchefstroom: Institute for Contemporary Christianity in Africa, 2006.

Vogl, Frank. *Waging War on Corruption: Inside the Movement Fighting the Abuse of Power*. Lanham, MD: Rowman & Littlefield, 2012.

Wallis, Jim. *The Soul of Politics: Beyond "Religious Right" and "Secular Left."* San Diego/New York/London: Harcourt, Brace & Co., 1995.

Walls, Andrew F. "Africa in History: Retrospect and Prospect," *Journal of African Christian Thought* 1, no. 1 (June 1998): 2–15.

Walton, John H. *The Lost World of Genesis One: Ancient Cosmology and the Origins Debate*. Downers Grove, IL: IVP Academic, 2009.

Ward, Kevin. "Introduction." In *The East African Revival: Histories and Legacies*, edited by Kevin Ward and Emma Wild-Wood, 3–10. Farnham: Ashgate, 2011.

Werbner, Richard. "Introduction." In *Postcolonial Identities in Africa*, edited by Richard Werbner and Terence Ranger, 1–23. London: Zed, 1996.

Westermann, Diedrich. "Cultural History of Negro Africa." *Cahiers d'histoire mondiale* 4 (1957).

"What Is African Evangelical Theology?" Editorial. *East Africa Journal of Evangelical Theology* 2, no. 1 (1983). http://biblicalstudies.gospelstudies.org.uk/pdf/ajet/02-1_001.pdf.

Wright, Christopher J. H. *God's People in God's Land: Family, Land, and Property in the Old Testament*. Grand Rapids, MI: Eerdmans, 1990.

———. *The Mission of God: Unlocking the Bible's Grand Narrative*. Downers Grove, IL: IVP Academic, 2006.

———. *The Mission of God's People: A Biblical Theology of the Church's Mission*. Grand Rapids, MI: Zondervan, 2010.

Yahya-Othman, Saida, and Joseph sinde Warioba. *Moving the Kenyan Constitution Review Process Forward: A Report of the Fact-Finding Mission to Kenya*. Kampala: Fountain, 2007.

Yoder, John Howard. *The Christian Witness to the State*. Newton, KS: Faith and Life, 1964.

———. *The Politics of Jesus: Vicit Agnus Noster*. Grand Rapids, MI: Eerdmans, 1994.

———. *The Priestly Kingdom: Social Ethics as Gospel*. Notre Dame, IN: University of Notre Dame Press, 1984.